the ultimate GIBSON book

PAUL DAY & WALTER CARTER

CHARTWELL
BOOKS

© 2010 by Outline Press (Book Publishers) Ltd.

This edition published in 2015 by

CHARTWELL BOOKS
an imprint of Book Sales
a division of Quarto Publishing Group USA Inc.
142 West 36th Street, 4th Floor
New York, New York 10018
USA

This edition published by arrangement with Outline Press Limited,
3.1D Union Court, 20-22 Union Road, London SW4 6JP, United Kingdom

COMMISSIONING EDITOR: Nigel Osborne
ART DIRECTOR: Paul Cooper Design
DESIGN: Elizabeth Owens

ISBN: 978-0-7858-3279-9

Printed by Regent Publishing Services, China

INTRODUCTION

Since the 1930s, Gibson electric guitars have been embedded in our culture as some of the most recognizable icons of jazz, blues, and rock'n'roll. The companies pioneering design work before World War II was followed by the 'classic' years under Ted McCarty's leadership before the much darker days of the Norlin period. Gibson's resurgence over the last twenty-five years resulted from the change in ownership in 1984 that eventually brought about a return to quality workmanship and traditional Gibson values.

"I am playing more smoothly now, I'm developing what I call my 'woman tone'. It's a sweet sound, something like the solo on 'I Feel Free' and it's more like the human voice than a guitar".
ERIC CLAPTON TALKING ABOUT HIS GIBSON LES PAUL STANDARD IN 1966.

Everyone from BB King and Zakk Wylde to Eric Clapton and Slash has played a Gibson electric guitar, but it is the millions of unknown guitarists regularly drawn to these stylish instruments who have ensured that Gibson remains the leading modern electric-guitar manufacturer.

The Ultimate Gibson Book is a complete guide to the electric guitars that Gibson has made since 1936. A detailed listing of the various models is illustrated with full color photographs.

The book is organized chronologically with the main model types dealt with as they appear in the story. Within each broad model category the variations of the model are fully listed. Each entry includes the guitar's full name and its production dates with a basic single-line identification followed by detailed specifications for the guitars neck, body, electronics, and hardware.

The Ultimate Gibson Book is a unique journey through the fascinating history and the present-day greatness of Gibson electric guitars. We hope you enjoy it.

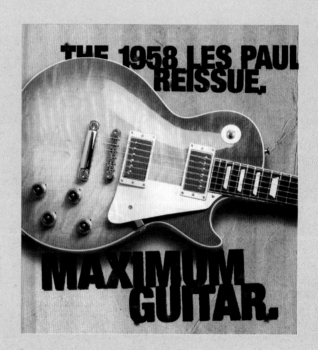

■ **1955** press advertisement

■ **1936** ES-150

ARCHTOP 1936-1940

ES-150 (pre-WWII) 1936–42
Non-cut archtop, dot inlays, pearl logo.
- Full-depth hollowbody, 16¼-inch wide, X-braced carved spruce top, flat back (arched from 1940), single-bound top and back, single-bound pickguard, Sunburst finish.
- Single-bound rosewood fingerboard (unbound from 1940), dot inlays, pearl logo.
- Charlie Christian blade pickup in hexagonal housing (rectangular metal-covered with screw-poles from 1940), single-ply binding around pickup and around blade (triple-ply 1938–9), two knobs, jack at tailpiece base.

Production: 1,629 (1937–41).

EST-150 1937–39 / ETG-150 1940–42
Tenor neck, arched back, jack on side.
Production: 95 (1937–41).

ES-100 1938–41/ ES-125 (pre-WWII) 1941–43
Non-cut archtop, one pickup, prewar script logo in paint.
- Full-depth hollowbody, 14¼-inch wide, X-braced carved spruce top, maple back and sides, flat back (arched from 1940), single-bound top and back, Sunburst finish.
- Unbound rosewood fingerboard (unbound from 1940), dot inlays, silkscreen logo.
- Blade pickup with white rectangular housing (rectangular metal-covered with screw-poles from 1940), pickup in neck position (bridge position from 1940), two knobs, jack on side.

Production: 585 (ES-100); 152 (ES-125, 1941).

EST-100 / ETG-100 1940–41
4-string tenor. Production: 19.

ESP-150 1939
Plectrum neck, arched back, jack on side. Production: 1.

ES-250 1939–40
Non-cut archtop, open-book inlays, Charlie Christian pickup.
- 17-inch wide, carved spruce top, maple sides and arched back, triple-bound pickguard, large tailpiece, Sunburst or Natural finish.
- Bound rosewood fingerboard, open-book inlay (some with double-parallelogram, some with fancy pattern in rectangular inserts), two-piece maple neck with center stripe, stairstep headstock (some with non-stairstep, bound or unbound), stinger on back of headstock, pearl logo (some with post-WWII logo).
- Triple-bound Charlie Christian pickup with 6 blades (some assembled post-WWII with P-90 pickup), two knobs, jack at tailpiece base.

Production: 70.

ES-300 (pre-WWII) 1940–42
Non-cut archtop, double-parallelogram inlays, prewar logo.
- 17-inch wide, parallel-braced carved spruce top, most with dowel supports under bridge, carved maple back, tailpiece with pointed ends and raised diamond and arrows, triple-bound top (some single-ply) and back, bound tortoiseshell celluloid pickguard.
- Two-piece maple neck with stripe down middle, double-parallelogram inlay, single-bound peghead, black stinger on back of peghead, crown peghead inlay (some with seven-piece split-diamond), pearl logo.
- 7-inch slant-mounted oblong pickup with adjustable poles (4⅛-inch pickup from 1941), jack on side.

Production: 194 (1940–41).

■ **1940** ES-300

ES-300 (post-WWII) 1945–52

Non-cut archtop, double-parallelogram inlays, postwar logo.

- 17-inch laminated maple body (a few early with 5-ply mahogany body), trapeze tailpiece with pointed ends and three raised parallelograms (early with plate tailpiece with two *f*-hole cutouts), laminated beveled-edge pickguard (early with bound tortoiseshell celluloid pickguard), triple-bound top and back, Sunburst or Natural finish (a few Black, 1945).
- One-piece mahogany neck, bound rosewood fingerboard, double-parallelogram inlay, bound peghead, crown peghead inlay, plastic keystone tuner buttons: mid 1946.
- P-90 pickup in neck position (2 pickups from 1948), two knobs (master tone knob added on upper treble bout, 1948).

Production: 826 (1948–56).

ES-125 (post-WWII) 1946–70

Non-cut archtop, one P-90 pickup, postwar logo, dot or trapezoid inlays.

- 16¼-inch full-depth hollowbody of laminated maple (some with all-mahogany body), tortoise pickguard, trapeze tailpiece, single-bound top and back, Sunburst finish.
- Unbound rosewood fingerboard (unbound from 1940), pearloid trapezoid inlay (some with dot inlay from 1946, all with dot inlay from 1950), decal logo.
- P-90 pickup in neck position (earliest with no non-adjustable poles or no poles), two knobs.

Production: 32,940.

■ **1945** ES-300

ES-150 (post-WWII) 1947–56

Non-cut archtop, 17-inch wide, single P-90 pickup, dot or trapezoid inlays.
- Full-depth laminated maple hollowbody, 17-inch wide, laminated beveled-edge pickguard, bound top and back.
- Unbound rosewood fingerboard (bound from 1950), dot inlay (trapezoid from 1950), silkscreen logo.
- P-90 pickup in neck position, jack on side.
Production: 3,447 (1948–56).

ETG-150 1947–71

Tenor neck, electric version of TG-50 acoustic, 16¼-inch hollowbody, one P-90 pickup, laminated beveled-edge pickguard, bound fingerboard, dot inlays, no peghead ornament.
Production: 476 (1948–60).

ES-350 (also ES-350 PREMIER) 1947–56

Single-cut archtop, rounded horn, double-parallelogram inlays.
- 17-inch wide, rosewood bridge (tune-o-matic 1956), trapeze tailpiece with pointed ends and three raised parallelograms, laminated beveled-edge pickguard (early with bound tortoiseshell celluloid pickguard), triple-bound top and back, gold-plated hardware, Sunburst or Natural finish.
- Two-piece maple neck with stripe down center, single-bound fingerboard, double-parallelogram inlay, single-bound peghead, black stinger on back of peghead, crown peghead inlay crown peghead inlay, plastic keystone tuner buttons.
- One P-90 pickup (2 pickups from 1948), two knobs (master tone control added on cutaway from 1948, four knobs and toggle switch from 1952).
Production: 1,056 (1948–56).

■ **1948** ES-350

■ **1949** ES-350 special prototype

THE BIRTH OF THE GIBSON ELECTRIC GUITAR

Working alone in his back-room workshop in Kalamazoo, Michigan, Orville Gibson invented the archtop guitar in the 1890s. In the 1920s and early '30s this was the most popular type of 'Spanish' style guitar with players in dance bands, swing orchestras, and western swing outfits – in short, with the guitarists who were finding themselves most in need of amplification. The form had reached its zenith in many players' and collectors' eyes with the Lloyd Loar-designed L-5 of 1922, an elaborately crafted instrument with a laboriously hand-carved solid spruce top. Designed for optimum performance and tone, the L-5 also had pretty good volume for an acoustic archtop, and quickly became the epitome of its type; but laboring away at the back of a stage crowded with horns, a piano, a drummer, and more often a singer with a microphone connected to a PA system, the type of guitarist who could afford an L-5 was rapidly finding he needed something louder to cut it at many playing dates. Enter the electric guitar, and a new era in both the instrument and the music that it helped to make possible.

Gibson wasn't the first to experiment with amplifying the guitar, but it was the first established company to offer an electric guitar as a standard production model. In 1936, the revolutionary ES-150 'Electric Spanish' guitar hit the scene. It had a 16¼-inch body with a carved, X-braced spruce top, a flat maple back, simple dot position markers in the fingerboard, and, most crucially, a single 'blade'-style magnetic pickup mounted in the body of the guitar and positioned near the end of the fingerboard, along with volume and tone controls to govern it. Although outwardly they appear to be just another single-coil pickup, these early Gibson pickups – which have forever after been known as 'Charlie Christian pickups' because of their use by the formative jazz guitarist – actually consist of a long bar magnet suspended under the top of the guitar by three adjustment screws, the magnet attached to a single blade pole-piece that protrudes through the visible surround.

Although rather basic, even crude by today's standards, the ES-150 was a considerable success and played a major part in ushering in the era of amplified music. It was a rather boomy, potentially bass-heavy sounding guitar, and prone to howling feedback if you weren't careful with volume levels and playing position, but it gave guitarists a means of escaping the ghetto of the rhythm section and even taking a spin in the spotlight now and then. This early bullseye gave Gibson the confidence to follow up with a succession of electric models in the prewar years, first looking down with the more affordable 14¼-inch ES-100 of 1938, then upscale with the 17-inch ES-250 of 1939. In 1940 the even more deluxe 17-inch-wide ES-300 was introduced, which also boasted a carved, arched maple back. But it would be the last Gibson electric to hit the scene before World War II put a halt to guitar production.

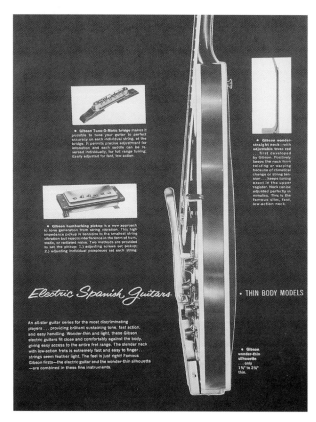

■ **1964** press advertisement

ARCHTOP 1949

ARCHTOP 1949

1949 press advertisement

1949 ES-5

ES-5 1949–55

Single-cut archtop, three pickups, four knobs.

- 17-inch wide, rounded cutaway, rosewood bridge (tune-o-matic from 1955) trapeze tailpiece with pointed ends and three raised parallelograms, laminated beveled-edge pickguard, triple-bound top and back (five-ply from 1955), bound *f*-holes (a few early unbound), gold-plated hardware, Sunburst or Natural finish.
- Two-piece maple neck with stripe down center, pointed-end rosewood fingerboard with five-ply binding, large pearl block inlays, single-bound peghead, black stinger on back of peghead, crown peghead inlay.
- Three P-90 pickups (Alnico V specified, 1955), three volume controls, one master tone knob on cutaway bout.

Production: 911 (includes some ES-5 Switchmasters 1955).

■ **1950** ES-5

ARCHTOP 1949

LAMINATED WOODS FOR SOLID TONES: THE ES-175

Having returned to the market with the ES-300, ES-125, ES-150, and ES-350 following the war, Gibson was already envisioning a future that took the electrified instrument a step further away from the constructional standards for quality acoustic archtop guitars. All of these models were still being made with carved solid-spruce tops. Gibson soon deduced, however, that once a guitar is amplified past its acoustic volume, considerations of acoustic tone take a back seat to amplified performance, and that amplified performance could be improved – arguably – with the use of a stiffer laminated top. Using laminated wood would also ease production and reduce expense, since the top could be pressed into its arched shape, rather than painstakingly carved by hand. The result was the ES-175, released in 1949 – Gibson's first archtop with a laminated maple top, and also the first with a pointed cutaway.

The model was born with a single P-90 pickup in the neck position, single volume and tone controls, and a body that was 16¼ inches wide and 3¼ inches deep. Two pickups were available from 1951. Gibson's hopes for the instrument bore fruit: the ES-175 was a little punchier and more cutting than traditional electric archtops, and also somewhat (if only slightly) more resistant to feedback. It quickly became a standard for many jazz players, and kicked off a line of laminated-wood electric archtops that remains popular to this day.

Not that Gibson was giving up on the carved-top archtop electric. In 1949 the company also introduced the ES-5, an upmarket model with 17-inch-wide body with rounded cutaway and – another first in the electric guitar world – three P-90 pickups (the model was modified into the ES-5 Switchmaster in 1955 to improve the selection facilities for these pickups). Gibson further reaffirmed its commitment to upscale archtop electrics with the introduction of the L-5CES and Super 400CES in 1951, but in the years to follow the laminated models would prove to be the greater popular success across the full range of electric guitar genres.

■ **1952** press advertisement

ES-175 SINGLE PICKUP 1949–72

Single-cut archtop, pointed horn, double-parallelogram inlay, one pickup.

- 16¼-inch wide, laminated maple body, pointed cutaway, laminated beveled-edge pickguard, rosewood bridge (tune-o-matic from 1977), hinged tailpiece with pointed ends and three raised parallelograms (T-center with zigzag tubes 1958–71), triple-bound top, single-bound back, Sunburst or Natural finish.
- Bound rosewood fingerboard, double-parallelogram inlay, crown peghead inlay, pearl logo.
- One P-90 pickup in neck position (some with two pickups and three knobs 1951–53; some with Alnico V pickup 1955, humbucker from 1957), two knobs.

Production; 9,964.

ES-175 DOUBLE PICKUP 1951–53, 1971–91, 2006–current / ES-175D 1953–70 / ES-175 REISSUE 1991–2005

Single-cut archtop, pointed horn, double-parallelogram inlay, two pickups.

- 16¼-inch wide, laminated maple body (mahogany back and sides 1983–90), pointed cutaway, laminated beveled-edge pickguard, rosewood bridge (tune-o-matic from 1977), hinged tailpiece with pointed ends and three raised parallelograms (T-center with zigzag tubes 1958–71, hinged from 1991), triple-bound top, single-bound back, Sunburst or Natural finish.
- Bound rosewood fingerboard, double-parallelogram inlay, crown peghead inlay, pearl logo.
- Two P-90 pickups (some with Alnico V, humbuckers from 1957), four knobs, toggle switch.

Production: 16,790.

ES-140 (¾-scale) 1950–56

Small single-cut archtop, pointed horn.

- 12¾-inch wide laminated maple hollowbody, *f*-holes, pointed cutaway, trapeze tailpiece, single-bound top and back.
- 22¾-inch scale, dot inlays, Sunburst finish (Natural finish rare).
- One P-90 pickup.

Production: 2,385.

1949 ES-175N

ARCHTOP 1949-1951

ARCHTOP 1951

1951 ES-175 Double Pickup

1958 ES-175D

1955 ES-140

SUPER 400CES

The acoustic Super 400 was introduced toward the end of 1934, an 18-inch wide archtop that cost $400 and was the largest and most expensive of its type. Production ceased during WWII and was resumed in 1947, the cutaway added in 1949. Unlike many post-war archtops, it retained its carved spruce top which was thickened for the electric version that appeared in 1951. This, and the L-5CES, were the first Gibson electrics to feature the now classic electronics layout: two pickups, three-way toggle pickup selector, and volume and tone controls for each pickup.

■ **1951** press advertisement

■ **1951** Super 400CES

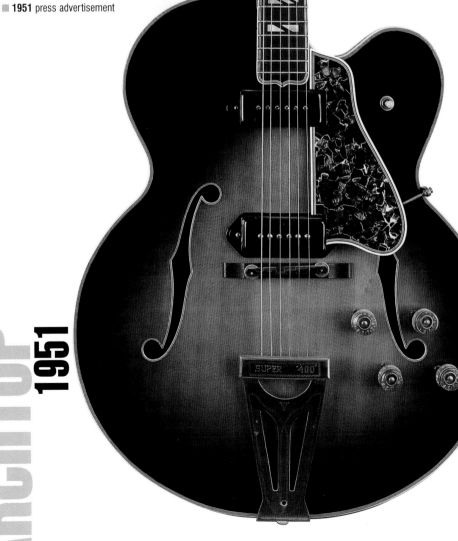

ARCHTOP 1951

SUPER 400CES 1951–current

Single-cut archtop, large flat tailpiece, split-block inlays.

- 18-inch wide maple body, rounded cutaway (pointed cutaway 1960–69), solid carved spruce top, carved maple back (laminated one-piece back 1960–69), maple sides, multiple-bound top, back and ƒ-holes.
- Ebony fingerboard with pointed end, split-lock inlay, multiple-bound fingerboard and peghead, five-piece split-diamond peghead inlay.
- Two P-90 pickups (Alnico V from 1954, humbuckers from late 1957), four knobs, selector switch.

Production: 1,476 (1951–79).

ARCHTOP 1951

■ **1960** Super 400CES

■ **1984** Super 400CES

17

L-5CES 1951–current

Single-cut archtop, block inlay.

- 17-inch wide, rounded cutaway (pointed cutaway 1960–69), solid carved spruce top, carved maple back (laminated one-piece back 1960–69), maple sides, single-bound *f*-holes, multiple-bound top and back.
- Ebony fingerboard with pointed end, block inlays, multiple-bound fingerboard and peghead, flowerpot peghead inlay.
- Two P-90 pickups (Alnico V from 1954, humbuckers from late 1957), four knobs, selector switch.

Production: 2,963 (1951–79).

L-5CEST 1954–62, 1983

Thinline body, rounded cutaway, two humbuckers (one floating humbucker in 1983).

L-5 CUSTOM See Super V p.27.

ES-295 1952–58, 1990–2000

Single-cut archtop, pointed horn, gold finish.

- 16¼-inch wide laminated maple body, pointed cutaway, clear pickguard back-painted with white background and gold floral design, trapeze bridge/tailpiece combo with strings looping over bridge (Bigsby vibrola 1992–97, optional 1998), triple-bound top, single-bound back, gold-plated hardware, gold finish.
- Bound rosewood fingerboard, 19 frets (20 from 1955), double-parallelogram inlay, crown peghead inlay.
- Two P-90 pickups with white covers (humbuckers from late 1958).

Production: 1,770 (1952–58).

■ **1951** L-5CES

ARCHTOP
1951-1954

ARCHTOP
1951-1954

1964 L-5CES

1952 ES-295

ES-130 FULL-DEPTH 1954–56, ES-135 1956–57
Non-cut archtop, one pickup, trapezoid inlays.
- 16¼-inch archtop body of laminated maple, trapeze tailpiece with raised diamond, laminated beveled-edge pickguard, single-bound top and back.
- One P-90 pickup mounted 1-inch from fingerboard, two knobs.
- Mahogany neck, 24¾-inch scale, single-bound fingerboard, trapezoid inlays, decal logo, no peghead ornament, Sunburst finish.

Production: 556.

SUPER 300CES 1954
Single-cut archtop, 18-inch wide, double-parallelogram inlays.
- 18-inch wide maple body, carved spruce top, triple-bound top and back, tailpiece with three cutouts, laminated beveled-edge pickguard.
- Single-bound fingerboard with square end, double-parallelogram inlay, single-bound headstock, crown headstock inlay.
- One or two P-90 pickups.

ES-5 SWITCHMASTER 1955–62
Single-cut archtop, three pickups, six knobs.
- 17-inch wide, rounded cutaway (pointed 1960–62), tune-o-matic bridge 1955, trapeze tailpiece (tubular with double loop from 1956), laminated beveled-edge pickguard, five-ply binding, gold-plated hardware, Sunburst or Natural finish.
- Two-piece maple neck with stripe down center, pointed-end rosewood fingerboard with five-ply binding, large pearl block inlays, single-bound peghead, black stinger on back of peghead, crown peghead inlay.
- Three P-90 pickups (humbuckers from 1957), six knobs (three volume, three tone), slotted pickup switch on cutaway bout.

Production: 498 (1956–71).

1955 ES-5 Switchmaster

ARCHTOP 1954-1955

■ **1956** ES-5 Switchmaster

■ **1958** ES-5 Switchmaster

■ **1960** ES-5 Switchmaster

BARNEY KESSEL CUSTOM 1961–73

Double-cut archtop, pointed horns, bowtie inlay.
- 17-inch wide, full-depth body, laminated spruce top (some with laminated maple 1961–64, standard from 1965), double pointed cutaways, gold-plated hardware, Cherry Sunburst finish.
- Maple neck, bound rosewood fingerboard, 25½-inch scale, bowtie inlay, bound peghead, musical note peghead inlay.
- Two humbucking pickups, tune-o-matic bridge, trapeze tailpiece with raised diamond, model name on wood tailpiece insert, laminated beveled-edge pickguard, triple-bound top and back.

Production: 740.

BARNEY KESSEL REGULAR 1961–73

Mahogany neck, double-parallelogram inlay, crown peghead inlay, nickel-plated hardware.
Production: 1,117.

1961 Barney Kessel Custom

ARCHTOP 1961

1964 Barney Kessel Regular

1961 press advertisement

JOHNNY SMITH 1961–88 / CHET ATKINS (JS) DOUBLE 1989–91 / LE GRAND 1993–current
Single-cut archtop, floating pickup, split-block inlays.
- 17-inch wide, 3⅛-inch deep (not as deep as L-5), single rounded cutaway, X-braced carved spruce top, maple back and sides, adjustable ebony bridge, L-5 style tailpiece with model name on center insert (TP-6 six-finger from 1979), multiple-bound top and back, gold-plated hardware, Sunburst or Natural finish.
- 25-inch scale, multiple-bound ebony fingerboard with square end, split-block inlays, multiple-bound peghead, five-piece split-diamond peghead inlay.
- One floating mini-humbucking pickup (some with experimental pickups 1989–91), knob on pickguard.
Production: 963 (1962–79).

JOHNNY SMITH DOUBLE 1963–89
Two floating mini-humbucking pickups.
Production: 625 (1962–79).

1961 Johnny Smith

ARCHTOP 1961-1962

ARCHTOP 1961-1962

"Gibson Boy" ...Tal Farlow

Truly a booster of his favorite guitar, Tal Farlow has written and recorded "Gibson Boy" in a newly released album. Heralded as the "brightest new star" among guitarists, Tal justifies this title in his brilliant recordings, his enthusiastic jazz sessions. For his fresh easy style, his wide ranges of moods and music, "Tal Farlow is a confirmed "Gibson-ite," as are so many other top stars.

GIBSON, INC., Kalamazoo, Michigan

■ **1964** press advertisement

TAL FARLOW SIGNATURE 1962–67, 1993–current
Single-cut archtop, simulated scroll in cutaway bout.
• Full-depth archtop of laminated maple, deep rounded cutaway, binding material inlaid in cutaway to simulate scroll, four-point single-bound pickguard, tune-o-matic bridge, trapeze tailpiece with raised diamond, model name on wood tailpiece insert, triple-bound top, Viceroy Brown finish (Wine Red added 1993).
• 25½-inch scale, bound fingerboard, fingerboard inlay like inverted J-200 crest inlay, bound peghead, double-crown peghead inlay.
• Two humbucking pickups, toggle switch just below pickguard.
Production: 215 (1962–67).

TF-7 1991
No specs available, possibly 7-string.

■ **1964** Tal Farlow Signature

TRINI LOPEZ SIGNATURE DELUXE 1964–71

Double-cut archtop, pointed horns, diamond soundholes.

- 16-inch laminated maple hollowbody, double pointed cutaways, tune-o-matic bridge, trapeze tailpiece with raised diamond, model name on wood tailpiece insert, bound pickguard, triple-bound top and back, Cherry Sunburst finish.
- Bound fingerboard and peghead, slashed-diamond inlay, 6-on-a-side tuner arrangement, no peghead ornament.
- 2 humbucking pickups, 4 knobs, 3-way pickup selector on treble cutaway bout, standby switch on bass cutaway bout.

Production: 302 (1964–70).

ES-125C 1966–70

Pointed cutaway, 1 P-90 pickup.
Production: 475.

ES-125CD 1966–70

Pointed cutaway, two P-90 pickups.
Production: 1,104.

ES-150DC 1969–74

Double-cut archtop, full-depth body, rounded horns.

- 16¼-inch archtop body of laminated maple, 3-inch deep, Natural, Walnut, or Cherry finish.
- Rosewood fingerboard, small block inlays, crown peghead inlay.
- Two humbucking pickups, four knobs on lower treble bout, master volume knob on upper treble bout.

Production: 2,801.

CITATION 1969–70, 1975, 1979–83, 1993–current

Single-cut archtop, fleur de lis on pickguard.

- 17-inch wide, full-depth body, rounded cutaway, solid spruce top, solid maple back and sides, wood pickguard with fleur-de-lis inlay, control knob(s) on pickguard, fancy tailpiece, multiple-bound top and back, gold-plated hardware, varnish (non-lacquer) finish in Sunburst or Natural.
- Bound ebony fingerboard with pointed-end, 25½-inch scale, cloud inlay, multiple-bound peghead, fleur-de-lis inlays on front and back of peghead and on bridge.
- One or two floating mini-humbucking pickups (some without visible polepieces), five-ply maple neck.

HOWARD ROBERTS CUSTOM 1970, 1974–80

Single-cut archtop, oval soundhole.

- 16-inch wide, full-depth body, pointed cutaway, laminated maple top, oval hole, height-adjustable ebony bridge, multiple-bound pickguard, multiple-bound top and back, chrome-plated hardware (some labeled Howard Roberts Artist, 1974–76).
- Bound ebony fingerboard (rosewood from 1974), slotted-block inlays, multiple-bound peghead, vine-pattern peghead inlay.
- One floating humbucking pickup.

Production: 1,152.

HOWARD ROBERTS DE 1970

Two pickups.
Production: 2.

Michael Ward's New Gibson is no Wallflower

If this were your gig, what would you play? You'll need a guitar that can cut through a screaming B-3 and a powerhouse rhythm section night after night. With a flip of a switch you'll go from rave-up rocker to bluesy ballad, from crisp and clean to soft and subtle. Your guitar cannot be a one-trick tone pony. You need a whole carousel of sounds at your command. Now, what guitar would you play?

Michael chose the Gibson Howard Roberts Fusion. An experienced player like Michael Ward doesn't categorize his guitars by musical style. The same open mind and ears that make his music special come into play when choosing an instrument. He listens to guitars to hear what they have to offer. The Howard Roberts Fusion has plenty to give: Fast action Maple neck, thinline body with expanded cutaway, versatile humbucking pickups, and a beautiful yet functional finger tailpiece. It just plain feels right. It's no Wallflower, even if Michael is.

Only a **Gibson** Is Good Enough

Gibson Guitar Corp. • Call 1-800-4-GIBSON for a free brochure "How to Buy an Electric Guitar." • Visit us @ http://www.gibson.com

ARCHTOP 1964-1978

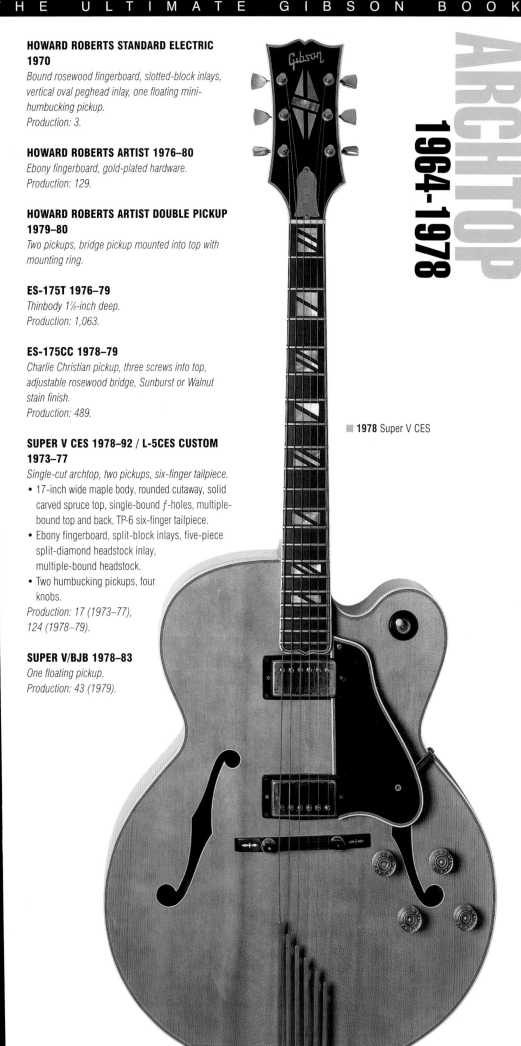

HOWARD ROBERTS STANDARD ELECTRIC 1970
Bound rosewood fingerboard, slotted-block inlays, vertical oval peghead inlay, one floating mini-humbucking pickup.
Production: 3.

HOWARD ROBERTS ARTIST 1976–80
Ebony fingerboard, gold-plated hardware.
Production: 129.

HOWARD ROBERTS ARTIST DOUBLE PICKUP 1979–80
Two pickups, bridge pickup mounted into top with mounting ring.

ES-175T 1976–79
Thinbody 1⅞-inch deep.
Production: 1,063.

ES-175CC 1978–79
Charlie Christian pickup, three screws into top, adjustable rosewood bridge, Sunburst or Walnut stain finish.
Production: 489.

SUPER V CES 1978–92 / L-5CES CUSTOM 1973–77
Single-cut archtop, two pickups, six-finger tailpiece.
* 17-inch wide maple body, rounded cutaway, solid carved spruce top, single-bound *f*-holes, multiple-bound top and back, TP-6 six-finger tailpiece.
* Ebony fingerboard, split-block inlays, five-piece split-diamond headstock inlay, multiple-bound headstock.
* Two humbucking pickups, four knobs.
Production: 17 (1973–77), 124 (1978–79).

SUPER V/BJB 1978–83
One floating pickup.
Production: 43 (1979).

■ **1978** Super V CES

ARCHTOP 1964-1978

KALAMAZOO AWARD 1978–84

Single-cut archtop, flying bird inlay on peghead.

- 17-inch wide, full-depth body, carved spruce top, maple back and side, adjustable ebony bridge with pearl inlays, wood pickguard with abalone inlay, knobs mounted on pickguard, multiple-bound top and back, bound *f*-holes, gold-plated hardware, Sunburst or Natural varnish (non-lacquer) finish.
- Bound ebony fingerboard, abalone block inlays, multiple-bound peghead, flying bird peghead inlay.
- One floating mini-humbucking pickup (some without visible polepieces).

KALAMAZOO AWARD 100TH ANNIVERSARY 1991

Two made for Japan.

SUPER 400C 50TH ANNIVERSARY 1984

BJB floating pickup, engraved heelcap, binding on back of peghead comes to point (similar to Citation binding but with no volute), Super 400 1935 50th Anniversary 1984 *engraved in abalone inlay on back of peghead, Kluson Sealfast tuners with pearl buttons.*

ES-775 CLASSIC BEAUTY 1990–93

Single-cut archtop, pointed horn, slotted-block inlay.

- 16¼-inch wide, figured laminated maple body, pointed cutaway, gold-plated hardware.
- Three-ply maple neck, bound ebony fingerboard, slotted-block inlay.
- Two humbucking pickups, four knobs, one selector switch.

■ **1978** Kalamazoo Award

ARCHTOP 1978-1994

HERB ELLIS SIGNATURE ES-165 1991–2004
Single-cut archtop, pointed horn, one humbucker.
- 16-inch full-depth archtop, pointed cutaway, tune-o-matic bridge on rosewood base, T-shaped tailpiece with zigzag wires, multiple top binding, single-bound back, gold-plated hardware.
- Mahogany neck, bound rosewood fingerboard, double-parallelogram inlay, decal model name and logo on peghead (crown peghead inlay, pearl logo from 2002).
- One humbucking pickup, two knobs (one floating mini-humbucking pickup, control knob in pickguard from 2002).

WES MONTGOMERY SIGNATURE 1993–current
Single-cut archtop, one humbucker.
- 17-inch single-cutaway archtop, maple back and sides, carved spruce top, gold-plated hardware, Vintage Sunburst or Wine Red finish.
- Bound ebony fingerboard, pearl block inlays.
- One humbucking pickup in neck position.

L-5CES CENTENNIAL (Dec. 1994 guitar of the month)
Ebony finish, serial number in raised numerals on tailpiece, numeral 1 of serial number formed by row of diamonds, letter i of logo dotted by inlaid diamond, gold medallion on back of peghead, gold-plated hardware, limited run of no more than 101 (serial-numbered from 1894–1994), packaged with 16x20 framed photograph and gold signet ring.

■ **1993** Wes Montgomery Signature

ARCHTOP CLASSIC

If the Les Paul Standard is the pinnacle of Gibson rock'n'roll electrics, then the ES-175 has the same standing in the jazz world. When it debuted in 1949 it was the first Gibson electric to feature a pointed Florentine cutaway and one of the first electric Spanish guitars to feature, in 1957, twin humbucking pickups. Its laminated construction ensured it remained affordable compared to the carved solid wood archtops; its trimmer dimensions meant it was more manageable, too. A true workhorse for jazz, fusion, and even rock players, the ES-175 is a true classic.

L-5 STUDIO 1996–current

Single-cut archtop, black binding, dot inlays.
- 17-inch wide maple body, rounded cutaway, solid carved spruce top, tune-o-matic bridge, trapeze tailpiece, "ice cube marble" pattern celluloid pickguard, black binding on top and back, Translucent Blue or Translucent Red finish.
- Unbound ebony fingerboard, dot inlays, pearl logo.
- Two humbuckers, four knobs, switch on cutaway bout.

ES-5 REISSUE 1996–2006

Three P-90 pickups.

SWITCHMASTER REISSUE 1996–2006

Three humbucking pickups.

SWITCHMASTER REISSUE ALNICO 1996–2006

Three Alnico V pickups.

WES MONTGOMERY HEART 1997

Reissue of one of Wes Montgomery's personal L-5s, heart-shaped pearl inlay with engraved Wes Montgomery in cutaway bout, special leather case, certificate.
Production: 25.

SWINGMASTER ES-175 1999

Two P-90 pickups, ebony fingerboard, pearloid trapezoid inlays, optional Bigsby vibrato, Custom Coral, Daddy-O Yellow, Mint Green, or Outa-Sight White finish.

STEVE HOWE SIGNATURE ES-175 2001–current

Based on Howe's 1964, multiple top binding, pearl-inlaid ebony bridge base, zigzag tailpiece, nickel-plated hardware.

L-5 SIGNATURE 2001–05

Single-cut archtop, rounded horn, scaled-down L-5.
- 15½-inch single-cutaway archtop, 2 ⅜-inch deep, rounded cutaway, tune-o-matic bridge, multiple top binding, single-bound back, gold-plated hardware.
- 25½-inch scale, bound ebony fingerboard, pearl block inlays, flowerpot peghead inlay.
- Two humbucking pickups.

ES-175 AGED REISSUE 2002–04

Zigzag tailpiece, aged hardware.

HERB ELLIS SIGNATURE ES-165 PLUS 2002–04

Curly top, removable f-hole inserts, two humbucking pickups mounted in top, four knobs, selector switch on upper bass bout.

LEE RITENOUR L-5 SIGNATURE 2003–current

Single-cut archtop, rounded horn, scaled-down L-5. As L-5 Signature with floating pickup, TP-6 fine-tune tailpiece.

LEE RITENOUR L-5 2003-current

Single-cut archtop, rounded horn, fingers-style tailpiece.
- 15 ½-inch wide maple body, rounded cutaway, solid carved spruce top, compensated ebony bridge, fingers-style tailpiece, multiple top binding, gold-plated hardware.
- 25 ½-inch scale, multiple bound ebony fingerboard, pearl block inlays, flowerpot peghead inlay.
- One BJB floating pickup, single volume on pickguard.

DUANE EDDY SIGNATURE 2005–current

Single-cut archtop, moustache inlays.
- 16-inch single-cutaway hollowbody of laminated maple, 3-inch deep, f-holes, tune-o-matic bridge, Bigsby vibrato, bound top and back, nickel-plated hardware, Rockabilly Brown finish.
- Maple/walnut neck, bond ebony fingerboard, pearl moustache inlay, pearl logo.
- Two custom single-coil pickups Baggs transducer pickup under bridge, four knobs.

L-4 CES MAHOGANY 2006-current

Single-cut archtop, single ply white binding, split parallelogram inlays.
- 16-inch wide mahogany body, pointed cutaway, solid carved spruce top, tune-o-matic bridge, L-4 T-shape trapeze tailpiece, gold-plated hardware.
- Bound ebony fingerboard, split parallelogram inlays, pearl logo.
- Two humbucking pickups, four knobs, switch on upper shoulder.

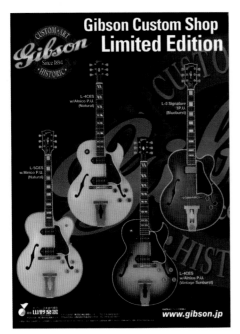

2003 press advertisement

HOWARD ROBERTS FUSION III 2006-2009
Single-cut archtop, fingers-style tailpiece.
- 14 ⅞-inch wide laminated maple body with arched top; top edge binding; large treble cutaway and thin horn; fingers-style tailpiece, tune-o-matic bridge.
- Bound rosewood fingerboard with dot inlays; Schaller Keystone tuners; "Howard Roberts Fusion" on truss-rod cover.
- Two humbuckers (490R & 490T), four knobs, switch on upper shoulder.
Gibson Custom.

ARCHTOP
1996-2011

■ **2008** ES-175 Classic

31

GOLDTOP (first version) 1952–53

*Crown fingerboard markers, two plastic-cover pickups,
bridge/tailpiece on long trapeze anchor.*

- Bound carved-top body; Gold only.
- Bound rosewood fingerboard, crown markers; "Les
  Paul Model" on headstock; plastic tuner buttons.
- Two plastic-cover six-polepiece single-coil pickups.
- Four controls (two volume, two tone) plus three-way
  selector.
- Cream plastic pickguard.
- Wrap-under bar bridge/tailpiece on long trapeze
  anchor.

*Some early examples do not have a bound fingerboard
and/or have a bridge pickup with fixing screws at two
corners rather than among polepiece screws.
Examples from 1952 have no serial number.
Some with all-gold body (rather than normal gold top
with brown back and sides) and gold back of neck.
Production: 1952 1,716; 1953 2,245 (includes some
Goldtop second version models).*

■ **1952** Les Paul Goldtop

LES PAUL GOLDTOP 1952

1952 press advertisement

1952 Les Paul Goldtop
(left-handed)

LES PAUL GOLDTOP
1952

A patent filed in 1952 by Les Paul (L.W. Polfuss) for his trapeze bridge/tailpiece, as used on the first-version Goldtop.

1952 Les Paul Goldtop

LES PAUL GOLDTOP

1952

LES PAUL: THE HEN THAT LAID THE GOLDEN LOG

Having only braved the concept of a hollowbodied archtop made from laminated woods three years before, Gibson threw itself head over heels into the concept of the electric guitar in 1952 with the release of the company's first solidbody guitar, the Les Paul. At the time it was a bold move for such a traditional guitar maker.

Scorned, laughed at, jeered, chided, and derided, the concept of the solidbody electric guitar was subject to such utter disdain in some corners that it's almost hard to believe it ever came to be at all. The ridicule and mockery would have been enough to send a less self-confident inventor running for the hills. Given our more than 55 years of perspective, though, we know it just had to be. A world without the solidbody guitar? Moreover, without the Gibson Les Paul? Unthinkable.

Of course, Rickenbacker had made limited numbers of solid electrics since the early 1930s, and Merle Travis and Paul A. Bigsby had together produced a few forward-looking, single-cutaway solidbodies in 1947–48, while Fender's coup in releasing the first mass-produced solidbody electric guitar in 1950 has been widely documented. Gibson, however, was one of the longest-established makers in the business, had set a standard with traditional players, and had a history and a reputation to consider. Little wonder its execs told young inventor, recording artist, and radio star Rhubarb Red to take a hike when he first started pestering them to turn his solid-cored electric into a reality in the early 1940s.

But you can't stop progress. Despite the mocking asides, the "canoe paddle" that an upstart company from California had introduced in 1950 was starting to catch on, and slowly but surely more guitarists were stepping toward the front of the stage alongside singers, lap-steel players, and horn soloists, and they wanted to be heard. Bright, cutting, feedback-resistant – the solidbody electric was the way to do it. You can almost hear the phone call: "Uh, Mr. Paul? This is Gibson. We were just wondering if you wouldn't mind popping back in for another little talk about that 'log' contraption of yours …?"

Rather than following Fender's bolt-together, plank-bodied standards, Gibson approached the solidbody electric from the perspective of a skilled, archtop guitar-maker. It used a carved maple cap atop the solid mahogany back, and a glued-in neck that, after the first few unbound examples, would carry a bound rosewood fingerboard. The model, therefore, was already more recognizable in feel and appearance to players familiar with Gibson's hollowbody archtops, but was entirely radical all the same—reflected in its gold metallic finish.

Over the course of the decade, the Les Paul would evolve into the most desirable collector's item on the vintage market: the Sunburst Standard of 1958–60. Along the way it gained an improved wrapover bridge (1953), then a tune-o-matic bridge (1955), humbucking pickups (1957), and finally that hallowed finish in 1958. Eight years down the road it finally proved just how far ahead of its time it was by failing to rack up satisfactory sales, and Gibson radically altered the Les Paul in 1961 to make it the double-cutaway, all-mahogany-bodied guitar that would soon and forever after be known as the SG. By the mid 1960s, however, the fat, plummy, full-throated, and long-sustaining Les Paul started to show what it could really do in the hands of a number of British and American blues-rockers, and by the late 1960s and early '70s was established as the favored tool of wailing, hard-rocking lead players in particular, a position from which it has never really been toppled.

■ **1954** Les Paul Goldtop

GOLDTOP (second version) 1953-55

Angled one-piece bridge/tailpiece.

- Bound carved-top body, Gold only.
- Bound rosewood fingerboard, crown markers: "Les Paul Model" on headstock; plastic tuner buttons.
- Two plastic-cover six polepiece single-coil pickups.
- Four controls (two volume, two tone) plus three-way selector.
- Cream plastic pickguard.
- Wrap-over bar bridge/tailpiece.

Some with all-gold body and back of neck.

Production: 1953 2,245 (includes some Goldtop first version model); 1954 1,504; 1955 862 (includes some Goldtop third version models).

■ **1953** Les Paul Goldtop

LES PAUL GOLDTOP 1953

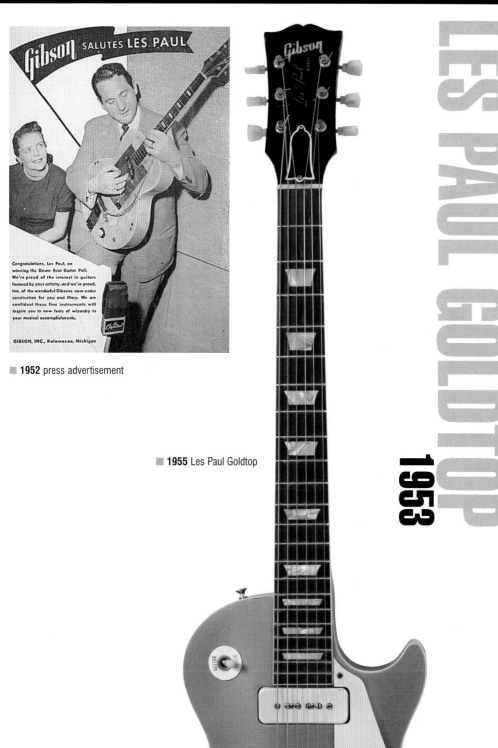

Gibson SALUTES LES PAUL

Congratulations, Les Paul, on winning the Down Beat Guitar Poll. We're proud of the interest in guitars fostered by your artistry, and we're proud, too, of the wonderful Gibsons now under construction for you and Mary. We are confident these fine instruments will inspire you to new feats of wizardry in your musical accomplishments.

GIBSON, INC., Kalamazoo, Michigan

1952 press advertisement

1955 Les Paul Goldtop

LES PAUL GOLDTOP

1953

Rear of all-gold version

1954 Les Paul
Goldtop all-gold

LES PAUL GOLDTOP 1953-1955

SOLID WOOD IS GOOD

Gibson could never have predicted the future success of the guitar that is now simply referred to as the Les Paul. The original mahogany/maple-topped solidbody electric guitar defines the Gibson electric sound to generation after generation of players. The construction style and materials marked Gibson as one of the foundations for modern guitar makers—the other, of course, was Fender.

There are few electric guitar makers today who don't reference the design in their catalogues of instruments: from Paul Reed Smith, to Schecter, ESP or Ibanez, you'll find designs based on the Les Paul recipe.

But in terms of wood supply, things are very different today from the 1950a. Companies struggle to find mahogany light enough to use for the bulky design; even Gibson now 'weight relieves' and 'chambers' many of its Les Pauls to combat this problem, and numerous other types of mahogany-like woods are used, especially by far-eastern manufacturers as the supplies of lightweight south American mahogany become more expensive by the day.

The Les Paul's maple cap, originally hidden under the goldtop finish, has come to signify opulence and quality. Famously, Paul Reed Smith put curly maple back on the map from the mid 1980s. Today, the quality of the figuring, often enhanced by colour-stained finish processes, determines the price and desirability of the instrument for many. Of course, that has nothing to do with the sound. Many lower-priced Les Paul-alikes simply use a very thin figured maple veneer to create the correct appearance; highly figured maple, like mahogany, is harder to find and more expensive today.

Yet the balance between the two different woods is crucial to the tone of a good Les Paul. The bulk of the mahogany body provides the dark, velveteen sustain; the maple cap expands the frequencies, adding highs and lows, clarity, and definition: a major reason why this design remains and indeed defines the sound of the solidbody electric guitar.

THEY'RE TOPS...LES PAUL, MARY FORD AND THEIR GIBSONS

Gibson Inc., Kalamazoo, Mich.

Its wondrous tone, unique features and beautiful styling have recorded a hit from coast to coast for the Les Paul Model. Guitarists marvel at the new design and playing ease. listeners enthuse over the exciting tonal qualities and sharp contrasts. Like its designer, the Gibson Les Paul Model is "star quality" in every respect.

1953 press advertisement

GOLDTOP (third version) 1955–57

Six-saddle bridge plus separate bar tailpiece, two plastic-cover pickups.
Similar to Goldtop second version, except:
• Six-saddle bridge plus separate bar tailpiece.
Production: 1955 862 (includes some Goldtop second version models); 1956 920; 1957 598 (includes some Goldtop fourth version models).

■ **1957** Les Paul Goldtop

LES PAUL GOLDTOP 1955

AN INTONATION REVELATION: THE TUNE-O-MATIC BRIDGE

Prior to the arrival of the tune-o-matic bridge in 1954, Gibson electrics carried either a floating bridge with compensated one-piece rosewood or ebony saddle, a rudimentary trapeze tailpiece with integral bridge bar, or a stud-mounted wraparound bridge, each of which offered only the crudest overall intonation and height-adjustment facilities. When the tune-o-matic bridge, also known as the ABR-1, first appeared—initially on the black Les Paul Custom and then on the Goldtop Les Paul "Standard" the following year—it was a true revelation in intonation and set a standard for simplicity and functionality for bridges of its ilk.

The tune-o-matic was designed by Gibson president Ted McCarty himself, and on solidbody guitars was partnered with a separate 'stud' or 'stop-bar' tailpiece, which was essentially a modified version of the wraparound bridge. The pair provided both a firm seating for the strings at the body-end termination point of their speaking length and a facility for adjusting the individual length of each via a sliding steel saddle and adjustment screw. Finally a player could fine-tune intonation for himself, in a matter of minutes, and easily adjust it again when atmospheric conditions required periodic alterations. This solid, well-anchored piece of hardware also yields good coupling between string and body, which results in solid tone and excellent sustain. Gibson has also employed the tune-o-matic bridge on a number of archtop

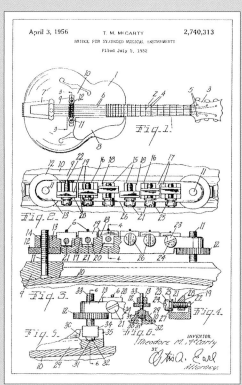

electrics over the years, where it is partnered either with a trapeze tailpiece on hollowbody models such as the ES-175, or a stop-bar tailpiece on semi-acoustic models with solid center blocks, such as the ES-335.

■ **1956** Tune-o-matic patent

■ **1956** Les Paul Goldtop

GOLDTOP (fourth version) 1957-58

Two humbuckers, six-saddle bridge plus separate bar tailpiece.

- Bound carved-top body, Gold only.
- Bound rosewood fingerboard, crown markers: "Les Paul Model" on headstock; plastic tuner buttons.
- Two metal-cover humbucker pickups.
- Four controls (two volume, two tone) plus three-way selector.
- Cream plastic pickguard.
- Six-saddle bridge plus separate bar tailpiece.

Finish changed to Sunburst in 1958: see later. Standard first version *entry.*

Production: 1957 598 (includes some Goldtop third version model); 1958 434 (includes some sunburst Standard models).

■ **1957** Les Paul Goldtop

LES PAUL GOLDTOP
1957

BUCKING THE HUM

At the urging of company president Ted McCarty, Gibson technicians Seth Lover and Walt Fuller began working on the idea of a hum-rejecting guitar pickup in 1955. Lover, a radio and electronics expert, had worked for Gibson on and off in the 1940s, and, after rejoining the company in 1952, had developed the single-coil Alnico pickup, as used briefly—but most famously—in the neck position of the Les Paul Custom, as well as on a few archtop models. Gibson's main pickup of the day, the P-90, had a full, fat, distinctive tone, but, like all single-coil pickups, was prone to picking up unwanted hum and noise from external electrical sources. Being familiar with tube amplifiers, Lover was well aware of how a 'choke' (a coil or small transformer) could help filter out hum induced by an amp's power supply, and began working toward applying the same logic to guitar pickups. His solution took the form of a double-coil pickup, in which the two coils were placed side by side, wired together out of phase with each other, and given opposite magnetic polarities. As a result, this configuration rejected much of the hum that single-coil pickups reproduce— which is eliminated when two like but reverse-phase signals are summed together—but passed along all of the guitar tone. Lover also added a thin nickel cover to the pickups, to further reject electrostatic interference. In addition to the benefits regarding noise rejection, the double-coil pickup's side-by-side coil alignment produced a bigger and rounder sound than that of the average single-coil pickup.

Gibson dubbed Lover's new creation the humbucker for its ability to "buck" electrical hum and, aware that it was a unique device in the fledgling industry, applied for a US patent to protect the design. The first humbucker used by Gibson in production was a triple-coil version that appeared on lap steel guitars in 1956. When the now-familiar double-coil humbuckers arrived in 1957 on the Goldtop and Custom Les Paul models, and on archtop electrics such as the ES-175, they carried stickers that read "Patent Applied For", to ward off would-be copyists while the company awaited the patent. Pickups of the era, therefore, are given the nickname PAF, which applies to any pickup carrying the "Patent Applied For" sticker all Gibson humbuckers wore between 1957 and late 1962.

The first patent-number pickups, as the post-PAF humbuckers have come to be known, were almost identical to the final stocks of PAFs, which had become fairly consistent in their construction by 1962. But earlier examples of the late 1950s had varied quite widely and, as any collector knows, there are great-greater-greatest versions out there. Gibson used a range of Alnico magnet types in constructing these pickups—from Alnico II through Alnico V, largely determined by whatever stocks the company could lay its hands on in the day—and, because coil winding was a hand-guided process, pickup coils were wound to different numbers of turns, too, and therefore differing strengths. In addition to these constructional variables, another purely cosmetic variable has sent many collectors in search of the rare and ultra-rare examples: when Gibson ran short of black plastic coil formers, or bobbins, it bought in cream stock, so double-cream and black-and-cream PAFs – dubbed "zebra stripes" – can also be found beneath some pickups' metal covers.

PAFs are not really much hotter, in electrical terms, than the average P-90, and the two different pickup types from the same era generally show similar DC resistance readings in the 7.5k to 8.5k ohms range. But the humbucker's broader sonic window sends a meatier spread of frequencies to the amp, which creates a fatter, warmer sound and can also drive an amp more easily into distortion if needed. However, a good PAF still has good treble response and excellent definition.

1978 press advertisement

GOLDTOP (fifth version) 1968-69

- Bound carved-top body, Gold only.
- Bound rosewood fingerboard, crown markers: "Les Paul Model" on headstock; plastic tuner buttons.
- Two plastic-cover six-polepiece single-coil pickups.
- Four controls (two volume, two tone) plus three-way selector.
- Cream plastic pickguard.
- Six-saddle bridge plus separate bar tailpiece.

With wide binding in cutaway. Confusingly referred to in Gibson literature as "Standard" model.
Production: 1968 1,224; 1969 2,751.

GOLDTOP (sixth version) 1971-72

- Bound carved-top body, Gold only.
- Bound rosewood fingerboard, crown markers: "Les Paul Model" on headstock; plastic tuner buttons.
- Two plastic-cover six-polepiece single-coil pickups.
- Four controls (two volume, two tone) plus three-way selector.
- Cream plastic pickguard.
- Wrap-over bar bridge/tailpiece.

Based on Goldtop second version (one-piece bridge/tailpiece), but with Gibson logo on pickups. Some examples with extra plastic ring around pickup covers. Also referred to in literature as "Standard 58."
Production: 1971 25; 1972 1,046; 1973 4; 1974 1.

1957 Les Paul Goldtop
(left-handed)

LES PAUL GOLDTOP 1968-1971

LES PAUL GOLDTOP

1968-1971

■ **1958** Les Paul Goldtop

■ **1968** Les Paul Goldtop

GOLDTOP 30TH ANNIVERSARY 1982–83

Anniversary model based on Goldtop fourth version but with "Thirtieth Anniversary" inlaid into position marker at 19th fret, Gold finish all-around. Serial-numbered with prefix A, B, or C.

■ **1982** Les Paul Goldtop 30th Anniversary

LES PAUL GOLDTOP 1982-1990

GOLDTOP 57 REISSUE 1983–90, 1993–current

Based on Goldtop fourth version. *"R7" stamped in control cavity from 1993. Known by various names through the years, including* Goldtop Reissue *(1983–90). Aged versions available, known as* Aged, *with optional reissue case and amplifier (2001),* Custom Authentic *(2002), and* VOS *Vintage Original Spec (2006–current). Also with optional dark-stained back, known as* Goldtop 57 Darkback *(2000–current); aged version available, known as* VOS *Vintage Original Spec (2006–current).*
Custom Shop.

GOLDTOP 56 REISSUE 1990–current

Based on Goldtop third version, *except plastic-covered humbucker pickups (visually identical to single-coils) through 1996, then single-coils. "R6" stamped in control cavity from 1993. Known by various names through the years, including* Goldtop Reissue *(1990). Aged versions available, known as* Custom Authentic *(2001) and* VOS *Vintage Original Spec (2006–current).*
Custom Shop.

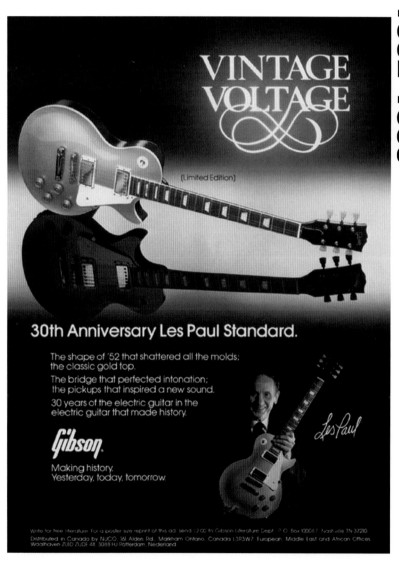

■ **1982** press advertisement

LES PAUL GOLDTOP 1982-1990

CLASSIC CENTENNIAL 1990–2008

"Classic" on truss-rod cover.

- Bound carved-top body; sunbursts or colours (Gold only in 1998).
- Bound rosewood fingerboard, crown markers; "Les Paul Model" on headstock; "Classic" on truss-rod cover; plastic tuner buttons.
- Two coverless humbuckers.
- Four controls (two volume, two tone) plus three-way selector.
- Cream plastic pickguard with "1960" logo.
- Six-saddle bridge plus separate bar tailpiece.

Vintage-style inked five or six-digit serial number, with first digit or first two digits corresponding to year of manufacture.

Also 1994 "100 Years" special.

Also Guitar Of The Week models 2007, production 400 each: Fireburst finish, Ripple-effect finish designed by artist Tom Morgan; antiqued appointments, H-90 pickups (stacked double-coil), Iced Tea Sunburst; antiqued appointments, zebra wood body; Mahogany top, antiqued appointments, faded cherry; Mahogany top, antiqued appointments, scroll logo, vintage sunburst.

40TH ANNIVERSARY GOLDTOP 1992–93

Similar to Goldtop third version, except:

- Black finish.
- Ebony fingerboard; "40th Anniversary" inlaid into position marker at 12th fret and on rear of headstock.
- Pickups, although visually similar to single-coils, are actually humbuckers.
- Gold-plated hardware.

Custom Shop.

1994 Les Paul Goldtop Classic Centennial 100 Years

LES PAUL GOLDTOP 1990-2010

GOLDTOP 54 REISSUE 1997–current

Based on Goldtop second version. "R4" stamped in control cavity. Known by various names through the years. Aged version available, known as VOS Vintage Original Spec (2006–current).
Custom Shop.

GOLDTOP 57 MARY FORD 1997

Based on Goldtop fourth version, except gold-stencilled leaves on pickguard, custom armrest.
Custom Shop.

GOLDTOP 52 REISSUE 1999–2005

Based on Goldtop first version. "R2" stamped in control cavity. Known by various names through the years. Aged version available, known as Aged (2002, production 50).
Custom Shop.

DICKEY BETTS 57 GOLDTOP 2001

Similar to Goldtop 57 reissue, except aged by Tom Murphy; replica Dickey Betts strap and faux alligator hardshell case included.
Custom Shop; production 114, numbered with DB prefix.

DICKEY BETTS 57 REDTOP 2002–03

Similar to Goldtop 57 reissue, except red top.
Custom Shop; production 55, numbered with DBR prefix.

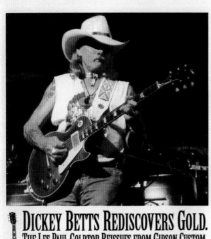

PETE TOWNSHEND DELUXE GOLDTOP 2006

Similar to Pete Townshend Deluxe #9 (p.201), except numeral "3" decal on front; gold top.
Custom Shop.

50TH ANNIVERSARY STANDARD GOLDTOP 2007–08

All-gold finish, gold pickguard, gold-plated head-plate with etched crown. "50th" serial numbered with 57S prefix.
Custom Shop; production 157.

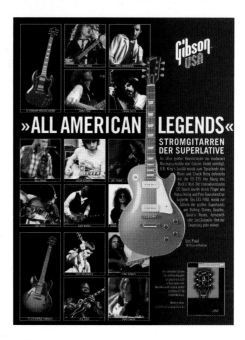

50TH ANNIVERSARY 1958 MURPHY-AGED GOLDTOP 2007–08

50th Anniversary banner on pickguard, Gold finish; aged by Tom Murphy.
Custom Shop; production 100.

JOE BONAMASSA 2008–current

"Bonamassa" on truss-rod cover. Similar to Goldtop 57 reissue, except:
- Antique gold finish.
- "Bonamassa" on truss-rod cover; Grover tuners with kidney-bean buttons.
- Black pickup surrounds, pickguard, and switch washer.
- Two amber knobs, two metal-capped knobs.
Custom Shop.

JOE BONAMASSA STUDIO 2011-current

Un-aged, full-gloss Studio version of Joe Bonamassa signature Goldtop with black back, sides, and neck. Burst Bucker 2 & 3 humbuckers; two amber knobs, two metal-capped knobs.
Limited run of 600 pieces.

SLASH GOLDTOP 2008

Coverless humbucking pickups, TonePro six-saddle bridge, vintage Kluson Deluxe-style tuners, Slash graphic with top hat on headstock (does not say "Les Paul"). Custom Shop; production 1,000.

LES PAUL TRIBUTE 1952 2010-11

- Modern replica of original 1952 Goldtop (first version). "Prototype" stamped on headstock back.

LES PAUL PIEZO 2010-11

Maple neck, active EMG humbuckers, LR Baggs piezo-loaded tune-o-matic bridge, gold hardware, dual outputs. Goldtop finish only.

1955 STOCK 1955 LES PAUL GOLDTOP 2010

- Two P-90 pickups; tune-o-matic bridge and stop bar tailpiece.
- Similar to Goldtop third version from run of guitars: 1955 Les Paul Custom Exclusives celebrating 1955, the "Year of Innovation."

Gibson Custom special run.

1955 LES PAUL GOLDTOP WRAPTAIL 2010

- Two P-90 pickups; wrap-over bridge.
- Similar to Goldtop third version from run of guitars: 1955 Les Paul Custom Exclusives celebrating 1955, the "Year of Innovation."

Gibson Custom special run.

■ **2008** Les Paul Goldtop Darkback

LES PAUL GOLDTOP 2010

LES PAUL GOLDTOP 2008-2010

2009 Les Paul Joe Bonamassa

2010 Les Paul Tribute 1952

2010 Les Paul Studio '60s Tribute Goldtop

REISSUES: PAY YOUR MONEY AND CHOOSE...

Unless you're lucky enough to have the money to buy an original 1950s Goldtop, you'll have to settle for some kind of reissue. Today, the line is very blurred, however, between historically accurate reissues, tribute models, even signatures and Inspired By… models, all based on Gibson's original Goldtop Les Paul.

Today, the most historically accurate goldtops are made by Gibson's Custom division. There's the 1954 Les Paul Goldtop with its wrap-over bridge and dual P90s. The 1956 Les Paul Goldtop VOS retains the P-90s but adds the historically correct tune-o-matic and stop tailpiece. Finally, the fully formed 1957 Les Paul Goldtop VOS features replicas of the fabled Gibson humbucker, and the model is also offered with the originally rare 'darkback' black finish.

If that's the second, third and fourth version of the 1950s Les Paul Goldtop covered, you have to move into Gibson USA to find the original first version, replicated as the Les Paul Tribute 1952 with its distinctive trapeze tailpiece/bridge. The famous disagreement between Les Paul and Gibson meant that the strings wrapped under the bridge on the original version; here, however, as a tribute to Les Paul, who passed away in 2009, the strings wrap over the bridge as Les intended so he could damp the strings with the palm of his right hand. It might not be totally accurate, but that's one thing about reissues: history can be changed … in this case for the better.

HOT-MOD 1955 LES PAUL GOLDTOP 2010

- Two humbucking pickups; tune-o-matic bridge and stop bar tailpiece.
- Similar to Goldtop third version but with retro-fitted humbuckers from run of guitars: 1955 Les Paul Custom Exclusives celebrating 1955, the "Year of Innovation."

Gibson Custom special run.

HOT-MOD 1955 LES PAUL GOLDTOP WRAPTAIL 2010

As Hot-Mod 1955 Les Paul Goldtop but with wraparound bridge.
Gibson Custom special run.

LES PAUL STUDIO 50S TRIBUTE 2010-current

- P-90s, unbound rosewood fingerboard, trapezoid inlays, worn Goldtop finish.
- Chambered mahogany body, carved maple top, natural edge "binding," Nashville tune-o-matic bridge and stop tailpiece, chrome-plated hardware.
- Unbound rosewood fingerboard, '50s profile mahogany neck, vintage-style tulip button tuners.
- P-90 distressed single-coils, four knobs, pickup toggle switch on upper shoulder.

Also available in four other worn colors. Limited run.

LES PAUL STUDIO 60S TRIBUTE 2011-current

As Les Paul Studio '50s Tribute but with 1960-style SlimTaper neck profile. Worn Goldtop finish plus four other worn colour finishes.
Limited run.

▓ **2010** press advertisement

LES PAUL GOLDTOP 2010-2011

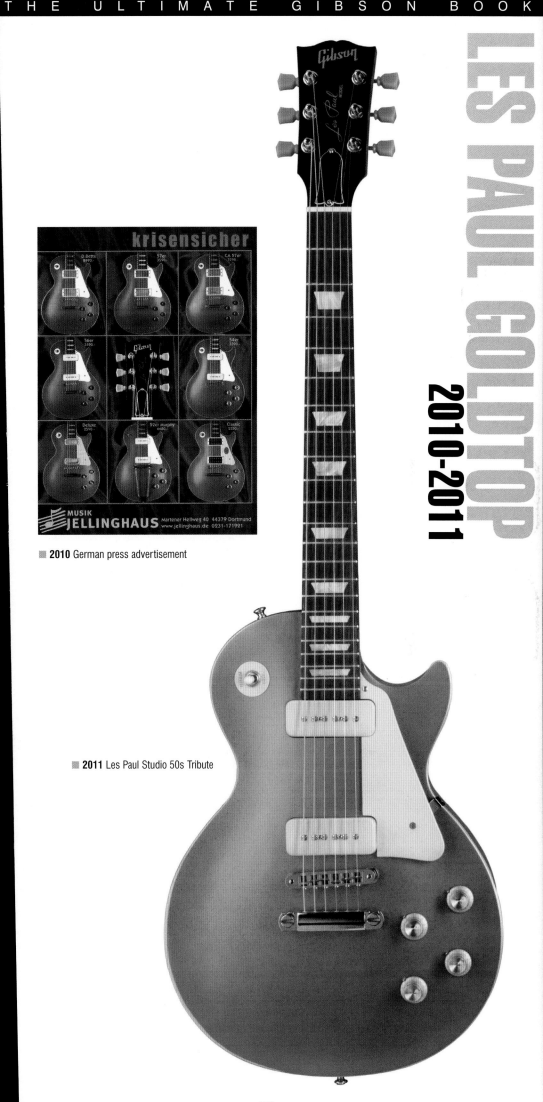

LES PAUL GOLDTOP 2010-2011

2010 German press advertisement

2011 Les Paul Studio 50s Tribute

CUSTOM (first version) 1954–57

Block fingerboard markers, split-diamond headstock inlay, "Les Paul Custom" on truss-rod cover, two plastic-cover pickups.

- Bound carved-top all-mahogany body; Black only.
- Bound ebony fingerboard, block markers; split-diamond inlay on headstock; "Les Paul Custom" on truss-rod cover.
- Two plastic-cover six-polepiece single-coil pickups (neck unit with oblong polepieces; bridge unit with round polepieces).
- Four controls (two volume, two tone) plus three-way selector.
- Black laminated plastic pickguard.
- Six-saddle bridge plus separate bar tailpiece.
- Gold-plated hardware.

Production: 1954 94; 1955 355; 1956 489; 1957 283 (includes some Custom second version models).

■ **1954** Les Paul Custom prototype

LES PAUL CUSTOM 1954

"The Fretless Wonder"
THE INCOMPARABLE
LES PAUL CUSTOM GUITAR

FLEXIBILITY FOR ANY DEMANDS

■ **1954** press advertisement

■ **1954** Les Paul Custom

CUSTOM (second version) 1957–61

Three humbucker pickups. Similar to Custom first
version, *except:*
• Three metal-cover humbucker pickups.
*Some with two humbucker pickups. Shape changed in
1961: see later* SG/Les Paul Custom *entry. Also 35th
Anniversary version with appropriate inlay on headstock
(1989–90): see later* 35th Anniversary *entry.
Production: 1957 283 (includes some Custom first
version models); 1958 256; 1959 246; 1960 189; 1961
513 (includes some SG/Les Paul Custom models).*

1957 press advertisement

■ **1957** Les Paul Custom
first version

LES PAUL CUSTOM 1957

1957 Les Paul Custom owned by Keith Richards

1957 Les Paul Custom second version

1960 Les Paul Custom

CUSTOM (third version) 1968–current

Two humbuckers. Similar to Custom second version, *except:*
• Maple top cap (53 made with Brazilian rosewood top, 1975–76), mahogany back; sunbursts, Natural, or colors.
• Two metal-cover humbucker pickups.

Also: three-humbucker version (various periods); versions with nickel-plated hardware (1976–83, 1996) or chrome-plated hardware (1983–87); maple fingerboard version (1975–81).

Production: Kalamazoo-made: 1968 433; 1969 2,353; 1970 2,612; 1971 3,201; 1972 4,002; 1973 7,232; 1974 7,563; 1975 7,448; 1976 4,323; 1977 3,133; 1978 10,744; 1979 1,624. Figures not available for large Nashville production started 1975 and continuing to current. At the time of writing this is a Custom Shop model.

1975 press advertisement

LES PAUL CUSTOM 1968

1968 Les Paul Custom

1997 Les Paul Custom

1990 Les Paul Custom

LES PAUL CUSTOM

1968

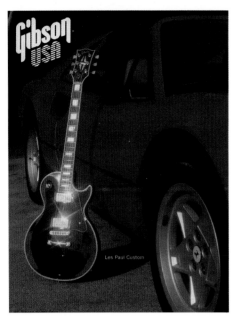

■ **1986** press advertisement

CUSTOM 54 LTD EDITION 1972–73

Reissue based on Custom first version, *identifiable by
serial number prefixed with LE.
Production: 1972 60; 1973 1090; 1975 3; 1977 1.*

CUSTOM 20TH ANNIVERSARY 1974

Anniversary model based on Custom third version *but
with "Twentieth Anniversary" inlaid into position marker
at 15th fret. Sunburst or colours.*

■ **1974** Les Paul Custom

LES PAUL CUSTOM 1972-1989

CUSTOM 25TH ANNIVERSARY 1977

Anniversary model based on Custom third version—
*even though 1977 was 25th anniversary of Les Paul
Standard—but with "25th Anniversary" engraved on
tailpiece, "Les Paul" signature on pickguard, chrome-
plated hardware, metallic silver.*

CUSTOM BLACK BEAUTY 82 1982–83

*Combines features of Custom and Standard, multiple
body binding, unbound ebony fingerboard with crown
inlay, gold-plated hardware.*

CUSTOM LITE 1987–89

Contoured, thinner body; block fingerboard markers.
- Bound carved-top thinner body with contoured back;
  Sunburst, Black, or Pink finishes.
- Bound ebony fingerboard, block markers; split-
  diamond inlay on headstock.
- Two metal-cover humbucker pickups.
- Three controls (two volumes, one tone) plus three-
  way selector (two controls plus three-way selector
  1989) and mini-switch.
- Black laminated plastic pickguard.
- Six-saddle bridge, separate bar tailpiece (locking
  vibrato option).
- Gold-plated hardware (black-plated 1989).

CUSTOM LITE SHOWCASE EDITION 1988

Similar to Custom Lite, *except plastic-cover EMG pickups,
active electronics, gold top, gold-plated hardware.
Production 250.*

CUSTOM SHOWCASE EDITION 1988

*Guitar Of The Month series, EMG pickups; ruby finish.
Custom Shop; production 200 for US distribution, 50
for overseas.*

35TH ANNIVERSARY CUSTOM 1989–90

Anniversary model based on Custom second version,
*but with "35th Anniversary" in bar of split-diamond
inlay on headstock.*

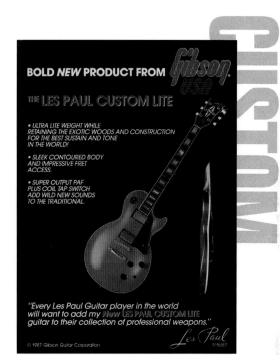

BOLD *NEW* PRODUCT FROM *Gibson* USA

THE LES PAUL CUSTOM LITE

- ULTRA LITE WEIGHT WHILE
  RETAINING THE EXOTIC WOODS AND CONSTRUCTION
  FOR THE BEST SUSTAIN AND TONE
  IN THE WORLD!

- SLEEK CONTOURED BODY
  AND IMPRESSIVE FRET
  ACCESS.

- SUPER OUTPUT PAF
  PLUS COIL TAP SWITCH
  ADD WILD NEW SOUNDS
  TO THE TRADITIONAL.

"Every Les Paul Guitar player in the world
will want to add my *New* LES PAUL CUSTOM LITE
guitar to their collection of professional weapons."

Les Paul 1/16/87

© 1987 Gibson Guitar Corporation

■ **1987** press advertisement

■ **1989** Les Paul 35th Anniversary Custom

■ **1988** press advertisement

CUSTOM 54 REISSUE 1991–current
Reissue based on Custom first version. *Optional Bigsby.
"R4" stamped in control cavity from 1993. Known by
various names through the years, including* Black
Beauty 54. *Aged versions available, known as* VOS
*Vintage Original Spec (2006–current).
Custom Shop.*

■ **1992** Les Paul Custom

LES PAUL CUSTOM
1991-1994

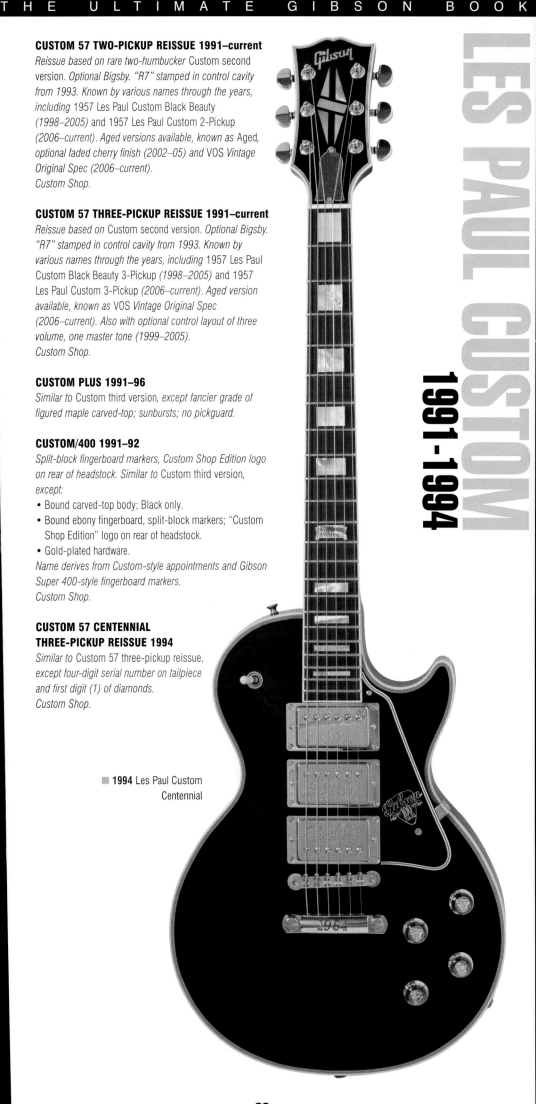

CUSTOM 57 TWO-PICKUP REISSUE 1991–current

Reissue based on rare two-humbucker Custom second version. Optional Bigsby. "R7" stamped in control cavity from 1993. Known by various names through the years, including 1957 Les Paul Custom Black Beauty *(1998–2005) and* 1957 Les Paul Custom 2-Pickup *(2006–current). Aged versions available, known as* Aged, *optional faded cherry finish (2002–05) and* VOS Vintage Original Spec *(2006–current).*
Custom Shop.

CUSTOM 57 THREE-PICKUP REISSUE 1991–current

Reissue based on Custom second version. *Optional Bigsby. "R7" stamped in control cavity from 1993. Known by various names through the years, including* 1957 Les Paul Custom Black Beauty 3-Pickup *(1998–2005) and* 1957 Les Paul Custom 3-Pickup *(2006–current). Aged version available, known as* VOS *Vintage Original Spec (2006–current). Also with optional control layout of three volume, one master tone (1999–2005).*
Custom Shop.

CUSTOM PLUS 1991–96

Similar to Custom third version, *except fancier grade of figured maple carved-top; sunbursts; no pickguard.*

CUSTOM/400 1991–92

Split-block fingerboard markers, Custom Shop Edition logo on rear of headstock. Similar to Custom third version, *except:*
- Bound carved-top body; Black only.
- Bound ebony fingerboard, split-block markers; "Custom Shop Edition" logo on rear of headstock.
- Gold-plated hardware.

Name derives from Custom-style appointments and Gibson Super 400-style fingerboard markers.
Custom Shop.

CUSTOM 57 CENTENNIAL
THREE-PICKUP REISSUE 1994

Similar to Custom 57 three-pickup reissue, *except four-digit serial number on tailpiece and first digit (1) of diamonds.*
Custom Shop.

■ **1994** Les Paul Custom
Centennial

LES PAUL CUSTOM 1991-1994

Ace Frehley and his
Signature LP4 Paul

Only a Gibson Is Good Enough™

The Ace Frehley Les Paul

• Lightning bolt inlays and Ace peghead image for the true Ace look

• Three DiMarzio pickups and ebony fingerboard for the ultimate Ace sound

• Figured maple top and '59 rounded neck for classic Gibson style and playability

Call 1-800-4-GIBSON for a free brochure: "How to Buy an Electric Guitar." Visit us @ http://www.gibson.com   641 Massman Drive • Nashville, TN 37210

■ **1997** press advertisement

■ **2000** Les Paul Custom

LES PAUL CUSTOM 1997-2008

ACE FREHLEY 1997–2000

Three white-coil pickups, Ace Frehley graphic on headstock. Similar to Custom, *except:*
- Bound carved-top body; flamed maple top cap; cherry sunburst.
- Lightning-bolt markers; signature inlaid at 12th fret; Ace playing-card on truss-rod cover (chrome for Custom Shop run; black plastic for production version); Frehley face on headstock.
- Three coverless pickups with white coils.
- Four controls (two volume, two tone) plus three-way selector.
- *Custom Shop version (1997), production 300, numbered with ACE prefix; USA factory version (1997–2000) numbered with regular eight-digit serial.*

MAHOGANY CUSTOM 1998

Similar to Custom second version, *except one-piece mahogany body (no top cap); faded cherry finish; three metal-cover humbucker pickups.*

CUSTOM 68 FIGUREDTOP 2000–current

Similar to Custom second version, *except figured maple top; Antique Natural, Butterscotch, Heritage Cherry Sunburst, or Triburst (only offered in Ebony or Vintage White; VOS Vintage Original Spec aging treatment, 2009–current). Aged version available, known as* Custom Authentic *(2002–05). Custom Shop.*

PETER FRAMPTON CUSTOM 2000–current

Three coverless humbucker pickups, "Peter Frampton" on 12th fret marker. Similar to Custom third version, *except:*
- "Peter Frampton" on 12th fret marker.
- Three coverless humbucker pickups.
- Custom-wired selector switch (no visible difference).
- No pickguard.
- Strap-locking endpin.
Numbered with PF prefix.
Custom Shop.

▨ **2000** press advertisement

JOHN SYKES CUSTOM 2007

Mirror pickguard, chrome pickup frames. Similar to 1978-period Custom third version, *except:*
- Ebony finish (aged or gloss).
- Brass nut.
- Two coverless humbucker pickups with chrome mounting frames.
- Mirror-finish pickguard.
- Bridge-pickup tone control disabled.
- *Custom Shop.*

SUPER CUSTOM 1984 prototypes, 2007 production

Curly maple top, back, and side veneers, one covered humbucker and one coverless humbucker, slashed-block markers.

CUSTOM 25 2008

Flame-maple headstock veneer, no headstock ornament.
- Bound carved-top body; Sunburst.
- Bound ebony fingerboard, slashed-block markers, flame-maple headstock overlay.
- Two metal-cover humbucker pickups.
- Four controls (two volume, two tone) plus three-way selector and mini-switch.
- Flame maple pickguard.
- Six-saddle bridge, fine-tune tailpiece.
- Gold-plated hardware.

JIMMY PAGE CUSTOM 2008

Similar to 1960-period Custom second version, *with three pickups, '60s-style thin neck profile, push/pull tone pot for bridge-pickup coil split; option of separate bar or Bigsby tailpiece; Vintage Original Spec aging treatment. Custom Shop; production 500.*

MICK JONES CUSTOM 2008–current

Two mini switches between standard control knobs. Similar to Custom third version, *except:*
- Aged Ebony finish.
- Schaller tuners.
- Schaller strap-lock buttons, black metal jackplate.
- Two coverless humbucker pickups.
- Two mini switches for pickup on/off selection.
Custom Shop.

STEVE JONES CUSTOM 2008–current

Two girlie decals on top. Similar to Custom third version, *except:*
- Carved maple top, decals of girl sitting on vinyl LP and girl playing uke; White finish aged to Ivory.
- Two coverless humbucker pickups.
- Late-'60s style 'witch hat' knobs.
- Aged hardware.
Custom Shop.

2008 press advertisement

2008 Jimmy Page Les Paul Custom With Bigsby

LES PAUL CUSTOM 2010

■ **2008** Steve Jones Custom Les Paul

■ **2008** Mick Jones Custom Les Paul

JIMMY PAGE LES PAUL CUSTOM WITH BIGSBY 2008

Replica of 1960 Custom used by Jimmy Page, stolen and never recovered in 1970. As Custom (second version) except:
• Three humbuckers; Bigsby.
• Three Jimmy Page Custom Burstbucker humbuckers.
• Push/pull switches on tone control splits bridge humbucker to single coil; six-position toggle pickup selector switch on upper shoulder.
• Gently-aged Ebony finish; worn gold-plated hardware.
500 only.
Gibson Custom.

50TH ANNIVERSARY 1960 LES PAUL CUSTOM BLACK BEAUTY 2010–current

Historically accurate reissue of dual-humbucker 1960 Les Paul Custom.
• Bound ebony fingerboard, block markers, split diamond inlay on headstock, 'Les Paul Custom' on truss-rod cover.
• Bound carved top, all-mahogany body, Black only.
• Two covered humbuckers (BurstBucker 1 at neck; BurstBucker 2 at bridge).
• Four controls (two volume, two tone), toggle pickup selector on upper shoulder.
• Black laminated plastic pickguard.
• Six saddle tune-o-matic bridge and stop tailpiece.
• Goldplated hardware.
Limited run of 200.
Gibson Custom.

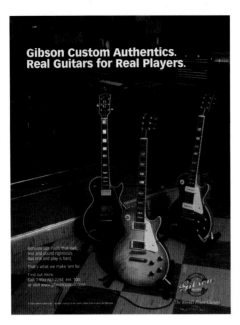

■ **2010** press advertisement

RANDY RHOADS LES PAUL CUSTOM
2010–current
*Yellowed White finish; 'Randy Rhoads' engraved on
pickguard; brass rhythm/lead toggle switch ring.
Similar to Custom (third version) except:*

- Mahogany/maple/mahogany back with carved maple
  top.
- Mahogany with maple spline neck with 'small D'
  Rhoads profile neck.
- Two Gibson Super'74 humbuckers.
- Randy Rhoads White VOS and Aged finish.
- Schaller tuners and strap locks.

*100 Aged finish; 200 VOS finish.
Gibson Custom.*

■ **2010** Randy Rhodes
Les Paul Custom

LES PAUL CUSTOM 2010-2011

1955 LES PAUL CUSTOM 2010

- Twin pickups, tune-o-matic bridge and stop bar tailpiece.
- As Custom (first version) but with Soft Shoulder '55 neck profile. From run of guitars: 1955 Les Paul Custom Exclusives celebrating 1955, the "Year of Innovation."

Gibson Custom special run.

HOT-MOD CUSTOM 2010

- Twin humbucking pickups, tune-o-matic bridge and stop bar tailpiece.
- As Custom (first version) but with dual humbuckers and Soft Shoulder '55 neck profile. From run of guitars: 1955 Les Paul Custom Exclusives celebrating 1955, the "Year of Innovation."

Gibson Custom special run.

HOT-MOD CUSTOM WRAPTAIL 2010

As Hot-Mod Custom but with wrap-over bridge.
Gibson Custom special run.

MARC BOLAN LES PAUL 2011

- Stripped top finish; block inlaid ebony finigerboard.
- Replica of Marc Bolan's much modified late '50s Les Paul retro-fitted with a '70s-style Les Paul Custom neck with ebony fingerboard and mother of pearl block inlays and stripped top finish.
- Bolan Chablis (orange) finish.
- Nickel-plated tune-o-matic bridge; gold-plated stopbar tailpiece from Les Paul Custom.

100 Aged finish; 350 VOS finish.
Gibson Custom.

LES PAUL CUSTOM 2010-2011

■ **2010** 50th Anniversary 1960 Les Paul Custom Black Beauty

JUNIOR SINGLE-CUT 1954–58, 2008–current

Slab single-cutaway body, one pickup.
- Unbound slab body; Sunburst.
- Unbound rosewood fingerboard, dot markers;
  "Les Paul Junior" on headstock ("Les Paul Model"
  on headstock, "Junior" on truss-rod cover,
  2008–current); plastic tuner buttons.
- One plastic-cover six-polepiece single-coil pickup.
- Two controls (volume, tone).
- Black or tortoiseshell plastic pickguard.
- Wrap-over bar bridge/tailpiece.

*Production: 1954 823; 1955 2,939; 1956 3,129; 1957
2,959; 1958 2,408 (includes some Junior double-cut
models). Figures not available for later years.*

TV SINGLE-CUT 1955–58

Similar to Junior single-cut *except:*
- TV Beige or Yellow finish.
- "Les Paul TV Model" on headstock.

*Production: 1954 5; 1955 230; 1956 511; 1957 552;
1958 429 (includes some TV double-cut models).*

■ **1957** Les Paul TV

LES PAUL JUNIOR 1954-1988

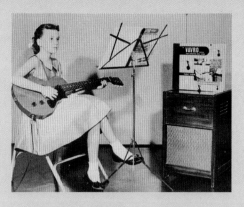

■ **1955** promotional photograph

JUNIOR SINGLE-CUT THREE-QUARTER 1956–58
Shorter 19–fret neck. Similar to Junior single-cut, *except:*
• Shorter neck (with 19 frets) and scale-length (two
inches less than normal).
*Production: 1956 18; 1957 222; 1958 181 (includes
some Junior double-cut three-quarter models).*

JUNIOR PRO 1988
*Single-cut solidbody, flat top, humbucker with black
cover, no Les Paul designation.*
• Single cutaway mahogany body (beveled waist on
treble side), small pickguard extends from treble-side
waist to end of fingerboard, Steingerber KB-X locking-
nut vibrato, black chrome hardware.
• Ebony fingerboard, dot inlays, decal logo.
• Slim-coil humbucking pickup with black cover and no
visible polepieces, two knobs.

■ **1954** Les Paul Junior

BILLIE JOE ARMSTRONG LES PAUL JR.
2006–current

As Junior single-cut *except:*

- H-90 humbucking P-90-style pickup.
- '60s Slim-Taper neck profile.
- Vintage Sunburst, Ebony, or Classic White finishes.

LES PAUL JR (SATIN), 2007–current

As Junior single-cut *except:*

- Lightning Bar Compensated Wrap-around bridge.
- Satin Vintage Burst, White, or Cherry finishes.

JOHN LENNON LES PAUL JUNIOR 2007–current

*Re-creation of the modified '50s Les Paul Jr owned by
John Lennon.*

As Junior single-cut *except:*

- Additional Charlie Christian-style single-coil in neck
  position.
- Aged Cherry finish.

■ **2008** Les Paul Junior

LES PAUL JUNIOR
2006-2011

2008 Les Paul Junior

LES PAUL JUNIOR 2006-2011

2006 Billy Joe Armstrong
Les Paul Jr

JUNIOR DOUBLE-CUT 1958–61, 1997–98

Slab double-cutaway body, one pickup.
- Unbound slab double-cutaway body; Cherry.
- Unbound rosewood fingerboard, dot markers; "Les Paul Junior" on headstock; plastic tuner buttons.
- One plastic-cover six-polepiece single-coil pickup.
- Two controls (volume, tone).
- Black or tortoiseshell plastic pickguard.
- Wrap-over bar bridge/tailpiece.

Shape changed in 1961: see later SG/Les Paul Junior entry.
Some examples in Sunburst.
Production: 1958 2,408 (includes some Junior single-cut models); 1959 4,364; 1960 2,513; 1961 2,151 (includes some SG/Les Paul Junior models). Figures not available for later years.
Also Guitar Of The Week version, 2007, with Satin White finish, wrap-over bridge, floral pattern (J-200 acoustic style) on pickguard.
Production 400.

TV DOUBLE-CUT 1958–59

Similar to Junior double-cut except:
- TV Yellow finish.
- "Les Paul TV Model" on headstock.

Name changed to SG TV in 1959 when Les Paul logo removed. Production: 1958 429 (includes some TV single-cuts); 1959 543 (includes some SG TVs).

■ **1958** Les Paul TV

LES PAUL JUNIOR 1958-2010

JUNIOR DOUBLE-CUT THREE-QUARTER 1958–61

Shorter 19-fret neck. Similar to Junior double-cut, *except:*
• Shorter neck (with 19 frets) and scale-length (two
   inches less than normal).
*Production: 1958 181 (includes some Junior single-cut
three-quarter models); 1959 199; 1960 96; 1961 71.*

JUNIOR 58 DOUBLE-CUT REISSUE 1987–95,
1998–current

Based on Junior double-cut *but six-saddle bridge plus
separate bar tailpiece; nickel-plated hardware and
plastic cover humbucker pickup (appears identical to
single-coil) 1990–92 only. Optional VOS Vintage
Original Spec aging treatment (2006–current).
Custom Shop.*

LES PAUL JR DOUBLECUT EXCLUSIVE
2010–current

*Slab double-cut body; compensated wrap-around
bridge.*
As Junior single-cut *except:*
• Lightning Bar Compensated Wrap-around bridge.
• Cherry or Gloss Yellow finish.

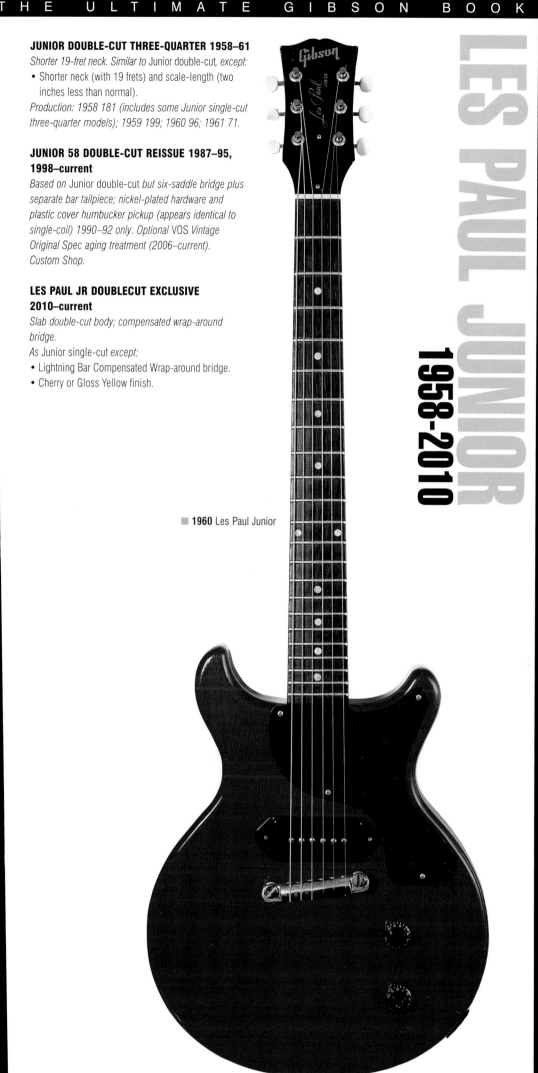

■ **1960** Les Paul Junior

LES PAUL JUNIOR 1958-2010

BIRTH OF THE THINLINE

Many attribute the birth of the Thinline electrics to 1950s studio guitarists Hank Garland and Billy Byrd, who, in collaboration with Gibson, came up with the Byrdland after they had suggested an L-5 style guitar but with a thinner body depth. The pair also requested a slightly narrower neck width, plus a shorter 23½-inch scale and 22 frets. As a result, this placed the pickups closer together than on the 25½-inch 20-fret L-5CES.

On its launch in 1955, the Byrdland was still a high-end guitar, including much of the L-5CES's style, including the carved spruce top. This meant that it was only $25 cheaper than the L-5CES.

1960 ES-350T

ARCHTOP THINLINES 1955

ES-350T 1955–63, 1977–80, 1992–93, 1998–99

Thinbody single-cut archtop, rounded horn, double-parallelogram inlays.

- 17-inch wide body of laminated maple, rounded cutaway (pointed cutaway 1960–63), tune-o-matic bridge, tailpiece with W-shape tubular design, laminated beveled-edge pickguard, triple-bound top and back, Sunburst or Natural finish, gold-plated hardware.
- 23½-inch scale (25½-inch from 1977), single-bound fingerboard and peghead, double-parallelogram inlay, crown peghead inlay.
- Two P-90 pickups (humbuckers from mid 1957).

Production: 1,041 (1955–63); 481 (1977–79).

■ **1955** ES-350T

ARCHTOP THINLINES 1955

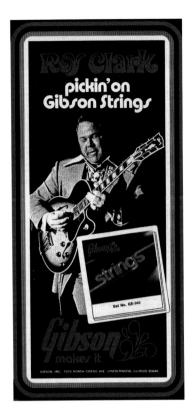

1979 press advertisment

 1955 Byrdland

ARCHTOP THINLINES 1955

78

BYRDLAND 1955–current

Thinbody archtop, short-scale version of L-5CES, pearl block inlays. Billy Byrd/Hank Garland model.

- 17-inch wide, rounded cutaway (a few double-cutaway 1958–62, pointed cutaway 1960–69), 2¼-inch deep, carved spruce top, carved maple back, triple-loop tubular tailpiece, tortoiseshell celluloid pickguard (a few early with pearloid), 7-ply top binding, triple-bound back, 7-ply pickguard binding, single-bound *f*-holes, gold-plated hardware, Sunburst or Natural finish.
- Two Alnico V pickups (humbuckers from late 1957, a few with one humbucker and one Charlie Christian).
- Ebony fingerboard with pointed end, 5-ply fingerboard binding, 23½-inch scale, pearl block inlays, flowerpot peghead inlay, 7-ply peghead binding.

Production: 2,670 (1955–79).

▓ **1955** press advertisement

▓ **1970** Byrdland

▓ **1967** Byrdland with custom body

THINLINE DEVELOPMENT

The solidbody Les Paul Goldtop may have been unleashed in 1952, but by the mid 1950s it was clear that many players still hankered for something more traditional, something that referenced the archtop. If the Byrdland is credited with the creation of Gibson's Thinline range, it was the more affordable all-laminate ES-225T model and the ES-350T, also released in 1955, that would have longer lasting appeal. Dual-pickup models were released the following year, along with the shorter-scale single-pickup cutaway ES-140T and the non-cutaway budget ES-125T model. But these archtop-inspired Thinline electrics were about to be usurped by one of Gibson's true classic guitars: the ES-335 (see p.94).

With its solid center block, the ES-335, launched in 1958, revolutionized the Thinline archtop genre, effectively merging the forward-looking electric solidbody with the classic style of a jazz archtop. But guitar players, then and now, are a conservative bunch when it comes to the instruments they play. As a result, the classic Thinline, in cutaway or non-cutaway styles, hollow or with the center-block pioneered by the ES-335, have remained a part of Gibson's production from the mid 1950s to the present day.

■ **1957** Press advertisment

ARCHTOP THINLINES 1956-1966

ES-225TD 1956–59

Two pickups.
Production: 2,754.

ES-225T 1956–58

Thinbody single-cut archtop, pointed horn,
dot inlay.

• 16¼-inch wide, pointed cutaway, trapeze
bridge/tailpiece combination with strings
looping over bridge, laminated beveled-edge
pickguard, single-bound top and back, Sunburst
or Natural finish.
• Bound rosewood fingerboard, dot inlays, pearl
logo, no peghead ornament.
• P-90 pickup in middle position, two knobs.
Production: 5,220.

ES-140T (¾-scale T) 1957–67

Thin body.
Production: 1,533.

ES-125TD 1957–63

Two pickups.
Production: 1,215.

ES-125TDC 1961–70

Two P-90 pickups:
Production: 5,556.

ES-125C 1966–70

Pointed cutaway, one P-90 pickup.
Production: 475.

ES-125CD 1966–70

Pointed cutaway, two P-90 pickups.
Production: 1,104.

ARCHTOP THINLINES

1956-1966

■ **1956** ES-140T

ES-330T 1959–63
Thinbody double-cut archtop, P-90 pickup.
- 16-inch hollow thinbody archtop of laminated maple, double rounded cutaways, tune-o-matic bridge, trapeze tailpiece, single-bound top and back, Sunburst or Natural finish.
- Neck joins body at 17th fret, bound rosewood fingerboard, dot inlay (small blocks from 1962), pearl logo, no peghead ornament.
- One black plastic-covered P-90 pickup in middle position (chrome cover from 1962).
Production: 2,510.

ES-330TD 1959–71, 1998–99
Two black plastic-covered P-90 pickups, neck joins at 20th fret from 1968.
Production: 21,379 (1959–75).

ES-125TCD 1960
Two P-90 pickups.
Production: 287.

ES-125TC 1961–69
Thinline body, pointed cutaway.
Production: 5,234.

ES-120T 1962–70
Thinbody archtop, pickup and controls in molded pickguard.
- 16¼-inch wide thinline body, one ƒ-hole, single-bound top and back, Sunburst finish.
- Unbound rosewood fingerboard, dot inlays, decal logo.
- Melody Maker pickup, knobs and jack all mounted in large molded pickguard.
Production: 8,895.

TRINI LOPEZ SIGNATURE DELUXE 1964–71
Double-cut archtop, pointed horns, diamond soundholes.
- 16-inch laminated maple hollowbody, double pointed cutaways, tune-o-matic bridge, trapeze tailpiece with raised diamond, model name on wood tailpiece insert, bound pickguard, triple-bound top and back, Cherry Sunburst finish.
- Bound fingerboard and peghead, slashed-diamond inlay, 6-on-a-side tuner arrangement, no peghead ornament.
- Two humbucking pickups, four knobs, 3-way pickup selector on treble cutaway bout, standby switch on bass cutaway bout.
Production: 302 (1964–70).

ES-320TD 1971–74
Thinbody double-cut archtop, dot inlays, oblong pickups.
- 16-inch double cutaway thinbody of laminated maple, tune-o-matic bridge, nickel-plated bridge cover with logo, black plastic pickguard, bound top and back (black-painted edges to simulate binding on Natural-finish models); Natural, Walnut, Cherry.
- Rosewood fingerboard, dot inlays, decal logo.

- Two Melody Maker pickups with embossed Gibson logo, oblong metal control plate with two knobs and two slide switches.
Production: 664.

ES-325TD 1972–79
Thinbody double-cut archtop, one ƒ-hole.
- 16-inch semi-hollow archtop, tune-o-matic, trapeze pointed-end tailpiece, single-bound top and back.
- Two mini-humbucking pickups with no visible poles (polepieces from 1976), semi-circular plastic control plate, four knobs.
- Rosewood fingerboard, dot inlays.
Production: 2,445.

ES-240 1977–1978
Thinbody double-cut archtop, rounded horns, same as ES-335 but with coil-tap switch.
- Thin double-cutaway semi-hollowbody, rounded horns, tune-o-matic bridge, stopbar tailpiece.
- Bound rosewood fingerboard, small block inlays, crown peghead inlay, pearl logo.
- Two humbucking pickups, four knobs, selector switch, coil-tap switch on lower bass treble bout near tone and volume knobs.
Production: 3.

CHET ATKINS COUNTRY GENTLEMAN 1986–2005
Thin single-cut archtop, red rectangular inlays on bass edge of fingerboard.
- 17-inch wide, rounded cutaway, thinline semi-hollowbody, tune-o-matic bridge, ebony bridge base with pearl inlay, Bigsby vibrato with curved tubular arm (optional from 1993), 7-ply top binding, 5-ply back binding, bound ƒ-holes.
- Laminated maple neck, 25½-inch scale, 21 frets, unbound ebony fingerboard, red rectangular (later white "thumbprint") inlays positioned on bass edge of fingerboard, 1¾-inch nut width, unbound peghead, crown peghead inlay, metal tuner buttons.
- Two humbucking pickups, three knobs (two volume, one master tone) and 3-way selector switch on lower treble bout, master volume knob on cutaway bout.

CHET ATKINS TENNESSEAN 1990–2005
Thinbody single-cut archtop, dot inlays near edge of fingerboard.
- 16¼-inch wide, 1⅝-inch deep, single rounded cutaway, laminated maple back and sides with Chromyte (balsa) center block, tune-o-matic bridge, stopbar tailpiece, clear pickguard with silver paint on back and model name stenciled in black, single-bound top and back.
- Unbound ebony fingerboard, 25½-inch scale, dot inlay positioned closer to bass edge of fingerboard, 1¾-inch nut width, clear plastic truss-rod cover back-painted silver, "Chet Atkins" signature peghead decal, plastic tuner buttons.
- Two humbucking pickups.

1998 Chet Atkins
Country Gentleman

ARCHTOP THINLINES

1959-1990

ES-135 (second version) 1991–2003

Thinbody single-cut archtop, pointed horn, dot inlays.

- 16-inch laminated maple/poplar/maple semi-hollowbody, 2¼-inch deep, pointed cutaway, ƒ-holes (no ƒ-holes from 2002), tune-o-matic bridge, trapeze tailpiece (stopbar from 2002), chrome-plated hardware (some gold-plated, 1998–99).
- Maple neck, unbound rosewood fingerboard, dot inlays, model name decal on peghead, decal logo.
- Two P-100 stacked-coil humbucking pickups (humbuckers optional, 1998–2002, standard from 2003), four knobs, selector switch on upper bass bout.

ES-135 GOTHIC 1998–99

Two humbucking pickups with no covers, black pickguard, ebony fingerboard, moon-and-star inlay at 12th fret, no other inlay, white outline of logo on peghead, black chrome hardware, Flat Black finish.

SWINGMASTER ES-135 1999

2 dog-ear P-90 pickups, ebony fingerboard, pearloid trapezoid inlays, optional Bigsby vibrato, Custom Coral, Daddy-O Yellow, Mint Green, or Outa-Sight White finish.

ES-350T CENTENNIAL (Mar. 1994 guitar of the month)

Vintage Sunburst finish, serial number in raised numerals on tailpiece, numeral 1 of serial number formed by row of diamonds, letter i of logo dotted by inlaid diamond, gold medallion on back of peghead, gold-plated hardware, limited run of no more than 101 serial numbered from 1894–1994, package includes 16x20-inch framed photograph and gold signet ring.

■ **1991** ES-135

ARCHTOP THINLINES 1991-2002

CHET ATKINS SUPER 4000 1995, 1997
Thinbody single-cut archtop, split-block inlays, floating pickup.

- 18-inch archtop, carved spruce top, figured maple back and sides, Heritage Cherry Sunburst finish.
- 5-piece maple neck, ebony fingerboard, split-block inlays, 5-piece split-diamond peghead inlay.
- Floating full-size humbucking pickup.

BYRDLAND FLORENTINE 1998–current
Pointed cutaway.

ES-137P (PREMIER) 2002–04
Thinbody single-cut archtop, pointed horn, half-trapezoid inlays.

- 16-inch laminated maple/poplar/maple semi-hollowbody, 2¼-inch deep, pointed cutaway, ƒ-holes, tune-o-matic bridge, black body binding, chrome-plated hardware, metallic finishes.
- Maple neck, unbound rosewood fingerboard, half-trapezoid inlays, *P* inlay at 12th fret, decal logo.
- Two exposed-coil humbucking pickups or two P-90 pickups, four knobs, selector switch on upper bass bout.

ES-137 CLASSIC 2002–current
Thinbody single-cut archtop, pointed horn, trapezoid inlays.

- 16-inch laminated maple/poplar/maple semi-hollowbody, 2¼-inch deep, pointed cutaway, ƒ-holes, tune-o-matic bridge, multiply top binding, single-bound back, chrome or gold-plated hardware.
- Maple neck, bound rosewood fingerboard, trapezoid inlays, *C* inlay at 12th fret, decal logo.
- Two humbucking pickups, four knobs, selector switch on upper bass bout.

■ **2008** ES-137 Classic

ARCHTOP THINLINES

1991-2002

THE ULTIMATE GIBSON BOOK

THE ULTIMATE GIBSON BOOK

ES-137 CUSTOM 2002–current

Thinbody single-cut archtop, pointed horn, split-diamond inlays.

- 16-inch laminated maple/poplar/maple semi-hollowbody, 2¼-inch deep, pointed cutaway, ƒ-holes, tune-o-matic bridge, multiply top binding, single-bound back, chrome or gold-plated hardware.
- 3-piece maple neck, bound ebony fingerboard, trapezoid inlays, pearl logo.
- Two humbucking pickups, four knobs, rotary Varitone switch, selector switch on upper bass bout.

ES-446S 2003–04

Thinbody single-cut archtop, pointed horn, spruce top.

- Single pointed cutaway, carved spruce top with integral braces, mahogany back, ƒ-holes, tune-o-matic bridge, trapeze tailpiece.
- Unbound rosewood fingerboard, dot inlay.
- Two humbucking pickups, four knobs, selector switch on upper bass bout.

JOHNNY A SIGNATURE 2003–current

Symmetrical double cutaway with pointed horns; Bigsby vibrato or tune-o-matic bridge and stop bar tailpiece.

- Thinline hollow mahogany body with carved figured maple top; multi-ply white and black binding, top and back; Bigsby vibrato or tune-o-matic bridge and stop bar tailpiece.
- 25½-inch scale length; bound ebony fingerboard with custom-designed pearl inlays; custom-design inlay on headstock and truss-rod cover.
- Two '57 Classic humbuckers, four knobs, toggle pickup selector switch by bridge.
- Gold-plated hardware.

Gibson Custom.

PAT MARTINO SIGNATURE 2003–2005

Single-cut carved top body; compact three-a-side headstock.

- Thinline mahogany body; carved figured maple top; tune-o-matic bridge and stop bar tailpiece.
- Bound ebony fingerboard; no face position markers; 'Pat Martino Signautre' on truss-rod cover.
- Two humbucking pickups, four knobs, toggle pickup selector switch on bass-side shoulder.

Gibson Custom.

■ **2003** press advertisement

ARCHTOP THINLINES 2002-2006

86

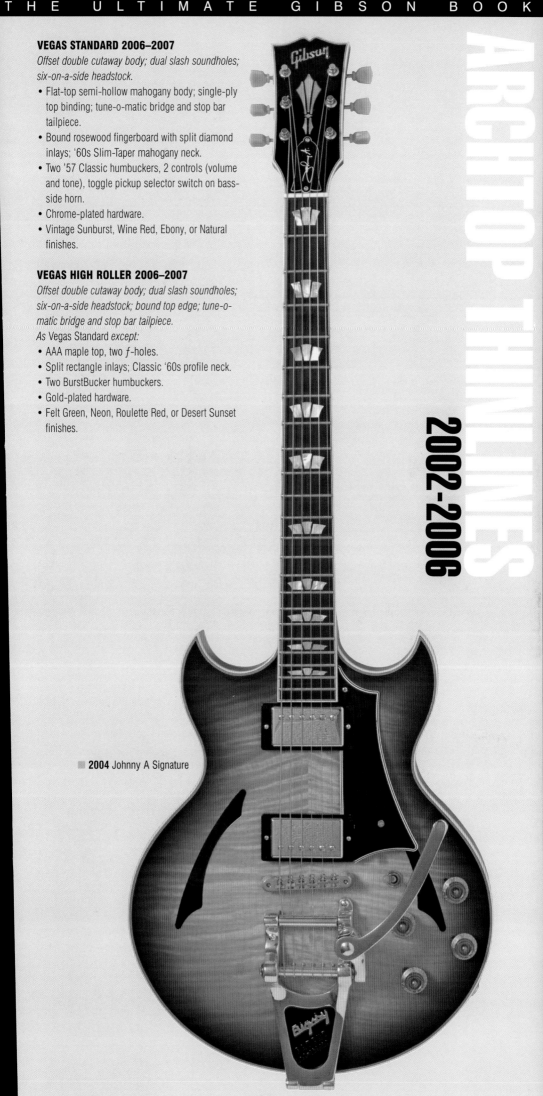

VEGAS STANDARD 2006–2007

Offset double cutaway body; dual slash soundholes; six-on-a-side headstock.

- Flat-top semi-hollow mahogany body; single-ply top binding; tune-o-matic bridge and stop bar tailpiece.
- Bound rosewood fingerboard with split diamond inlays; '60s Slim-Taper mahogany neck.
- Two '57 Classic humbuckers, 2 controls (volume and tone), toggle pickup selector switch on bass-side horn.
- Chrome-plated hardware.
- Vintage Sunburst, Wine Red, Ebony, or Natural finishes.

VEGAS HIGH ROLLER 2006–2007

Offset double cutaway body; dual slash soundholes; six-on-a-side headstock; bound top edge; tune-o-matic bridge and stop bar tailpiece.
As Vegas Standard except:

- AAA maple top, two *f*-holes.
- Split rectangle inlays; Classic '60s profile neck.
- Two BurstBucker humbuckers.
- Gold-plated hardware.
- Felt Green, Neon, Roulette Red, or Desert Sunset finishes.

■ **2004** Johnny A Signature

ARCHTOP THINLINES

2002-2006

SPECIAL SINGLE-CUT 1955–58, 1972, 1998

Slab single-cutaway body, two pickups.
- Unbound slab body; Beige (SL urethane colors 1998 only).
- Bound rosewood fingerboard (unbound on SL version 1998), dot markers (small blocks 1972); "Les Paul Special" on headstock; plastic tuner buttons.
- Two plastic-cover six-polepiece single-coil pickups.
- Four controls (two volume, two tone) plus three-way selector.
- Black laminated plastic pickguard.
- Wrap-over bar bridge/tailpiece.

Some early examples with brown plastic parts (knobs, pickguard, etc).
Production: 1955 373; 1956 1,345; 1957 1,452; 1958 958. Figures not available for later years.

SPECIAL 55 1974, 1977–80

Based on Special single-cut: earliest examples with wrap-over bar bridge/tailpiece; majority have six-saddle bridge plus separate bar tailpiece. Sunbursts or colors. Earlier examples have plastic tuner buttons.
Production: Kalamazoo-made: 1974 1925; 1976 2; 1977 331; 1978 293; 1979 224. Figures not available for 1980 nor for any later Nashville production.

■ **1955** Les Paul Special

LES PAUL SPECIAL 1955-2006

SPECIAL 400 1985
Based on Special single-cut, *except one humbucker and two single-coil pickups; two knobs (master tone and master volume), three switches (on/off pickup selector), vibrato, most with ebony fingerboard.*

JUNIOR II 1989
Similar to Special single-cut, *except humbucker pickups (not visibly different from single-coils) and six-saddle bridge with separate tailpiece (renamed* Special *in 1989: see* Special single-cut reissue).

SPECIAL SINGLE-CUT REISSUE 1989–current
Similar to Special single-cut, *except:*
- Sunburst, Cherry, Yellow, or Black (Faded Cherry or TV Yellow from 1998).
- Metal tuner buttons (white plastic from 1998).
- Pickups, although visually similar to originals, are actually humbuckers (single-coils from 1998).
- Six-saddle bridge plus separate bar tailpiece (wrap-over from 1998).

Originally and erroneously referred to in Gibson literature as Junior II. Also available (2006–current) with VOS Vintage Original Spec aging treatment.

SPECIAL SINGLE-CUTAWAY CENTENNIAL 1994
Gold or TV Yellow, four-digit serial number on tailpiece with first digit (1) in diamonds. Custom Shop; production no more than 101, promotional prototypes only.

JUNIOR SPECIAL 1999–2005
Similar to Special single-cut, *except humbucker pickups (at first not visibly different from single-coils), six-saddle bridge with separate tailpiece, unbound fingerboard, half-size crown markers (dots from 2001), contoured back of body.*

JUNIOR SPECIAL HUM (or HB) 2001–08
Similar to Special single-cut, *except metal-cover humbucker pickups; six-saddle bridge with separate tailpiece; unbound fingerboard, contoured back of body.*

JUNIOR SPECIAL PLUS 2001–05
Similar to Special single-cut, *except figured maple top cap; metal-cover humbucker pickups; six-saddle bridge with separate tailpiece; selector switch on upper bass bout; unbound fingerboard; gold-plated hardware; Trans Amber or Trans Red finishes.*

BOB MARLEY SPECIAL 2002–04
Elliptical switch washer.
Similar to Special single-cut, *except:*
- Aged Cherry finish appears stripped.
- Small-block fingerboard markers, wide binding on headstock.
- Elliptical switch washer.
- Aluminum pickguard.
Custom Shop; production 200.

BILLIE JOE ARMSTRONG JUNIOR 2006–current
50s-specification Junior Single-Cut *with one plastic-cover six-polepiece stacked double-coil pickup, wrap-over bridge-tailpiece; Sunburst, Black, or White; signature on back of headstock.*

PETER FRAMPTON SPECIAL 2006
Three plastic-cover six-polepiece single-coil pickups, "Peter Frampton" on truss-rod cover.
- Unbound slab all-mahogany body; Sunburst.
- Bound ebony fingerboard, dot markers, "Peter Frampton" on truss-rod cover, Grover tuners with gold-plated kidney-bean buttons, thin neck profile.
- Three plastic-cover six-polepiece single-coil pickups.
- Four controls (three volume, one tone) plus three-way selector.
- Red tortoiseshell plastic pickguard.
- Six-saddle bridge plus separate bar tailpiece.
- Strap-locking endpin.
Numbered with PF prefix. Custom Shop.

■ **2002** Les Paul Bob Marley Special

2009 Robot Les Paul Jr Special

LES PAUL SPECIAL 2007-2011

JOHN LENNON 2007

Dog-eared P-90 and Charlie Christian pickups. Similar to Junior single-cut, except:
- Natural mahogany finish.
- "Custom" on truss-rod cover.
- Plastic-cover six-polepiece single-coil pickup (bridge), 'Charlie Christian' bar pickup (neck).
- Two controls (tone and volume) plus three-way selector.
- Six-saddle bridge with two thumbwheels on treble side; separate bar tailpiece.
- Aged chrome-plated hardware.

Custom Shop.

LES PAUL JR SPECIAL EXCLUSIVE 2007–current

Slab single-cut body; tune-o-matic bridge and stop bar tailpiece.
As Special Single-cut except:
- Tune-o-matic bridge and stop bar tailpiece.
- Cherry, Alpine White, or Gloss Yellow finishes.

ROBOT LES PAUL JR SPECIAL 2009–2010

Slab single-cut body; tune-o-matic bridge and stop bar tailpiece.
As Special Single-cut except:
- Tune-o-matic bridge and stop bar tailpiece.
- Multi-Control Knob; Neck Central Processing Unit on back of headstock; Robot locking tuners.
- TV Yellow finish.

LES PAUL SPECIAL 2007-2011

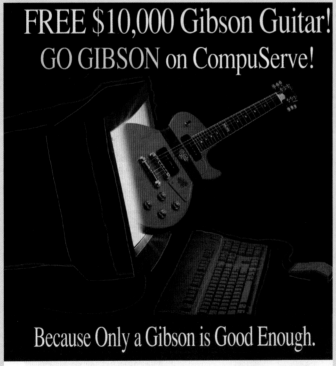

FREE $10,000 Gibson Guitar!
GO GIBSON on CompuServe!

Because Only a Gibson is Good Enough.

- Buy a Gibson and receive a FREE CompuServe membership!
- Type "GO GIBSON", then interview Gibson endorsees and receive product information 24 hours a day "on-line"!
- Enter to win a $10,000 Gibson Centennial Guitar on CompuServe today!

 CompuServe To join CompuServe call 1-800-524-3388 and ask for Rep. 54!
Gibson Guitar Corp. • 641 Massman Drive • Nashville, TN 37210-3781 • (800)4-GIBSON

■ **2001** press advertisement

SPECIAL DOUBLE-CUT 1959–60, 1998

Slab double-cutaway body, two pickups.
- Unbound slab double-cutaway body; Yellow or Cherry.
- Bound rosewood fingerboard, dot markers; "Les Paul Special" on headstock; plastic tuner buttons.
- Two plastic-cover six-polepiece single-coil pickups.
- Four controls (two volume, two tone) plus three-way selector.
- Black laminated plastic pickguard.
- Wrap-over bar bridge/tailpiece.

Later '59–60 examples with neck pickup moved further down body, away from end of fingerboard, and selector moved next to bridge.
Model name changed to SG Special in 1960 when Les Paul logo removed.
Production: 1959 1,821; 1960 1,387 (includes some SG Special models). Figures not available for 1998.

SPECIAL DOUBLE-CUT THREE-QUARTER 1959–60

Shorter 19-fret neck. Similar to Special double-cut, *except:*
- Cherry finish only.
- Shorter neck (with 19 frets) and scale-length (two inches less than normal).

Model name changed to SG Special three-quarter in 1960 when Les Paul logo removed.
Production: 1959 12; 1960 39 (includes some SG Special three-quarter models).

SPECIAL 58 1976–85, 1998

Based on Special double-cut *but six-saddle bridge plus separate bar tailpiece; sunbursts or colours.*
Production: Kalamazoo-made: 1976 162; 1977 1,622; 1978 803; 1979 150. Figures not available for any Nashville production.

■ **1959** Les Paul Special

LES PAUL SPECIAL 1959-2007

SPECIAL DOUBLE CMT 1979
Curly maple top. Custom Shop; production 133.

SPECIAL DOUBLE-CUTAWAY CENTENNIAL 1994
Heritage cherry finish.
Custom Shop; production of no more than 101, four-digit serial number on tailpiece with first digit (1) in diamonds.

SPECIAL 60 DOUBLE-CUT REISSUE
1998–current
Similar to Special double-cut, except nickel-plated hardware; Faded Cherry or TV Yellow finish (Ebony, Cinnamon, or Natural from 2001). Also available (2006–current) with VOS Vintage Original Spec aging treatment.
Custom Shop.

STANDARD LITE 1999–2000
This model has the Special double-cut's body shape but with a carved-top; see Standard: Other Models.

JUNIOR LITE 1999–2002
Based on Special double-cut but with two stacked humbucker pickups (not visibly different from single-coils), six-saddle bridge with separate tailpiece, unbound fingerboard, half-size crown markers, contoured back of body.

FADED DOUBLE CUTAWAY 2007–08
Unbound fingerboard; Worn Cherry, Worn Yellow, or Worn Brown finish.
Custom Shop.

▓ **1959** Les Paul Special
three-quarter

LES PAUL SPECIAL
1959-2007

THINLINE SEMIS

The thinline archtop style that Gibson introduced in 1955 with the Byrdland and ES-225T provided guitarists with more playing comfort, but these instruments still behaved like full-depth archtops when it came to feeding back. The solid body of Gibson's Les Paul models eliminated the vibration of the top of the guitar, which reduced the tendency to generate an ear-splitting squeal at high volumes, but many guitarists did not want to abandon the look of a traditional f-hole archtop guitar.

Gibson president Ted McCarty, an engineer by training, personally took on the task of bringing solidbody performance together with archtop aesthetics. McCarty took the thinline archtop concept and added a solid block down the center of the body to stabilize the top. To modernize the appearance, he gave the body a double-cutaway shape.

Gibson introduced the ES-335, featuring this revolutionary semi-hollowbody concept, in 1958, the same year as the Flying V, the Explorer, and the Cherry Sunburst finish on the Les Paul Standard. Despite the legendary status that those solidbodies would eventually attain, the ES-335 was the most successful of all, and Gibson followed quickly with two fancier models, the ES-345 and ES-355. The V, Explorer, and Cherry Sunburst Les Paul were gone within two years, but the ES-335 has never gone out of production.

■ **1958** ES-355TD

THINLINE SEMIS 1958-1959

ES-335TD 1958–81 / ES-335 DOT 1981–90 / ES-335 REISSUE 1991–98 / ES-335 DOT 1999–current

Thinbody double-cutaway archtop, two humbuckers, dot or small block inlays.

- 16-inch semi-hollowbody of laminated maple, 1⅝-inch deep, double-cutaway, rounded horns, tune-o-matic bridge, stop tailpiece (trapeze from 1964), Bigsby vibrato optional (most models with Bigsby have CUSTOM MADE plate covering original tailpiece holes; some without holes or plate), laminated beveled-edge pickguard extends below bridge

(shorter guard from 1961), single-bound top and back, plain or figured top optional from 2006, satin or gloss finish optional from 2006.
- Single-bound rosewood fingerboard, neck-body joint at 19th fret, dot inlay (small pearloid blocks from 1962; some with single-parallelogram 1960s), crown peghead inlay (early with unbound fingerboard and no peghead ornament).
- Two humbucking pickups, two tone and two volume knobs, one switch; coil tap switch 1977–81.
Production: 23,571 (1958–70); 26,781 (1971–79).

■ **1958** ES-335TD

■ **1958** ES-335TD

95

Gibson thin-body guitars feel just right

Whenever guitar players get to talking about their favorite instrument there's one thing they'll always say: *the feel is right!* And that's just what they've all been saying about Gibson's great new series of thin-body electrics. Yes, every one of these models—each with the Gibson *wonder-thin silhouette*—really does have that certain "feel" to it. And fitting so close and comfortably to your body, it'll let you reach many chords easily you've never played before.* You'll find the slender Gibson neck feels just right in your hand, and it's so easy to finger. That extremely fast, low action will make the strings seem feather-light to your touch. If you haven't done so already, be sure to find out all about this new all-star line of light-weight low-action thin-body Gibsons . . . each model so easy to handle, so easy to play. All have that quick response, balanced tone that always says instantly—Gibson.

Gibson INC.
KALAMAZOO, MICHIGAN

the Gibson wonder-thin silhouette . . . only 1³⁄₄″ thin . . . in a full series of Gibson guitars, priced from $115 to $695.

* Especially with Gibson's beautiful, cherry-red ES-355T double cutaway model, you'll reach right down to the very last fret with the greatest of ease (shown here, along with the GA-400 amp, by Gibson artist-enthusiast, Andy Nelson).

1959 press advertisement

1959 ES-345TD

THINLINE SEMIS 1958-1959

THINLINE SEMIS 1958-1959

■ **1959** ES-355TDN

■ **1959** ES-355TD custom

■ **1959** ES-345TDN

1960 ES-335TDN
with Bigsby

1960 ES-335TDN

THINLINE SEMIS
1958-1959

THINLINE SEMIS

1958-1959

■ **1960** press advertisement

■ **1960** ES-355TD

ES-355TD 1958–71, 1994, 1997, 2004

Thinbody double-cut archtop, two humbuckers, block inlays.

- 16-inch semi-hollowbody of laminated maple, 1⅝-inch deep, double-cutaway, rounded horns, tune-o-matic bridge, Bigsby vibrato (SW sideways-action vibrato optional, lyre vibrato 1963–68), multiple-bound pickguard extends below bridge, multiple-bound top, triple-bound back, single-bound *f*-holes.
- Single-bound ebony fingerboard, large block inlays, multiple-bound peghead, 5-piece split-diamond peghead inlay, Grover Rotomatic tuners.
- Two humbucking pickups, mono circuitry standard but stereo with Varitone more common.

Production: 3,151 (1958–70); 2,029 (1971–79).

ES-345TD 1959–82, 2002 / ES-345 REISSUE 2003–current

Thinbody double-cut archtop, two humbuckers, double-parallelogram inlays.

- 16-inch semi-hollow body of laminated maple, 1⅝-inch deep, double rounded cutaways, tune-o-matic bridge, stop tailpiece (trapeze from 1964, stopbar from 1982), laminated beveled-edge pickguard extends below bridge (shorter guard from 1961), single-bound top and back, gold-plated hardware.
- Single-bound rosewood fingerboard, neck-body joint at 19th fret, double-parallelogram inlay, crown peghead inlay (early with unbound fingerboard and no peghead ornament).
- Two humbucking pickups, two tone and two volume knobs, one selector switch switch, stereo electronics with two jacks, Varitone rotary tone selector, black ring around Varitone switch (gold ring from 1960).

Production: 7,240 (1958–70); 4,348 (1971–79).

The critics gave our new amps a real cool reception.

■ **1960** ES-345TD

THINLINE SEMIS 1958-1959

THINLINE SEMIS 1958-1959

■ **1960** ES-345TD custom

■ **1963** ES-345TDC with Custom Made plate

■ **1964** ES-335TDC owned by Eric Clapton

 1963 catalogue cover

1965 ES-335-12

THINLINE SEMIS 1964-1965

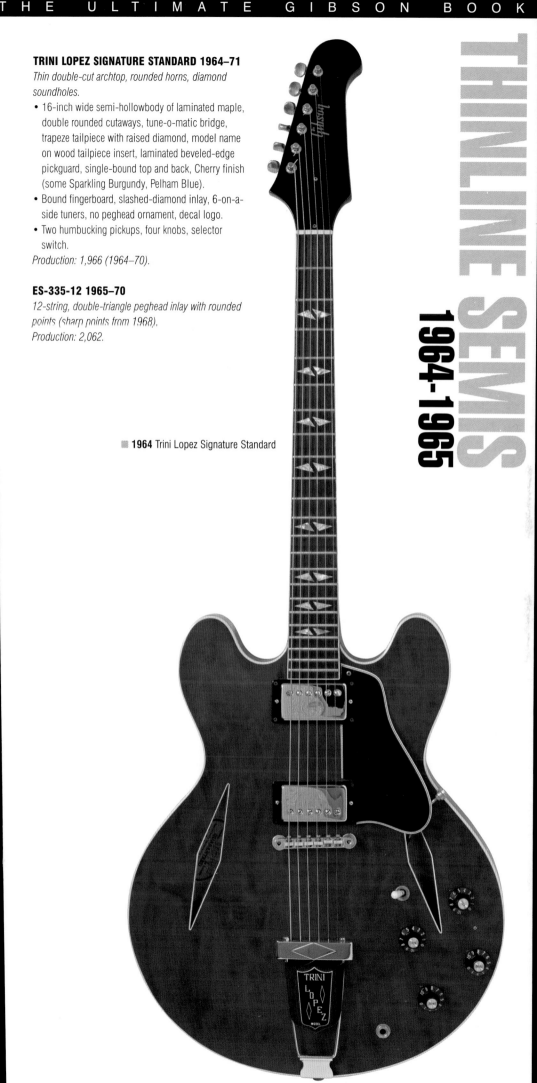

TRINI LOPEZ SIGNATURE STANDARD 1964–71

Thin double-cut archtop, rounded horns, diamond soundholes.

- 16-inch wide semi-hollowbody of laminated maple, double rounded cutaways, tune-o-matic bridge, trapeze tailpiece with raised diamond, model name on wood tailpiece insert, laminated beveled-edge pickguard, single-bound top and back, Cherry finish (some Sparkling Burgundy, Pelham Blue).
- Bound fingerboard, slashed-diamond inlay, 6-on-a-side tuners, no peghead ornament, decal logo.
- Two humbucking pickups, four knobs, selector switch.

Production: 1,966 (1964–70).

ES-335-12 1965–70

12-string, double-triangle peghead inlay with rounded points (sharp points from 1968).
Production: 2,062.

1964 Trini Lopez Signature Standard

THINLINE SEMIS

1964-1965

■ **1981** press advertisement

ES-340TD 1969–73

Same as ES-335 except for maple neck (ES-335 has mahogany neck during ES-340 production period).

- 16-inch semi-hollowbody of laminated maple, 1⅝-inch deep, double-cutaway, rounded horns, tune-o-matic bridge, trapeze tailpiece, single-bound top and back, Walnut or Natural finish.
- 3-piece maple neck, single-bound rosewood fingerboard, small block inlays, crown peghead inlay.
- Two humbucking pickups, four knobs, master volume control and master mixer control (rather than two volume controls).

Production: 1,561.

■ **1998** B.B. King Lucille

THINLINE SEMIS 1969-1981

ES-347TD 1978–85 / ES-347S 1987–93

Thinbody double-cut archtop, two humbuckers, TP-6 tailpiece.

- 16-inch semi-hollowbody of laminated maple, 1⅝-inch deep, double rounded cutaways, tune-o-matic bridge, TP-6 fine-tune tailpiece, laminated beveled-edge pickguard, single-bound top and back, chrome-plated hardware (gold-plated from 1987).
- Bound ebony fingerboard, large block inlays, bound peghead (multiple binding from 1987), crown peghead inlay, pearl logo.
- Two humbucking pickups, four knobs and one pickup selector switch on lower treble bout, coil-tap switch on upper treble bout. *Production: 1,896 (1978–79).*

ES-335 CRR 1979

Country Rock Regular, two exposed-coil Dirty Fingers humbuckers, coil tap, brass nut, Antique Sunburst finish. Production: 300

ES-335 CRRS 1979

Country Rock Stereo, stereo electronics, master volume control, coil tap, TP-6 fine-tune tailpiece, brass nut, Country Tobacco or Dixie Brown (pink-to-brown sunburst) finish. Production: 300

ES-335 PRO 1979–81

Two Dirty Fingers humbucking pickups with exposed coils.

ES-ARTIST 1979–85

Thinbody double-cut archtop, winged-ƒ peghead inlay.

- 16-inch semi-hollow archtop body of laminated maple, 1¾-inch deep, no ƒ-holes, tune-o-matic bridge, TP-6 tailpiece, laminated beveled-edge double pickguard, multiple-bound top and back, gold-plated hardware, Cherry Sunburst, Ebony, or Antique Fireburst finish.
- Single-bound ebony fingerboard, off-center dot inlay near bass edge of fingerboard, pearl logo.
- Two humbucking pickups, active electronics, three knobs (bass, treble, volume), 3-way selector switch, three mini-toggle switches (bright, compression/expansion, active on/off).

B.B. KING STANDARD 1980 / LUCILLE STANDARD 1981–85

Thinbody double-cut archtop, no ƒ-holes, dot inlays, Lucille on peghead.

The man and the woman.

■ **1970** press advertisement

- Thin double-cutaway semi-hollowbody of laminated maple, no ƒ-holes, Nashville tune-o-matic bridge, TP-6 tailpiece, laminated beveled-edge pickguard, multiple-bound top and back, chrome-plated hardware, Ebony or Cherry finish.
- Single-bound rosewood fingerboard, dot inlays, *Lucille* peghead inlay.
- Two PAF humbucking pickups, stereo electronics with two jacks.

B.B. KING CUSTOM 1980 / LUCILLE 1981–85 / B.B. KING LUCILLE 1986–current

Thinbody double-cut archtop, no ƒ-holes, block inlays, Lucille on peghead.

- Thin double-cutaway semi-hollowbody of laminated maple, no ƒ-holes, TP-6 tailpiece, multiple-bound top and back, single-bound pickguard, tune-o-matic bridge, gold-plated hardware, Ebony or Cherry finish.
- Bound ebony fingerboard, large block inlays, *Lucille* peghead inlay.
- Two PAF humbucking pickups, Varitone rotary tone selector switch, stereo wiring with two jacks.

■ **1979** ES Artist

ES-335 DOT 1981–90

Dot inlays, stopbar tailpiece, gold-plated hardware optional with white finish.

ES-369 1982

Thinbody double-cut archtop, narrow peghead, pre-war script logo.
- 16-inch semi-hollow archtop body of laminated maple, tune-o-matic bridge, TP-6 tailpiece, single-ply cream-colored pickguard, single-bound top and back.
- Single-bound rosewood fingerboard, pearloid trapezoid inlays, snakehead peghead, old-style script logo.
- Two Dirty Fingers pickups with exposed coils, four speed knobs, one selector switch, one mini-toggle coil-tap switch.

ES-335 DOT CMT 1983–85

Custom Shop model, highly figured maple top and back, two PAF humbucking pickups, full-length maple centerblock, mahogany neck.

ES-357 1983–84

Thinbody double-cut archtop, three pickups, Mitch Holder model.
- 16-inch semi-hollowbody of laminated maple, 2-inch deep, curly maple top, no *f*-holes, TP-6 fine-tune tailpiece, single-bound top and back, Natural finish.
- 3-piece maple neck, bound ebony fingerboard, pearl block inlays, crown peghead inlay, bound peghead, gold-plated hardware.
- Three P-90 pickups with black soapbar covers or humbucking covers (polepieces across center), four knobs (three volume, one master tone), selector switch, mini-toggle switch for middle pickup control.

Production: 7 from Kalamazoo Custom Shop (1983); a few more made in Nashville (1984).

2005 Eric Clapton ES-335

THINLINE SEMIS 1981-1983

LARRY CARLTON
and the GIBSON TP-6

Precision Performers

Larry Carlton doesn't settle for anything less than the very best. And you shouldn't either. The Gibson TP-6 fine tuning tailpiece gives you performance perfection, in concert or in the studio, with fingertip ease.
For the first time, you can fine tune with one hand while you're playing. And you don't have to own a Gibson to get the benefit of precision tuning at the touch of your fingers as you play. Because Gibson designed it to fit most instruments with a stop-bar tailpiece.
See your authorized Gibson dealer and check out the Gibson TP-6. It's available in both Chrome and Gold. For precision tuning and top performance—Gibson is the only name in genuine Replacement Parts. And only authorized Gibson parts dealers carry them.

Gibson
A Division of Norlin Industries, Inc.
7373 N. Cicero Avenue, Lincolnwood, IL 60646 In Canada: 51 Nantucket Boulevard, Scarborough, Ont. M1P 2N6

■ **1981** press advertisement

■ **2008** BB King Super Lucille

THINLINE SEMIS

1981-1983

ES-335 STUDIO 1986–91

ES-Studio (1991): No f-holes, two Dirty Fingers humbucking pickups with covers (earliest with exposed-coil PAF humbuckers), mahogany neck, unbound rosewood fingerboard (earliest with ebony), dot inlays, no peghead ornament, decal logo, Ebony or Cherry finish.

ES-335 SHOWCASE EDITION (Apr. 1988 guitar of the month)

EMG pickups, Beige finish. Production: 200 for U.S., 50 for overseas.

ES-335 REISSUE 1990–current

Dot inlay (some limited runs with black binding, ebony fingerboard, small block inlays, 1998–99), stopbar tailpiece.

ES-335 CENTENNIAL (Aug. 1994 guitar of the month)

Cherry finish, serial number in raised numerals on tailpiece, numeral 1 of serial number formed by row of diamonds, letter i of logo dotted by inlaid diamond, gold medallion on back of peghead, gold-plated hardware, limited run of no more than 101 serial numbered from 1894–1994, packaged with 16x20-inch framed photograph and gold signet ring.

ES-355 CENTENNIAL (June 1994 guitar of the month)

Vintage Sunburst finish, serial number in raised numerals on tailpiece, numeral 1 of serial number formed by row of diamonds, letter i of logo dotted by inlaid diamond, gold medallion on back of peghead, gold-plated hardware, Vintage Sunburst finish, limited run of no more than 101 serial numbered from 1894–1994, package includes 16x20-inch framed photograph and gold signet ring.

ES-335 CENTENNIAL (Aug. 1994 guitar of the month)

Cherry finish, serial number in raised numerals on tailpiece, numeral 1 of serial number formed by row of diamonds, letter i of logo dotted by inlaid diamond, gold medallion on back of peghead, gold-plated hardware, limited run of no more than 101 serial numbered from 1894–1994, packaged with 16x20-inch framed photograph and gold signet ring.

CUSTOM SHOP ES-335 1995–2001

Figured maple back, long pickguard, thick 1959-style neck, replica orange oval label.

ES-336 1996–98 / CS-336 2002–current

Thinbody double-cut archtop, smaller than ES-335, dot inlays.

- 13¾-inch double-cutaway semi-hollowbody, routed mahogany back with solid center area, arched (routed) maple top available with plain or figured grain, f-holes, rounded double cutaways, body lines similar to ES-335, back beveled on bass side, tune-o-matic bridge, bound top and back, chrome-plated hardware.
- Offset-V neck profile, bound rosewood fingerboard with compound radius, dot inlays, tapered peghead with straight string-pull (standard peghead from 2002), decal logo, Custom Shop decal logo on peghead, sealed-back tuners, inked-on serial number.
- Two '57 Classic humbucking pickups, four knobs.

ES-346 1997–98 / PAUL JACKSON JR. ES-346 1999–2006

Thinbody double-cut archtop, smaller than ES-335, double-parallelogram inlay.

- 13¾-inch double-cutaway semi-hollowbody, routed mahogany back with solid center area, arched (routed) maple top available with plain or figured grain, f-holes,

THINLINE SEMIS 1986-1997

2002 press advertisement

rounded double cutaways, body lines similar to ES-335, back beveled on bass side, tune-o-matic bridge, bound top and back, gold-plated hardware, Emberglow, Faded Cherry, or Gingerburst finish.
• Offset-V neck profile, bound rosewood fingerboard with compound radius, double-parallelogram inlay, tapered peghead with straight string-pull, pearl logo, Custom Shop decal logo on peghead, sealed-back tuners, chrome-plated hardware, inked-on serial number.
• Two '57 Classic humbucking pickups, four knobs.

2008 press advertisement

2008 Lee Ritenour ES-335

2008 ES-335
Light Burst

2008 ES-335 Desert Burst

THINLINE SEMIS 1998-2001

ES-335 BLOCK 1998–2000
Unbound ebony fingerboard, small block inlays.

ES-335 GOTHIC 1998
Two '57 Classic humbucking pickups with no covers, black pickguard, ebony fingerboard, moon-and-star inlay at 12th fret, no other inlay, white outline of logo on peghead, black chrome hardware, Flat Black finish.

B.B. KING LITTLE LUCILLE 1999–current
Single-cut solidbody, pointed horn, Little Lucille *on top.*
- Semi-hollow poplar body, flat top, *f*-holes, TP-6 fine-tune tailpiece, gold-plated truss-rod cover engraved with *B.B. King*, black finish, *Little Lucille* on upper bass bout next to fingerboard, black finish.
- 25½-inch scale, unbound rosewood fingerboard, diamond inlay, stacked-diamond peghead inlay, pearl logo.
- Two special design Blues 90 pickups with cream soapbar covers and non-adjustable poles, two knobs

(with push/pull to disable Varitone), slide switch, 6-position Varitone control.

PAT MARTINO CUSTOM / PAT MARTINO SIGNATURE 1999–2006
Thinbody single-cut archtop, no fingerboard inlay, curly top.
- 16-inch thin semi-hollowbody, single pointed cutaway, carved flamed maple top, routed mahogany back, *f*-holes, tune-o-matic bridge, stopbar tailpiece, Caramel or Heritage Cherry Sunburst finish.
- Mahogany neck, bound ebony fingerboard, no inlay, narrow peghead with straight string-pull, pearl logo.
- Two humbucking pickups, four knobs, selector switch on upper bass bout.

ANDY SUMMERS 1960 ES-335 2001
Replica of Summers' personal guitar, 1960 specs, aged Cherry finish.
Production: 50.

■ **2010** 50th Anniversary 1960 ES-335TDN

■ **2010** 50th Anniversary 1960 ES-335TDC

111

ES-335 BLOCK REISSUE 2002–current
Custom shop model, small block inlays, nickel-plated hardware, double-ring tuner buttons.

LARRY CARLTON ES-335 2002–current
Chrome-plated hardware, small block inlays, slim neck profile, Carltonburst finish (yellow-to-red sunburst).

1959 ES-335 DOT REISSUE 2002–current
Custom Shop model, dot inlays, plain top, nickel-plated hardware, single-ring tuner buttons.

TOM DELONGE SIGNATURE 2003–current
Thinbody double-cut archtop, rounded horns, one pickup, racing stripe.
• ES-335 style semi-hollowbody, tune-o-matic bridge, bound top and back, Brown finish with cream racing stripes.
• Bound rosewood fingerboard, dot inlays, Natural finish peghead.
• One exposed-coil Dirty Fingers humbucking pickup, one volume knob.

ES-333 2003–05
Thin double-cut archtop, rounded horns, no pickguard.
• Thin double-cutaway semi-hollowbody of laminated maple/poplar/maple, tune-o-matic bridge, bound top and back, nickel-plated hardware.
• Bound rosewood fingerboard, dot inlays, no peghead ornament, decal logo.
• Two exposed-coil humbucking pickups, four knobs.

2010 ES-345 Alpine White

THINLINE SEMIS 2002-2005

112

2010 Trini Lopez ES

2010 ES-339

LEE ROY PARNELL CS-336 2004
Custom fat-profile neck, aged nickel hardware.

ES-335 PLAIN 60s BLOCK 2005
Regular production model, plain top, block inlays, thin 1960s neck profile.

ERIC CLAPTON ES-335 2005
Tune-o-matic bridge with white plastic saddles, small block inlays, long neck tenon, aged chrome and gold hardware, Cherry finish.
Production: 250.

ALVIN LEE BIG RED ES-335 2005–current
Based on Lee's 1959 with replaced fingerboard, small block inlays, two exposed-coil humbuckers and one Seymour Duncan uncovered single-coil in middle position, three volume knobs, two tone knobs, one switch, peace symbol and other Woodstock era graphics, Custom Authentic faded Cherry finish.
Production: Limited run of 50 with signed certificate, then unlimited production.

ES-335 1960 50TH ANNIVERSARY 2010
Nickel-plated hardware, low-profile neck, dot inlays, tortoise side dots; Antique Faded Cherry, Antique Faded Sunburst, or Antique Natural finish, all with VOS (Vintage Original Spec) finish treatment; two '57 Classic humbuckers.

2010 VOS ES-335 Black Cherry

THINLINE SEMIS 2005-2011

2010 VOS ES-335 Block
Light Caramel Burst

2010 VOS ES-335 Block
Antique Faded Cherry with Maestro

2010 VOS ES-335 Block
Antique Ebony with Bigsby

THINLINES WITHOUT CENTER BLOCKS

The double-cutaway body of the ES-335 not only introduced the concept of a semi-hollowbody, it opened the door for new designs in the line of fully hollow thinlines. Prior to the ES-335, all of Gibson's thinlines appeared, from the front view, to be traditional full-depth models, with a rounded cutaway (Byrdland, ES-350T), pointed cutaway (ES-225), or with no cutaway (ES-125T), but in 1959, only a year after the ES-335's smashing debut, Gibson introduced a new model with the look of the 335 but without the ES-335's center block.

The model name of the ES-330TD suggests that it was a step down from the ES-335, which it was—but not because of its fully hollow body. In order to offer a less expensive alternative to the 335, Gibson fitted the 330TD with single-coil P-90 pickups rather than the newly developed humbuckers that were standard on all the semi-hollow models (an even less expensive, single-pickup ES-330T was also available). At $210 for sunburst and $225 for natural, the double-pickup 330 was about $55 cheaper than the 335.

Due to the ES-330's assigned price point below the ES-335, step-up versions were never introduced. Demand fell off as the 1960s progressed, but Gibson gave the thin, double-cut hollowbody style a big sendoff in 1969 with the super-deluxe Brazilian rosewood Crest model.

THINLINE HOLLOWBODY 1959-1969

1971 Crest Gold

ES-330T 1959–63
Thinbody double-cut archtop, P-90 pickup.
- 16-inch hollow thinbody archtop of laminated maple, double rounded cutaways, tune-o-matic bridge, trapeze tailpiece, single-bound top and back, Sunburst or Natural finish.
- Neck joins body at 17th fret, bound rosewood fingerboard, dot inlay (small blocks from 1962), pearl logo, no peghead ornament.
- One black plastic-covered P-90 pickup in middle position (chrome cover from 1962).
Production: 2,510.

ES-330TD 1959–71, 1998–99
Two P-90 pickups, neck joins at 20th fret from 1968.
Production: 21,379 (1959–75).

CREST SPECIAL 1961–63, 1969
Thinbody single-cut archtop, crest on peghead.
- Thin hollowbody, carved spruce top, pointed cutaway, crest-shaped insert in trapeze tailpiece, gold-plated

hardware, some labeled L-5CT Spec.
- Ebony fingerboard, slashed-block (Super 400 style) inlay, crest peghead inlay with three crescent moons and castle.
- Two humbucking pickups, Varitone control.

CREST 1969–71
Thinbody double-cut archtop, Brazilian rosewood body.
- 16-inch hollow thinbody archtop body of laminated Brazilian rosewood, double rounded cutaways, flat back (some arched), multiple-bound rosewood pickguard, adjustable rosewood bridge, multiple-bound top, triple-bound back, single-bound *f*-holes, backstripe marquetry, gold-plated (Crest Gold) or silver-plated (Crest Silver) hardware.
- Neck-body joint at 17th fret, fingerboard raised off of top, block inlays, multiple-bound peghead, 5-piece split-diamond peghead inlay.
- 2 floating mini-humbucking pickups.
Production: 162.

■ **1959** ES-330TD

■ **1960** ES-330TDN

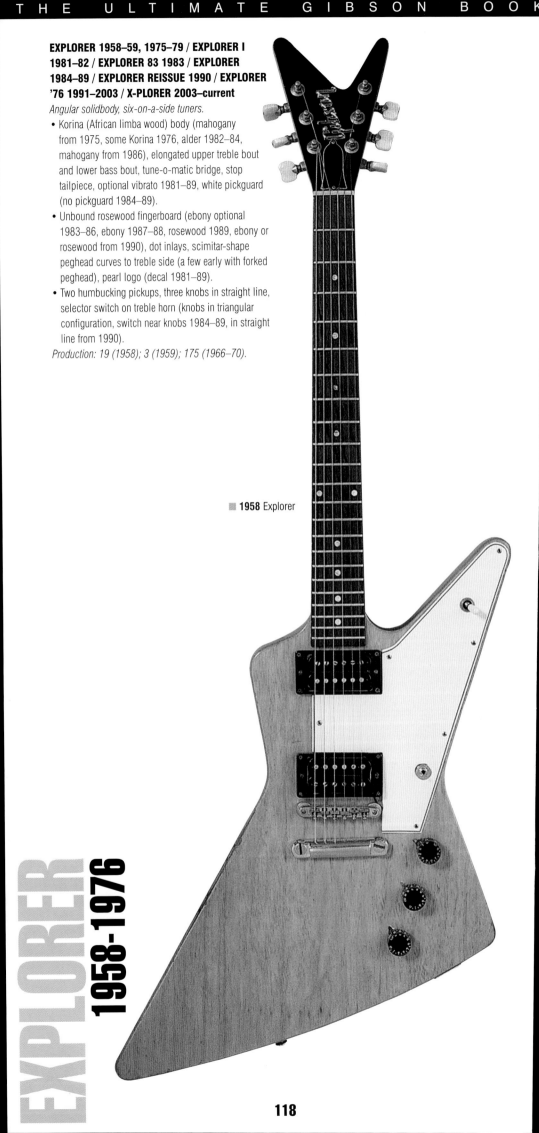

EXPLORER 1958–59, 1975–79 / EXPLORER I 1981–82 / EXPLORER 83 1983 / EXPLORER 1984–89 / EXPLORER REISSUE 1990 / EXPLORER '76 1991–2003 / X-PLORER 2003–current

Angular solidbody, six-on-a-side tuners.

- Korina (African limba wood) body (mahogany from 1975, some Korina 1976, alder 1982–84, mahogany from 1986), elongated upper treble bout and lower bass bout, tune-o-matic bridge, stop tailpiece, optional vibrato 1981–89, white pickguard (no pickguard 1984–89).
- Unbound rosewood fingerboard (ebony optional 1983–86, ebony 1987–88, rosewood 1989, ebony or rosewood from 1990), dot inlays, scimitar-shape peghead curves to treble side (a few early with forked peghead), pearl logo (decal 1981–89).
- Two humbucking pickups, three knobs in straight line, selector switch on treble horn (knobs in triangular configuration, switch near knobs 1984–89, in straight line from 1990).

Production: 19 (1958); 3 (1959); 175 (1966–70).

■ **1958** Explorer

EXPLORER 1958-1976

EXPLORER 1958-1976

American-made.
World-played.

Gibson: The first name in guitars. The final word in quality.

Two examples of this enduring excellence are the Flying V, for rock at the highest altitudes, and the Explorer, a traveller along the farthest frontiers of sound.

Like every Gibson since 1894, these instruments are created from a unique marriage of materials and expertise.

A Gibson® is mass and density crafted into brilliance and sustain. It is electronics on the edge of today's sound, destined to be tomorrow's classic.

Gibson. Made in America. Best in the world.

Gibson the first name in guitars. Yesterday, today, tomorrow.

1983 press advertisement

THE EXPLORER/EXPLORER CM 1976, 1981–84
Angular solidbody, curly maple top, fine-tune tailpiece.
- Angular maple solidbody, bound curly maple top, tune-o-matic bridge, TP-6 fine-tune tailpiece, gold-plated hardware, Antique Sunburst, Vintage Cherry Sunburst, or Antique Natural finish.
- Maple neck, unbound ebony fingerboard, dot inlays, some with *E/2* on truss-rod cover, pearl logo.
- Two exposed-coil Dirty Fingers humbucking pickups, three knobs in straight line, knobs mounted into top, 3-way selector switch on upper treble horn.

1963 Explorer

EXPLORER II 1979–83

Angular multi-layer solidbody with beveled edges.
- 5-layer walnut and maple body with walnut or maple top, beveled body edges, tune-o-matic bridge, TP-6 tailpiece, gold-plated hardware, Natural finish.
- 22 frets, 24¾-inch scale, unbound ebony fingerboard, dot inlays, E/2 on truss-rod cover.
- Two humbucking pickups with exposed coils, three knobs in straight line, knobs mounted into top, 3-way selector switch into pickguard on upper treble horn.

EXPLORER KORINA 1982–84

Reissue of 1958 version, Korina body, Nashville wide-travel tune-o-matic bridge, gold knobs, metal tuner buttons, standard 8-digit serial number, Candy Apple Red, Ebony, Ivory, or Antique Natural finish.

EXPLORER HERITAGE 1983

Reissue of 1958 version, Korina body, black knobs, 3-piece Korina neck (first eight with one-piece neck), pearloid keystone tuner buttons, serial number of 1 followed by a space and four digits, Antique Natural, Ebony, or Ivory finish.
Production: 100.

EXPLORER LEFT HAND 1984–87

Left-handed.

EXPLORER III 1984–85

Angular solidbody, three pickups.
- Alder body, tune-o-matic bridge, locking nut vibrato system optional, Alpine White or military-style Camouflage finish.
- Maple neck, unbound rosewood fingerboard, dot inlays, metal tuners, decal logo.
- Three soapbar pickups, two knobs, two selector switches.

EXPLORER 400/400+ 1985–86

400-series electronics, one Dirty Fingers humbucking pickup and two single-coil pickups, master tone and master volume knob, three mini-switches for on/off pickup control, push/pull volume control for coil tap, Kahler Flyer vibrato, black chrome hardware, Alpine White, Ebony, Ferrari Red, or Pewter finish.

EXPLORER SYNTHESIZER 1985

Roland 700 synthesizer system, Alpine White or Ebony finish.

EXPLORER BLACK HARDWARE 1985

Kahler vibrato standard, black hardware.

EXPLORER 90 1988

Angular solidbody, strings through body.
- Angular mahogany solidbody, tune-o-matic bridge, lightning-bolt tailpiece with strings through body, Floyd Rose vibrato optional, black chrome hardware, Alpine White, Ebony, or Luna Silver finish.
- 25½-inch scale, ebony fingerboard, split-diamond inlays, pearl logo.
- One humbucking pickup, two knobs.

EXPLORER 90 DOUBLE 1989–90

Single-coil neck pickup, humbucking bridge pickup, two knobs, push/pull volume knob for coil tap, selector switch between knobs.

1958 KORINA EXPLORER 1993–current

Replica of 1958 version (5 with "split V" peghead shape), Korina body and neck, gold-plated hardware, Antique Natural finish.

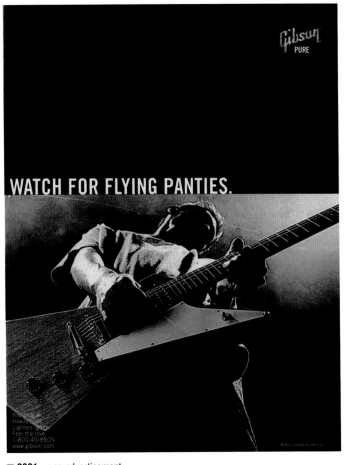

■ **2001** press advertisement

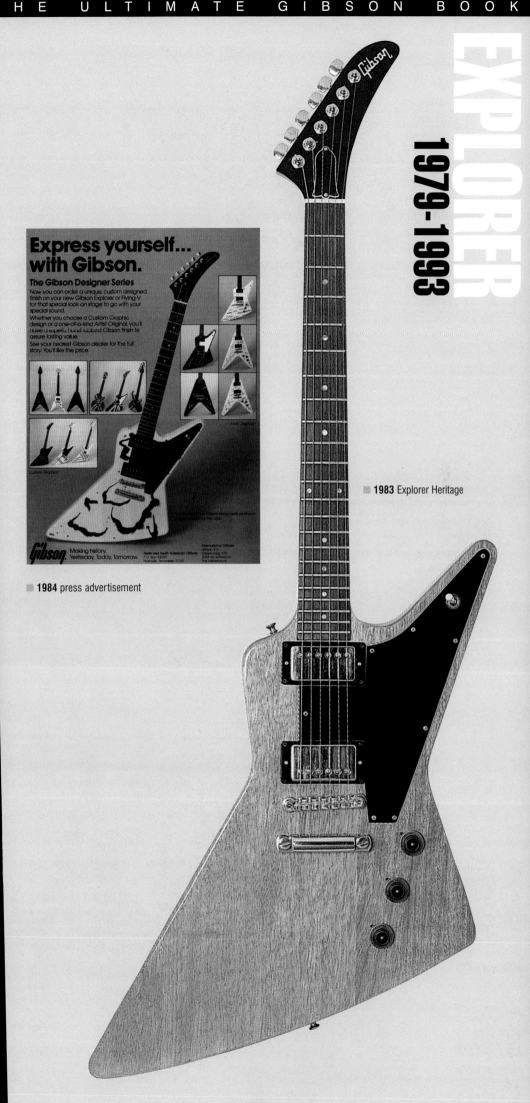

1983 Explorer Heritage

1984 press advertisement

EXPLORER CENTENNIAL (Apr. 1994 guitar of the month)

Serial number in raised numerals on tailpiece, numeral 1 of serial number formed by row of diamonds, letter i of logo dotted by inlaid diamond, gold medallion on back of peghead, gold-plated hardware, Antique Gold finish, limited run of no more than 101 serial numbered from 1894–1994, package includes 16x20 framed photograph and gold signet ring.

EXPLORER GOTHIC 1998–2001 / X-PLORER GOTHIC 2001

No pickup covers, black pickguard, ebony fingerboard, moon-and-star inlay at 12th fret (no other inlay), white-outline headstock logo, black chrome hardware, Flat Black finish.

EXPLORER PRO 2002–05, 2007–current

Angular body, smaller than standard Explorer size, flame maple top.

- Angular-design mahogany solidbody, seven-eighths of standard Explorer size, flame maple top optional, tune-o-matic bridge, Antique binding, chrome-plated hardware.
- Mahogany neck, bound rosewood fingerboard, dot inlays, curved peghead with 6-on-a-side tuner configuration, pearl logo.
- Two exposed-coil humbucking pickups, three knobs in line parallel to edge, selector switch on treble horn.

EXPLORER VOODOO 2002–04

Swamp ash body, Juju finish (black with red wood filler), ebony fingerboard, voodoo doll inlay at 5th fret (no other inlays), red logo, red/black pickup coils.

MAHOGANY EXPLORER 2002–03

Green, Copper, Blue, or Silver satin metallic finishes. Production: 15 in each finish.

MAHOGANY EXPLORER SPLIT HEADSTOCK 2003–04

Mahogany body and neck, V-shaped headstock.

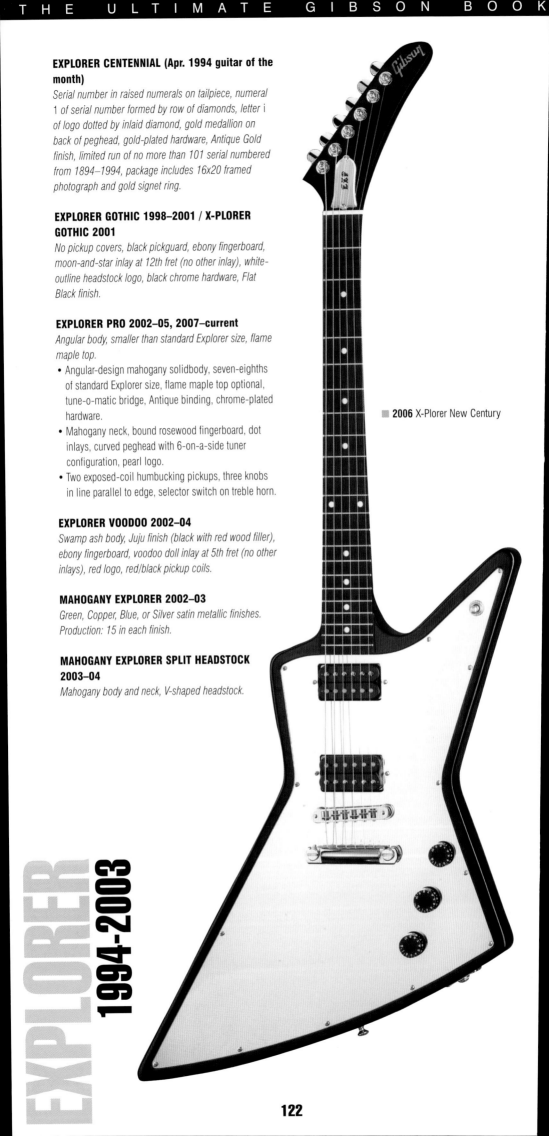

2006 X-Plorer New Century

EXPLORER 1994-2003

EXPLORER 1994-2003

2010 The Holy Explorer
Limited Run

2009 Robot Explorer

GIBSON MODERNE

The Gibson Moderne is, arguably, the most famous guitar that never existed. Its fame is not arguable, but the possibility of its existence has made the closest thing the guitar world has to a holy grail. Like the Biblical holy grail, the Moderne has been depicted in art—in a painting by a guitar designer, and in Gibson president Ted McCarty's patent drawing. It was to be the third member of the Modernistic Trio of 1958 that included the Flying V and Explorer. But, the legend goes, the V and Explorer were so poorly received that no Modernes were ever shipped.

Attendees at a trade show in 1958 have said, albeit 35 years later, that they saw the Moderne with their own eyes. Despite testimony from a Gibson employee who says they never even made a "soft prototype," from which the production tooling would be developed, collectors have turned the Moderne into the holy grail of the guitar world. And like the biblical Holy Grail, no original Moderne has ever been found.

The search for the Moderne has inspired numerous fakes and forgeries, and Gibson only added to the Moderne mystique in 1982 by "reissuing" it, with a design inspired by the patent drawings. To date these Moderne Heritage models are the only authentic Modernes.

1982 Moderne

EXPLORER SATIN FINISH 2003–04
Non-gloss finish.

ALLEN COLLINS EXPLORER 2003
Based on 1958 version, signature model for Lynyrd Skynyrd band member, Korina body and neck, Maestro vibrato, additional strap button on neck heel, aged Natural finish, belt buckle wear on back.
Production: 100.

X-PLORER STUDIO 2004
Angular body smaller than standard Explorer size.
- Angular-design poplar solidbody, seven-eighths of regular Explorer size, tune-o-matic bridge, no pickguard.
- Mahogany neck, unbound rosewood fingerboard, dot inlays, curved peghead with 6-on-a-side tuner configuration, pearl logo.
- Two exposed-coil humbucking pickups, three knobs in line parallel to edge of guitar, selector switch on treble horn.

X-PLORER NEW CENTURY 2006–current
Full-body mirror pickguard, rosewood fingerboard, mirror dot inlays, two exposed-coil humbuckers.

EXPLORER 2003-2006

■ **2010** Melody Maker
Explorer

■ **2009** Tribal Explorer
Limited Run

The Flying V is winging your way again

Gibson's original Flying V's are considered the most valuable electric guitars around—so valuable that their owners won't part with them for any price.

The demand to bring back the Flying V has gotten so out of hand, Gibson is now offering a Special Edition of this famous guitar. If you weren't around in the 50's to get a Gibson Flying V, or if you simply passed up the chance of a lifetime, you'd better jump at this second chance now while this Special Edition is available. You'll be glad you did—even twenty years from now.

Gibson

A Product of Norlin Music, Inc.
7373 N. Cicero Ave.
Lincolnwood, Illinois 60646

■ **1975** press advertisement

■ **1957** Flying V prototype

FLYING V
1958-1981

FLYING V 1958–59, 1965–69, 1971–79, 1984–89 / FLYING V I 1981–82 / FLYING V 83 1983 / FLYING V REISSUE 1990 / FLYING V '67 1991–2003 / X-FACTOR V 2003–current

V-shaped solidbody.

- Korina (African limba wood) V-shaped solidbody (mahogany 1965–79, alder 1981–89, mahogany from 1990), some with *Limited Edition Reissue* medallion on top 1971–74, strings anchor through body in V-shaped anchor plate (stopbar or vibrato from 1965), white pickguard (a few early with black, no pickguard 1981–89), body shoulders square at neck, gold-plated hardware (chrome from 1965).
- Unbound rosewood fingerboard (ebony 1981–83, rosewood or ebony 1981–88), dot inlays, triangular peghead with rounded top, raised plastic peghead logo (logo on truss-rod cover from 1965–79, decal from 1981).
- Two humbucking pickups (exposed-coil 1975–79), three knobs in straight line (triangular knob configuration from 1965.

Production: 81 (1958); 17 (1959); 2 (1965); 111 (1966); 15 (1969); 47 (1970); 350 (1971); 2 (1973); 1 (1974), 3,223 (1975–79).

FLYING V II 1979–82

V-shaped layered body, boomerang pickups.

- 5-layer maple/walnut body with walnut or maple top, beveled top and back body edges, tune-o-matic bridge, gold-plated hardware, Natural finish.
- Unbound ebony fingerboard, dot inlays.
- Two boomerang-shaped pickups.

FLYING V CMT / THE V 1981–85

V-shaped solidbody, curly maple top.

- Maple body (earliest with mahogany body), curly maple top, no pickguard, bound top, vibrato optional, gold-plated hardware, Antique Sunburst, Antique Natural, or Vintage Cherry Sunburst finish.
- Maple neck, ebony fingerboard, dot inlays, pearl logo.
- Two Dirty Fingers humbucking pickups with exposed cream coils, three knobs in curving line, selector switch between upper knobs.

FLYING V FF 8 1981

Made for Frankfurt (Germany) trade show, same specs as Flying V I.

FLYING V HERITAGE 1981–82

Reissue of 1958 version, 3-piece Korina neck, Antique Natural, Ebony, Candy Apple Red, or White finish, serial number of letter followed by three digits (example: A 123).

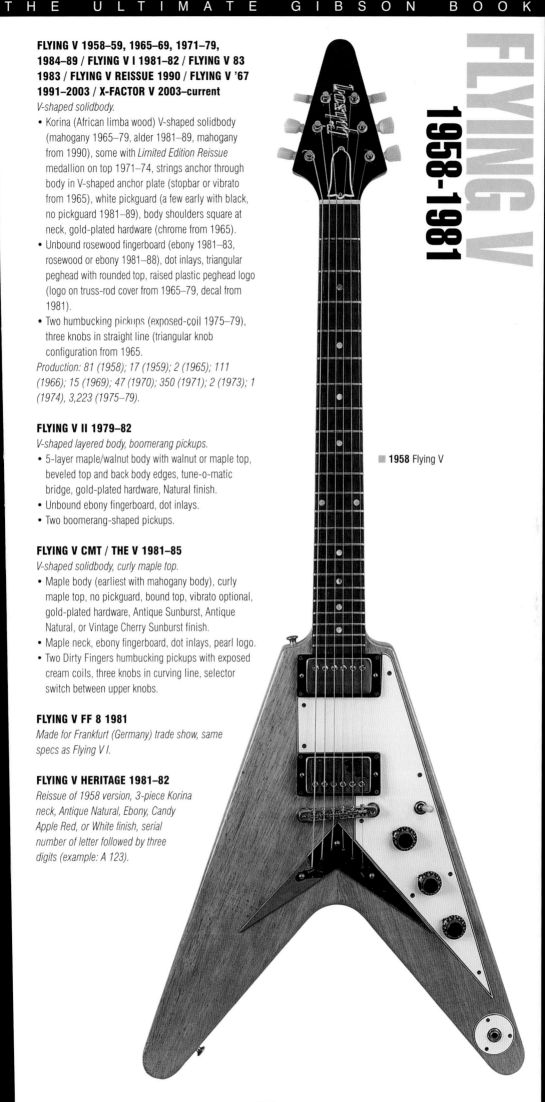

1958 Flying V

127

FLYING V KORINA 1983

Same as Flying V Heritage except for black barrel knobs, 8-digit serial number.

FLYING V LEFT HAND 1984–87

Left-handed, Ebony or Red finish.

FLYING V XPL 1984–86

Kahler vibrato or combination bridge/tailpiece with individual string adjustments (tune-o-matic optional from 1985), maple neck, unbound ebony fingerboard, Explorer-style peghead, 6-on-a-side tuner arrangement.

FLYING V XPL BLACK HARDWARE 1985

Black hardware, Kahler vibrola standard, Ebony, Alpine White, or Red finish.

FLYING V 400/400+ 1985–86

400-series electronics, one Dirty Fingers humbucking pickup and two single-coil pickups, master tone and master volume knob, three mini-switches for on/off pickup control, push/pull volume control for coil tap, Kahler Flyer vibrato, black chrome hardware, Alpine White, Ebony, Ferrari Red, or Pewter finish.

FLYING V BLACK HARDWARE 1985

Kahler vibrato standard, black hardware.

FLYING V 90 1988

V-shaped solidbody, split-diamond inlays.
- Floyd Rose vibrato optional, black chrome hardware, Alpine White, Ebony, or Nuclear Yellow finish.
- 25½-inch scale, unbound ebony fingerboard, split-diamond inlays, pearl logo.
- One humbucking pickup.

FLYING V 90 DOUBLE 1989–90

One single-coil and one double-coil pickup, two knobs, push/pull volume knob for coil tap, tune-o-matic bridge, Floyd Rose vibrato optional, pearl logo, Alpine White, Ebony, or Luna Silver finish.

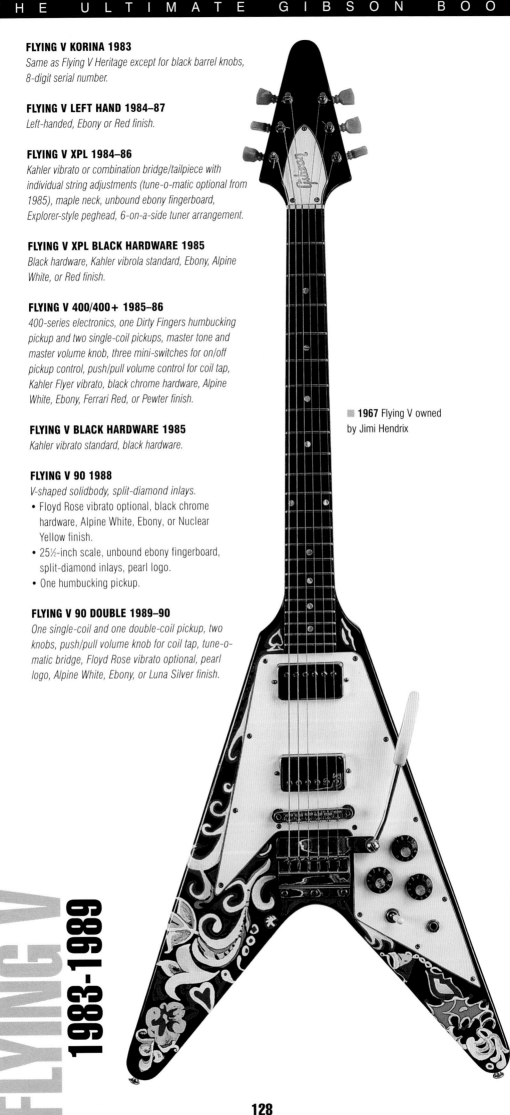

1967 Flying V owned by Jimi Hendrix

FLYING V 1983-1989

■ **1981** press advertisement

■ **1979** Flying V

■ **1981** Flying V-II

1958 KORINA FLYING V 1991–current / 1959 KORINA FLYING V 1994–current

Replica of 1958/59 style, Korina body and neck, gold-plated hardware, Antique Natural finish.

JIMI HENDRIX '69 FLYING V CUSTOM 1991–1993

Based on 1969 model, mahogany body, 490R and 490T humbucking pickups, signature on pickguard, mahogany neck, split-diamond inlays, gold-plated hardware, first run of 400 numbered on truss-rod cover, Hall of Fame series logo on back of peghead, Ebony finish.
Production: 25 promotional instruments for RCA Records.

LONNIE MACK FLYING V 1993–94

Mahogany body, 1958-style control arrangement, Bigsby vibrato with anchor bar between lower bouts.

FLYING V CENTENNIAL (July 1994 guitar of the month)

Serial number in raised numerals on tailpiece, numeral 1 of serial number formed by row of diamonds, letter i of logo dotted by inlaid diamond, gold medallion on back of peghead, gold-plated hardware, Antique Gold finish, limited run of no more than 101 serial numbered from 1894–1994, package includes 16x20 framed photograph and gold signet ring.

FLYING V PRIMAVERA 1994

Primavera wood (light mahogany), gold-plated hardware with Antique Natural finish, chrome-plated hardware with translucent and metallic finishes.

FLYING V '98 GOTHIC 1998–2001

Two '57 Classic humbucking pickups with no covers, Flying V '98 control configuration with 3-in-line knobs, black pickguard, ebony fingerboard, moon-and-star inlay at 12th fret, no other inlay, white outline of logo on peghead, black chrome hardware, satin Ebony finish.

1998 Flying V '98 Gothic

FLYING V 1991-2008

FLYING V '98 1998

Two ceramic-magnet humbucking pickups with exposed coils, 1958-style controls (3-in-line knob configuration, switch above knobs, jack in lower treble bout), Grover tuners with metal buttons, Natural or Naturalburst finish with gold-plated hardware, or Translucent Purple finish with chrome-plated hardware.

LENNY KRAVITZ 1967 FLYING V 2001–04

Mirror pickguard, Black finish with sparkles, Maestro vibrato.
Production: 125.

MAHOGANY FLYING V 2002–04

Mahogany neck and body, Green, Copper, Blue, or Silver satin metallic finishes.
Production: 15 in each finish.

FLYING V MIRROR PICKGUARD 2002

Mirror pickguard, Cherry, Ebony, or Classic White finishes.

FLYING V CUSTOM 2002, 2004

Knobs in straight line, ebony fingerboard, pearl block inlays, Ebony (2002) or Classic White (2004) finish.
Production: 40 (2002).

FLYING V VOODOO 2002

Swamp ash body, Juju finish (black with red wood filler), ebony fingerboard, voodoo doll inlay at 5th fret (no other inlays), red logo, red/black pickup coils.

X-FACTOR V FADED 2003–current

Rosewood fingerboard, two exposed-coil humbuckers, three knobs in triangular configuration, Worn Cherry finish.

FLYING V STANDARD QUILT TOP 2004–06

Quilted maple top cap.

JUDAS PRIEST FLYING V 2005–current

1960s styling, tune-o-matic bridge with plastic saddles, two exposed-coil 57 Classic humbuckers, three knobs in triangular configuration, Custom Authentic Candy Apple Red finish, certificate signed by K.K. Downing and Glenn Tipton.
Production: 30 (sold as a set with Judas Priest SG).

X-FACTOR V NEW CENTURY 2006–current

Mirror dot inlays, full body mirror pickguard.

JIMI HENDRIX PSYCHEDELIC FLYING V 2006

Based on 1967 version hand-painted by Hendrix, Maestro vibrato, chrome-plated hardware, witch hat knobs.
Production: 150.

FLYING V FADED 3-PICKUP 2007

Three uncovered humbuckers, two standard knobs, 6-way rotary selector switch with pointer knob, Worn Black or Worn White finish.

REVERSE FLYING V 2007

V opens toward neck, asymmetrical V-shaped headstock, Trans Amber finish, guitar of the week.
Production: 400.

50-YEAR COMMEMORATIVE FLYING V (Mar. 2008 guitar of the month)

Curly maple top cap with beveled edges, 2 knobs, 1 switch, bound ebony fingerboard, slashed block inlays, gold fretwire, bound peghead, "50th" on truss-rod cover, inverted red V on peghead, thin script Gibson logo (from early 1950s BR-series lap steels), Steinberger gearless tuners, gold-plated hardware, Brimstone Burst finish, guitar of the month.
Production: 1,000.

ROBOT FLYING V 2008–CURRENT

Auto tune system, two knobs, uncovered humbuckers, bound ebony fingerboard, trapezoid inlays, Metallic Red finish.

SHRED V (Aug. 2008 guitar of the month)

Two EMG humbuckers, two knobs, Kahler vibrato, '50s rounded neck profile, unbound ebony fingerboard, black dot inlays, locking Grover tuners, black chrome hardware, Ebony finish, guitar of the month.
Production: 1,000.

2003 press advertisement

2009 Tribal V

2010 Melody Maker Flying V

FLYING V 2008-2011

ZAKK WYLDE FLYING V BULLSEYE 2008–09 / ZAKK WYLDE FLYING V CUSTOM FLOYD ROSE 2010–current

Bullseye finish.

- Mahogany body, Floyd Rose vibrato, black and white bullseye graphic on body.
- Bound ebony fingerboard, pearl block inlay, bound peghead, 5-piece split-diamond peghead inlay, pearl logo.
- Two EMG humbucking pickups, four knobs, selector switch.

THE HOLY V (Jan. 2009 guitar of the month)

Triangular hole through body in each wing, boomerang-shaped hole between pickup and fingerboard, one uncovered humbucking pickup, one knob, bound ebony fingerboard, split-diamond inlays, Gibson logo on truss rod cover, Steinberger Gearless tuners, chrome-plated hardware, guitar of the month.
Production: 1,000.

TRIBAL V 2009–10

Two uncovered pickups, two knobs, Kahler tremolo, unbound ebony fingerboard, White finish with abstract black art, Limited Run series.
Production: 350.

7-STRING FLYING V 2011–current

Two EMG active humbuckers, V-shaped string anchor plate, three knobs in straight line, black pickguard, unbound rosewood fingerboard, no inlays, gold-plated hardware, Steinberger gearless tuners, Black finish.

MELODY MAKER FLYING V 2011–current

One uncovered humbucker, one knob, satin finish.

■ **2011** 7-string Flying V

TWICE AS MANY NECKS

Gibson made doubleneck guitars before World War II but only for Hawaiian-style players. It wasn't until the 1950s, when West Coast country artists began using custom-made doublenecks, that Gibson recognized a market for "two guitars in one."

To distinguish a Gibson from the competition, the company came up with a unique design, featuring a hollow body with Gibson's traditional carved spruce top and no soundholes. Pointed cutaways on both sides of the body predated the SG body shape by three years.

Two doubleneck models debuted in 1958: the six-string/twelve-string EDS-1275 and six-string/short-scale EMS-1235 (called "double mandolin" even though both necks had six strings). They were available by custom order only, with any combination of necks, including tenor, plectrum, or bass.

The hollow, hole-less bodies produced a sound unlike any Gibson electric before or since, but they were heavy and unwieldy, and in 1961, Gibson gave the doublenecks the same thinner, lighter, solid mahogany body of the new SG models. The six/twelve remained in production through the 1960s and, thanks to its onstage use by Led Zeppelin's Jimmy Page in the early 1970s, was put back into production in 1977. The EDS-1275 received another boost in the 1980s when Slash of Guns N' Roses became associated with the model, and it is still in production today.

EDS-1275 DOUBLE 12 1958–68, 1974–current
Six-string neck and twelve-string neck.
- Hollowbody with maple back and sides and carved spruce top, double cutaway with pointed horns (SG-style solidbody with pointed horns from c.1962), no soundholes, tune-o-matic bridges, triple-bound top and back (unbound with change to SG shape), nickel-plated hardware (gold on Alpine White finish from 1988).
- 12-string and 6-string necks, 24¾-inch scales, bound rosewood fingerboards, double-parallelogram inlay, pearl logo (decal from 1977).
- Two humbucking pickups for each neck, two knobs for each neck, one switch on treble side, one switch on bass side, one switch between bridges (with change to SG body): four knobs on lower treble bout, one switch between tailpieces, one switch on upper treble bout).
Production: 110 (1958–68); 1,145 (1974–79).

DOUBLENECK STYLES
Any combination of necks was available by custom order from 1958–68.

EMS-1235 DOUBLE MANDOLIN 1958–68
Short six-string guitar neck and standard six-string guitar neck.
- Double pointed cutaways, hollow maple body with carved spruce top, no soundholes (SG-style solidbody with pointed cutaways from c1962), tune-o-matic bridge for standard neck, height-adjustable bridge for short neck.
- Standard guitar neck and short six-string neck with 15½-inch scale, bound rosewood fingerboards, double-parallelogram inlay, no peghead ornament.
- One humbucking pickup for short neck, two humbucking pickups for standard neck, four knobs on lower treble bout, one switch between tailpieces, one switch on upper treble bout.
Production: 61.

1958 EDS-1275 Double 12

MELODY MAKER / MM 1959–70, 1986–92, 2007–current

Thin single- or double-cut solidbody, oblong pickup.

- Single rounded cutaway (symmetrical double cutaway with rounded horns, 1961–62; horns slightly more open, 1963–64; SG shape with pointed horns, 1965–70; single cutaway 1986–92, 2007–current), body 1⅜-inch deep, wraparound bridge/tailpiece, pickguard surrounds pickups, vibrato optional from 1962.
- Unbound rosewood fingerboard, dot inlays, narrow (2¼-inch) peghead (standard width 1970, narrow 1986–92), decal logo.
- Oblong pickup ⅞-inch-wide (⅝-inch-inch from 1960) with black plastic cover and no visible poles, two knobs; single-coil pickup with visible polepieces (2007–current); two-pickup option (2007–08).

Production: 23,006 (1959–70).

MM ¾-scale 1959–70

22¾-inch scale, 12 frets clear of body.
Production: 3,356.

 **1961** Melody Maker

MELODY MAKERS

1959

MELODY MAKERS

MELODY MAKERS: STUDENT GUITARS, MASS APPEAL, TIGHT ECONOMIES—THEY'RE BACK TODAY

Through most of the 20th century, the best-selling Gibsons were the lowest-priced models. That pattern held true in the 1950s in the Les Paul line, where Gibson sold more Juniors than all the other Les Pauls combined. It stood to reason that an even cheaper model would sell even better, and to that end, Gibson debuted the Melody Maker, in full-scale and three-quarter-scale versions, in 1959.

The Melody Maker was obviously cheaper than a Les Paul Junior, with a thinner body and a thinner pickup with no individual polepieces. A double-pickup version followed in 1960, and later a triple-pickup and a 12-string Melody Maker also joined the flock.

The Melody Makers' prices made them irresistible to buyers on a budget. In 1960, the single-pickup model was $99.50, compared to $132.50 for the Les Paul Junior. In 1962, the two-pickup MM-D listed at $147.50—the exact same price as the SG Junior, which had only one pickup. By 1965, the Melody Makers were outselling the SGs in significant numbers, but the resurgence of interest in Les Paul Standards in the late 1960s marked the beginning of that model's domination of Gibson sales and the end of the Melody Makers.

To counteract the flood of cheap Japanese imports, Gibson revived its pre-World War II budget brand Kalamazoo in the late 1960s. The appeal of essential features at a rock-bottom price never completely died, however, and Gibson brought back the Melody Maker—equipped with a single humbucker—for brief return engagements in 1988 and again in the mid 1990s.

1968 press advertisement

MM-D/MELODY MAKER DOUBLE (first version) 1960–70, 1976

Two pickups, four knobs, standard peghead size.
Production: 19,456 (1960–70).

MELODY MAKER DOUBLE (second version) 1977–83

Rounded horns, horns point away from neck, two pickups, tune-o-matic bridge (earliest with stud-mounted wraparound bridge/tailpiece), four knobs, earliest with bolt-on neck, narrow peghead, metal tuner buttons, Cherry or Sunburst finish.
Production: 1,085 (1977–79).

MM-III 1967–71

Three pickups.
Production: 352.

MM-12 1967–71

12-string, two pickups, no vibrato.
Production: 210.

2007 Melody Maker

MELODY MAKERS 1960-2011

2010 Jonas Brothers Melody Maker

2011 Joan Jett Melody Maker

STANDARD (first version) 1958

- Bound carved-top body with red to yellow sunburst.
- Bound rosewood fingerboard, crown markers; "Les Paul Model" on headstock; plastic tuner buttons.
- Two metal-cover humbucker pickups.
- Six-saddle bridge plus separate bar tailpiece.
- Four controls (two volume, two tone) plus three-way selector.
- Cream plastic pickguard.

Small profile frets on standard chunky round-backed neck.

Production: 434 (including some Goldtop models).

■ **1958** Les Paul Standard

LES PAUL STANDARD 1958

1958 Les Paul Standard

1958 Les Paul Standard

1958 Les Paul Standard

STANDARD (first version) 1959
- Bound carved-top body with red to yellow sunburst.
- Bound rosewood fingerboard, crown markers; "Les Paul Model" on headstock; plastic tuner buttons.
- Two metal-cover humbucker pickups.
- Six-saddle bridge plus separate bar tailpiece.
- Four controls (two volume, two tone) plus three-way selector.
- Cream plastic pickguard.

Larger profile frets on standard round-backed neck.
Production: 643.

■ **1959** Les Paul Standard

LES PAUL STANDARD 1959

LES PAUL STANDARD

■ **1959** Les Paul Standard

■ **1959** Les Paul Standard

■ **1959** Les Paul Standard custom finish

STANDARD (first version) 1960

- Bound carved-top body with red to yellow sunburst.
- Bound rosewood fingerboard, crown markers; "Les Paul Model" on headstock; plastic tuner buttons.
- Two metal-cover humbucker pickups.
- Six-saddle bridge plus separate bar tailpiece.
- Four controls (two volume, two tone) plus three-way selector.
- Cream plastic pickguard.

Larger profile frets on slimmer flat-profiled neck.
Production: 635.

■ **1960** Les Paul Standard

LES PAUL STANDARD 1960

LES PAUL STANDARD: A LEGEND IS BORN

On May 28, 1958, two Les Pauls were entered into Gibson's shipping log with the cryptic note "2 LP Spec Finish." The special finish was a sunburst style, with amber-yellow in the middle, graduating to cherry red around the edges. It was the final evolutionary step from the original Goldtop Les Paul Model to the sunburst Les Paul Standard, which would become the most coveted model in the history of the electric guitar.

The original 1952 Les Paul was pretty close to perfect, but the neck angle didn't work with the trapeze-style bridge/tailpiece. The tune-o-matic bridge with stopbar tailpiece, introduced on the Les Paul Custom in 1954 and adopted by the Goldtop in 1955, solved the problems in that area. Gibson's powerful new humbucking pickups replaced the original single-coil P-90s in 1957—although guitarists wouldn't tap their full potential until well into the 1960s. In 1958, the sunburst finish allowed the wood grain of the maple top to show through, adding an aesthetic element that, like a fingerprint, gave every sunburst Les Paul its own unique identity.

To distinguish this new Les Paul from the three others in the line, Gibson upgraded the old, generic model name ("Model") to Standard. That small name change proved to be prophetic in a big way, as the Les Paul Standard would come to set the standard for the electric guitar in rock'n'roll music.

■ **1960** Les Paul Standard

LES PAUL STANDARD 1960

1960 Les
Paul Standard

1960 Les Paul Standard
Paul McCartney's left-handed example

LES PAUL STANDARD 1960

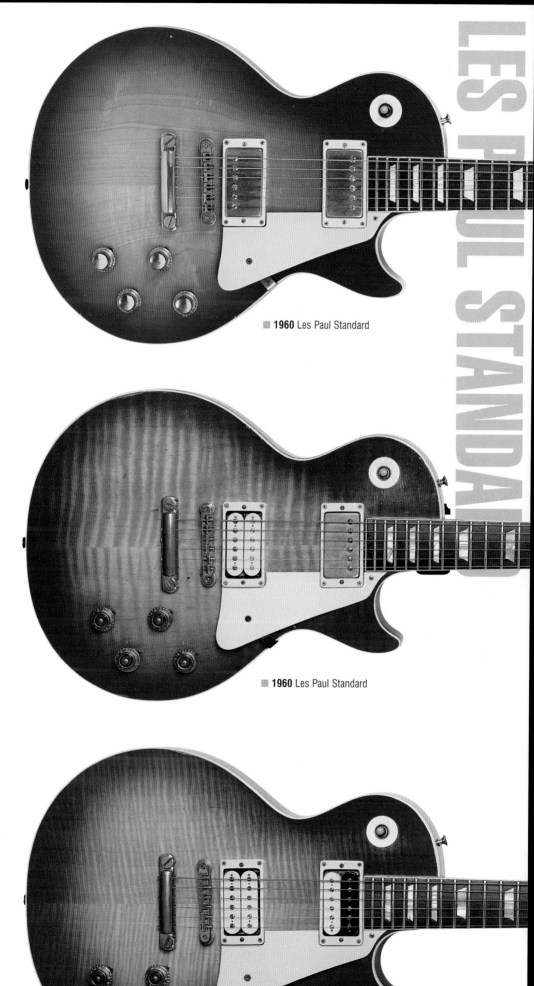

LES PAUL STANDARD

■ **1960** Les Paul Standard

■ **1960** Les Paul Standard

■ **1960** Les Paul Standard

DELUXE 1969–84, 1992–97, 1999–2008
"Deluxe" on truss-rod cover.
- Bound carved-top body; sunbursts, Natural, or colors.
- Bound rosewood fingerboard, crown markers; "Les Paul Model" on headstock; "Deluxe" on truss-rod cover; plastic tuner buttons (later metal).
- Two mini-sized metal-cover humbucker pickups.
- Four controls (two volume, two tone) plus three-way selector.
- Cream plastic pickguard.
- Six-saddle bridge plus separate bar tailpiece.

Earliest examples with plastic-cover six-polepiece single-coil pickups.
Some mini-humbucker-equipped examples with extra plastic ring around pickup covers.
Also 30th Anniversary version (2000).
Also Guitar Of The Week model 2007, Gold top finish with antiqued binding.
Production: Kalamazoo-made: 1971 4,466; 1972 5,194; 1973 10,484; 1974 7,367; 1975 2,561; 1976 172; 1977 413; 1978 4,450; 1979 413. Figures not available for 1969, 1970, and 80s, nor for any Nashville production.

DELUXE HALL OF FAME EDITION 1991
Similar to Deluxe, *except Gold finish all around (sides, back, back of neck).*
Custom Shop.

STRINGS & THINGS REISSUE 1975–78
Reissue based on 1959-period original; special order by Strings & Things store in Memphis, TN; production 28 (four of which destroyed).

■ **1969** Les Paul Deluxe

1969 Les Paul Deluxe

1976 Les Paul Artisan

1978 Les Paul Artisan

149

ARTISAN 1976–82

Ornate fingerboard markers.

- Bound carved-top body; Sunburst, Brown, Black, or White.
- Bound ebony fingerboard, ornate markers; script Gibson logo and ornate inlay on headstock; "Artisan" on truss-rod cover.
- Two or three metal-cover humbucker pickups.
- Four controls (two volume, two tone) plus three-way selector.
- Black laminated plastic pickguard.
- Six-saddle bridge plus separate bar tailpiece (some with six fine-tuning knobs).
- Gold-plated hardware.

Some without fine-tuners on tailpiece.

Production: 1976 2; 1977 1,469; 1978 641; 1979 108. Figures not available for 80s.

PRO DELUXE 1976–82

Bound ebony fingerboard with crown markers.

- Bound carved-top body; sunbursts or colors.
- Bound ebony fingerboard, crown markers; "Les Paul Model" on headstock; "Pro" on truss-rod cover.
- Two plastic-cover six-polepiece single-coil pickups.
- Four controls (two volume, two tone) plus three-way selector.
- Cream plastic pickguard.
- Six-saddle bridge plus separate bar tailpiece.

■ **1980** Les Paul Pro Deluxe

LES PAUL STANDARD 1976

THE LES PAUL RETURNS

A demand for the original Les Paul design that was fueled by the blues-rock boom of the mid and late 1960s inspired Gibson to reissue two versions of the model in 1968. Oddly enough, these took the form of the two-humbucker Les Paul Custom, known as the Black Beauty, and the Goldtop with P-90s and tune-o-matic bridge, patterned after the Les Paul circa 1955. Neither was a detail-perfect reproduction, but they fit the bill very well and helped to satisfy players' cravings for a readily available Les Paul.

The following year, the Les Paul Deluxe with two mini-humbucking pickups was introduced, becoming the "non-standard Standard" of sorts for many years. Given that the original PAF-style humbucking pickup was a major ingredient in the Les Paul's booming popularity, it remains eternally puzzling that Gibson didn't see fit to release a Standard with these pickups until a range of models returned to the form in the late '70s. Some Deluxes were issued with P-90s and, purportedly, a few were also special-ordered with standard-sized humbuckers, but the mini-humbucker remained far and away the most-seen pickup on the Les Paul of the 1970s (and perhaps the most swapped-out pickup of all time, given the number of players who "Standardized" their Deluxes).

Gibson also played around with the wood formula over the course of the decade, building the models for a time with four-piece mahogany/maple-fillet/mahogany/maple-top 'pancake' bodies instead of simply the solid mahogany back and carved maple top, and using a maple neck in place of the traditional mahogany for a time. Regardless, the Deluxe sold well, and if a player was seen with the iconic single-cutaway Gibson solidbody in the 1970s or early '80s, chances are it was one of these variations on the form.

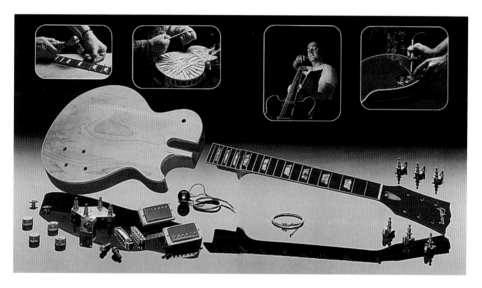

■ **1983** press advertisement

■ **1978** The Les Paul

■ **1978** The Les Paul

LES PAUL STANDARD
1976-1978

STANDARD (second version) 1976–2007

(continues as 2008 Standard, *see p.205, and* Traditional, *see p.205)* "Standard" on truss-rod cover.

- Bound carved-top body; sunbursts, Natural, or colors.
- Bound rosewood fingerboard, optional '50s fat or '60s thin neck-profile from 2002, crown markers; "Les Paul Model" on headstock; "Standard" on truss-rod cover.
- Two metal-cover humbucker pickups.
- Four controls (two volume, two tone) plus three-way selector.
- Cream plastic pickguard.
- Six-saddle bridge plus separate bar tailpiece.
- Chrome-plated hardware (gold optional in many years, nickel from 2002).

Also: natural-finish version with gold-plated hardware (1991–92); Antique Vintage Sunburst finish with '50s neck, 2007 Guitar Of The Week model, production 400.
Production: Kalamazoo-made: 1975 1; 1976 24; 1977 586; 1978 5,947; 1979 1,054. Figures not available for large Nashville production started in 70s and continuing to current.
For 80s Standard-80 models, see Heritage *entry p.158. Model changed in 2008 to* 2008 Standard *(see p.205) and* Traditional *(see p.205).*

THE LES PAUL 1976–79

"The Les Paul" on truss-rod cover.

- Bound carved-top body; Natural or Wine Red.
- Bound ebony fingerboard, block markers; split-diamond inlay on headstock; "The Les Paul" on truss-rod cover.
- Two metal-cover humbucker pickups.
- Four controls (two volume, two tone) plus three-way selector.
- Wooden pickguard.
- Six-saddle bridge plus separate bar tailpiece.
- Gold-plated hardware.

Some examples with fine-tuning tailpiece. Most examples have carved wooden components (pickup surrounds, pickguard, knobs, etc) rather than plastic.
Production: 1976 33; 1977 10; 1979 11. Total not available for 1978.

NORTH STAR 1978

Star inlay on headstock. Similar to Standard second version, *except:*

- Multi-layer (Custom-style) body binding.
- "North Star" on truss-rod cover, star inlaid in headstock.

■ **1976** The Les Paul

LES PAUL STANDARD

1976-1978

JIMMY WALLACE REISSUE 1978–97

*Reissue based on 1959-period original; special order by
Arnold & Morgan store in Dallas, TX (1978–81), then by
Sound Southwest store in Sunnyvale, TX; "Jimmy Wallace"
on truss-rod cover.*

THE PAUL STANDARD 1978–81

Thin carved walnut body.
- Unbound single-cutaway walnut body; natural.
- Unbound ebony fingerboard, dot markers, decal logo
  ("Firebrand" logo, routed but with no pearl inlay, from mid
  1981).
- Two coverless humbucker pickups.
- Four controls (two volume, two tone) plus three-way selector.
- No pickguard.
- Six-saddle bridge plus separate tailpiece.

25/50 ANNIVERSARY 1978–79

"25 50" inlay on headstock.
- Bound carved-top body; Sunburst, Natural, Red, or Black.
- Bound ebony fingerboard, split-block markers; "Les Paul 25
  50" on headstock; "Les Paul Anniversary" on gold-plated
  metal truss-rod cover; brass nut; four-figure number on back
  of headstock in addition to normal serial number.
- Two metal-cover humbucker pickups.
- Four controls (two volume, two tone) plus three-way
  selector and mini-switch.
- Black laminated plastic pickguard.
- Six-saddle bridge plus separate bar tailpiece with six fine-
  tuning knobs.
- Gold/chrome-plated hardware.

Production: 1978 1,106; 1979 2,305.

LES PAUL STANDARD 1978

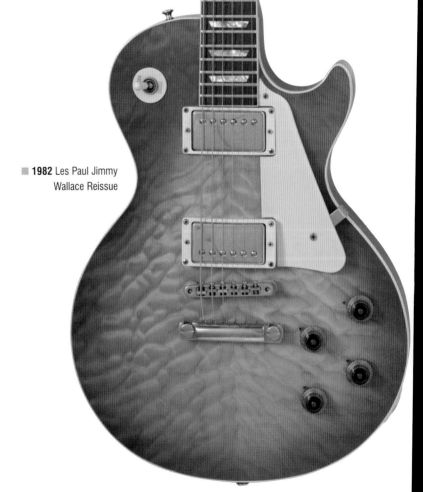

■ **1982** Les Paul Jimmy
Wallace Reissue

LES PAUL STANDARD

■ **1979** Les Paul 25/50 Anniversary

■ **1978** Les Paul 25/50 Anniversary

■ **1978** press advertisement

And now for my next number…

Gibson and Les Paul are two tough
names to live up to. Now there's a
new guitar that lives up to both.
The Paul by Gibson. It's an
ingenious variation of a theme
that's a masterpiece in itself,
the Gibson Les Paul guitar.
You get brilliant sustain from
the solid sculptured body. Plus
rich, warm tones from one of
the most beautiful musical woods,
walnut. And to put a bright edge on the
sound, there's two powerful Humbucking
pickups with exposed black coils. The Paul by
Gibson. The kind of guitar you should get to
know on a last name basis.

The Paul by *Gibson*

Another quality
product from Norlin

7373 N. Cicero Ave., Lincolnwood, Illinois 60646
51 Nantucket Blvd., Scarborough, Ontario Canada

ARTIST 1979–81

Block fingerboard markers, "LP" headstock inlay, three controls and three mini-switches.
- Bound carved-top body; sunbursts or Black.
- Bound ebony fingerboard, block markers; "LP" inlay on headstock; metal truss-rod cover; brass nut.
- Two metal-cover humbucker pickups.
- Three controls (volume, bass, treble) plus three-way selector, three mini-switches (brightness, expansion, compression); active circuit.
- Black laminated plastic pickguard.
- Six-saddle bridge plus separate bar tailpiece with six fine-tuning knobs.
- Gold-plated hardware.

Also known as Active *model.*
Production: 1979 234. Figures not available for 1980 and 1981.

KM 1979

"Les Paul KM" on truss-rod cover. Similar to Standard second version, *except:*
- Sunbursts or Natural.
- "Les Paul KM" on truss-rod cover.
- Two coverless cream-coil humbucker pickups.
- Larger rectangular six-saddle bridge plus separate bar tailpiece.

Made in Kalamazoo (hence KM) after Les Paul production moved to Nashville.
Early examples with "Custom Made" plastic plate on body face below tailpiece.
Production 1,052.

1979 Les Paul KM

LES PAUL STANDARD 1980

1980 Les Paul Artist

1979 Les Paul Artist

LES PAUL STANDARD

1980 press advertisement

HERITAGE STANDARD 80 1980–82
"Heritage Series Standard-80" on truss-rod cover; extra four-figure number on back of headstock.
- Bound carved-top body; sunbursts.
- Bound rosewood fingerboard, crown markers; "Les Paul Model" on headstock; "Heritage Series Standard-80" on truss-rod cover.
- Two metal-cover humbucker pickups.
- Four controls (two volume, two tone) plus three-way selector.
- Cream plastic pickguard.
- Six-saddle bridge plus separate bar tailpiece.

Four-figure series number on back of headstock in addition to regular serial.

HERITAGE STANDARD 80 ELITE 1980–82
"Heritage Series Standard-80 Elite" on truss-rod cover; additional four-figure serial number on back of headstock. Similar to Heritage Standard 80, *except:*
- Quilted maple carved-top.
- Bound ebony fingerboard; "Heritage Series Standard-80 Elite" on truss-rod cover.

K-II 1980
Carved-top double-cutaway body, two humbucker pickups, "K-II" on truss-rod cover.

1980 Les Paul Heritage Standard 80

1980 Les Paul Heritage Standard 80

1981 Les Paul Heritage Standard 80 Award

1982 Les Paul Heritage Standard 80 Elite

SM 1980

Dot markers, "SM" on truss-rod cover, coil tap.

- Multiple-bound carved-top body, silverburst.
- Bound rosewood fingerboard, dot markers; "SM" on truss-rod cover.
- Two metal-cover humbucker pickups.
- Four controls (two volume, two tone) plus selector and coil-tap switch.
- Six-saddle bridge plus separate bar tailpiece.

LP XRI 1981–82

"XR-I" on truss-rod cover.

- Unbound carved-top body; sunbursts.
- Unbound rosewood fingerboard, dot markers; "Les Paul Model" on headstock; and with "XR I" on truss-rod cover.
- Two coverless humbucker pickups.
- Four controls (two volume, two tone) plus three-way selector and mini-switch.
- No pickguard.
- Six-saddle bridge plus separate bar tailpiece.

LP XRII 1981–82

"XR-II" on truss-rod cover. Similar to LP XRI, *except:*

- Bound slab body; sunbursts or Natural.
- "XR II" on truss-rod cover.
- Two mini-sized metal-cover humbucker pickups.

LP XRIII 1982

"XR-III" on truss-rod cover. Similar to LP XRI, *except:*

- Possibly only Red-finish body.
- "XR III" on truss-rod cover.

■ **1982** Les Paul
Guitar Trader Reissue

LES PAUL STANDARD 1980-1982

GUITAR TRADER REISSUE 1982–84
Reissue based on 1959-period original; special order by Guitar Trader store in Redbank, NJ; serial number begins with 9, except for a few beginning with 0 (with thinner 1960-style neck). Production around 53.

LEO'S REISSUE 1982–84
Reissue based on 1959-period original; special order by Leo's music store in Oakland, CA; serial number begins with L.

■ **1982** Les Paul Leo's Reissue

LES PAUL STANDARD
1980-1982

1983 LES PAUL SPOTLIGHT SPECIAL

The three-piece tops of the 1970s Les Pauls have always been considered aesthetically inferior to the two-piece tops of the 1950s sunbursts, but in 1983 Gibson turned the tables with a model that made the three-piece top an asset. The selling point was a center section of walnut between two pieces of maple, complemented by a walnut peghead veneer that matched the center piece of the body. Multi-ply cream-brown-cream top binding, gold-plated hardware, and oval-shaped pearloid tuner buttons added to the model's visual appeal.

Gibson called the model the Les Paul Spotlight Special and offered it in Antique Natural or Antique Sunburst finish. A unique serial number configuration, with a space separating the year 83 from the limited-edition ranking, made it seem even more special. No production figure was ever announced, but the serial numbers go as high as 211.

The Spotlight Special was probably created to use up small pieces of maple and walnut that otherwise would have been scrapped. Nevertheless, it became such a special model that Gibson's Custom Shop re-created it in a limited run in 2008 as the Les Paul Spotlight Flame, again featuring highly flamed maple top pieces.

LES PAUL STANDARD 1982-1983

1983 Les Paul Spotlight Special ANT

STANDARD 82 1982

Reissue made in Kalamazoo, "Standard 82" on truss-rod cover.

SPOTLIGHT SPECIAL 1983

Contrasting wood stripe down center of body.

- Bound carved-top body with darker contrasting wood stripe down center; Natural (ANT) or Sunburst (ASB).
- Bound rosewood fingerboard, crown markers; "Les Paul Model" on headstock; "Custom Shop Edition" logo on rear of headstock; plastic tuner buttons (Natural versions) or metal tuner buttons (Sunburst versions).
- Two metal-cover humbucker pickups.
- Four controls (two volume, two tone) plus three-way selector.
- Usually no pickguard.
- Six-saddle bridge plus separate bar tailpiece.
- Gold-plated hardware.

Serial number consists of "83" plus three-figure number, on back of headstock, instead of regular serial. Custom Shop marking; production around 200 (records indicate 211).

SPOTLIGHT FLAME 2008

Similar to Spotlight Special, except: brown binding on top and fingerboard, does not say "Les Paul" on headstock or truss-rod cover, "Gibson Custom" logo on rear of headstock, inked serial number prefixed with CS.

■ **1983** Les Paul Spotlight Special ASB

LES PAUL STANDARD 1982-1983

STANDARD 59 REISSUE 1983–current

Based on Standard first version *from 1959 period, with
figured top and relatively "fat" neck profile. Over the
years, more "accurate" features: longer neck tenon,
smaller headstock. "R9" stamped in control cavity from
1993. Known by various names through the years,
including* Standard Reissue *(1983–90),* Les Paul
Reissue *(1983–93),* Standard 59 Flametop *(1991–99),*
Standard 59 Figuredtop *(2000–02). Aged versions
available, known as* Aged *(1999–2003),* Custom
Authentic *(2004–05), and VOS* Vintage Original Spec
*(2006–current). Also 50th Anniversary version (2009):
see* 50th Anniversary 1959 Standard *p.207, 209.
Custom Shop.*

■ **1993** Les Paul
Standard 59 Flametop

LES PAUL STANDARD 1983

■ **1983** Les Paul Standard Reissue

■ **1984** Les Paul Standard Reissue

■ **1985** Les Paul Standard Reissue signed by Les Paul

THE ULTIMATE GIBSON BOOK

STANDARD SPECIAL 1983
Similar to Standard second version, *except ebony fingerboard, pearl inlay, gold-plated hardware, Cardinal Red finish.*

STANDARD 83 1983
PAF Reissue pickups, pearl crown markers, nickel-plated hardware, Natural and sunbursts.

STUDIO 1983–current
"Studio" on truss-rod cover.
- Unbound carved-top body; Sunburst, Natural, or colors.
- Unbound rosewood fingerboard (rosewood or ebony 1987–98, rosewood 1999–current), dot markers (crown markers 1990–98, three-quarter-size crown markers 1999–2000, full-size crown markers 2001–current); "Les Paul Model" on headstock; "Studio" on truss-rod cover.
- Two metal-cover humbucker pickups.
- Four controls (two volume, two tone) plus three-way selector.
- Cream or laminated black plastic pickguard.
- Six-saddle bridge plus separate bar tailpiece; optional bridge/vibrato unit.
- Optional gold-plated hardware (from 1986).

Also: version with P-90 pickups, White finish, gold-plated hardware, 1997 only; Platinum version (2003–04) with "monochrome" look, ebony fingerboard with no markers, silver-color pickguard.
Guitar Of The Week version with EMG pickups, satin Ebony finish, 2007.
Production 400.

1990 Les Paul Studio Lite second version

LES PAUL STANDARD 1983-1988

STUDIO CUSTOM 1984–85
Similar to Studio, except gold-plated hardware.

STUDIO STANDARD 1984–87
Similar to Studio, except bound rosewood fingerboard, bound carved-top body.

DOUBLE-CUTAWAY XPL 1984–86
Carved-top, double cutaway, headstock with six tuners on bass side.
• Bound carved-top body, double-cutaway; Heritage Cherry Sunburst or Heritage Dark Sunburst.
• Bound ebony fingerboard, dot markers, 'scimitar' headstock with six tuners on bass side, decal logo.
• Two humbucker pickups.
• Four controls (two volume, two tone) plus three-way selector.
• Six-saddle bridge or Gibson/Kahler vibrato.

DOUBLE-CUTAWAY XPL/400 1984
Two knobs and three mini-switches. Similar to Double-Cutaway XPL, except:
• One coverless humbucker pickup and two single-coil pickups.
• Two knobs (master tone and master volume/coil-tap) and three mini switches.

XPL 1984
Similar to Standard second version, with regular single-

cut Les Paul shape, except 'scimitar' headstock with 6-on-a-side tuner configuration.

STUDIO SYNTHESIZER 1985
Similar to Studio, except Roland 700 synthesizer system.

STANDARD CMT 1986–89
Similar to Standard 59 reissue except wide binding in cutaway, metal jack plate. CMT stands for curly maple top.

STANDARD SHOWCASE EDITION 1988
Similar to Standard second version, except black-cover poleless EMG pickups, Silverburst.

STUDIO LITE (first version) 1988–90
Unbound ebony fingerboard, dot markers.
• Unbound carved-top thinner body with contoured back; sunbursts or colors.
• Unbound ebony fingerboard, dot markers; thistle-style inlay on headstock.
• Two plastic-cover humbucker pickups.
• Two controls (volume, tone) plus three-way selector and mini-switch.
• No pickguard.
• Six-saddle bridge plus separate bar tailpiece; optional bridge/vibrato unit (1988–89).
• Black-plated or gold-plated hardware.

■ **1987** catalogue spread

STANDARD VARIATIONS IN THE 90s

The Les Paul had been a bona fide model line since the 1950s, when the Custom, Special, and Junior joined the original Goldtop. By the 1990s, the Standard was such a dominating force in the guitar world that Gibson focused much of its line expansion on creating variations of the Standard.

The Classic kicked off the movement in 1990, with a modern take on the Standard, featuring the thin, fast neck of a 1960 Standard and hotter open-coil pickups. That same year, Gibson upgraded the Les Paul Studio's sub-Standard identity by changing the inlays from dots to the Standard's trapezoids. The Studio Lite followed suit a year later. By mid-decade, the Les Paul Standard had become the flagship of what was essentially a model line within a model line.

STANDARD P-100 1989

Two P-100 stacked humbucker pickups with 'soapbar' covers; Gold top.
Custom Shop.

■ **1991** Les Paul Classic/MIII

LES PAUL STANDARD 1989-1990

STUDIO LITE (second version) 1990–98
Unbound ebony fingerboard, crown markers. Similar to Studio Lite first version, except:
- Lightweight carved-top flat-back body.
- "Les Paul Model" on headstock.
- Crown markers.
- Two coverless humbucker pickups.
- Four controls (two volume, two tone) plus three-way selector.

Also version with three-piece figured maple top, Amber or Red finish (1991).

CLASSIC 1990–2008
"Classic" on truss-rod cover.
- Bound carved-top body; sunbursts or colors (Gold only in 1998).
- Bound rosewood fingerboard, crown markers; "Les Paul Model" on headstock; "Classic" on truss-rod cover; plastic tuner buttons.
- Two coverless humbuckers.
- Four controls (two volume, two tone) plus three-way selector.
- Cream plastic pickguard with "1960" logo.
- Six-saddle bridge plus separate bar tailpiece.

Vintage-style inked five or six-digit serial number, with first digit or first two digits corresponding to year of manufacture.

Also Guitar Of The Week models 2007, production 400 each: Fireburst finish; Ripple-effect finish designed by artist Tom Morgan; antiqued appointments, H-90 pickups (stacked double-coil), Iced Tea Sunburst; antiqued appointments, zebra wood body; Mahogany top, antiqued appointments, Faded Cherry; Mahogany top, antiqued appointments, scroll logo, Vintage Sunburst.

■ **1990** Les Paul Classic

LES PAUL STANDARD 1989-1990

ORVILLE 1988-1998

The forename of the founder of the American company was used by Gibson on a line of Japanese-made guitars that officially "copied" Gibson's most famous designs, launched in 1988 and lasting until about 1998 (when Gibson began making some Epiphone-branded guitars in Japan). While the cheaper models carried the Orville logo, the higher-priced versions were branded Orville By Gibson. The 'By Gibsons' bore the Les Paul logo when appropriate, and models included Custom, Standard, and Junior, equipped with US-made Gibson pickups. Both Orville brands were high-quality, accurate repros sold only on the Japanese market.

1989 Orville Les Paul Standard

LES PAUL STANDARD

STANDARD 60 REISSUE 1991–current

Reissue based on Standard first version *from 1960 period, with figured top and relatively slimmer neck profile. Over the years, more "accurate" features: longer neck tenon, smaller headstock. "R0" stamped in control cavity from 1993. Known by various names through the years, including* Standard 60 Flametop *(1991–99) and* Standard 60 Figuredtop *(2000–02). Aged versions available, known as* Custom Authentic *(2004–05) and* VOS *Vintage Original Spec (2006–current).* Custom Shop.

CLASSIC/MIII 1991–92

Additional central single-coil pickup; bound fingerboard. Similar to Classic, *except:*

- Sunburst only.
- Two coverless humbuckers plus one central six-polepiece single-coil pickup.
- Two controls (volume, tone) plus five-way selector and mini-switch.
- No pickguard.

1992 Les Paul 40th Anniversary

LES PAUL STANDARD 1991

171

CLASSIC CELEBRITY 1992

"Celebrity" on pickguard. Similar to Classic, *except:*

- Bound ebony fingerboard.
- Black only.
- Two coverless humbuckers.
- White plastic pickguard with "Celebrity" logo.
- Gold-plated hardware.

Production 200.

STUDIO LITE/MIII 1992–94

Similar to Studio Lite second version, *except:*

- Two coverless humbuckers plus one central six-polepiece single-coil pickup.
- Two controls (volume, tone) plus five-way selector and mini-switch.

MILLER GENUINE 1992

Similar to Studio, *except Miller Genuine beer logo. Custom Shop. Production approximately 20.*

STANDARD MAHOGANY 1993

Similar to Standard second version, *except solid mahogany body (no top cap), plastic-covered single-coil pickups.*

LES PAUL STANDARD 1992-1993

■ **1995** Les Paul Classic Plus

■ **1996** Les Paul Classic
Premium Plus Limited
Edition Trans Red

■ **1996** Les Paul Classic
Premium Plus Limited Edition
Trans Green

■ **1996** Les Paul Classic
Premium Plus Limited Edition
Trans Brown

LES PAUL STANDARD 1991-1996

CLASSIC PLUS 1992–95, 1999–2000
CLASSIC PREMIUM PLUS 1993–97
CLASSIC BIRDSEYE 1993
CLASSIC PREMIUM BIRDSEYE 1993
CLASSIC QUILT TOP 1998

All similar to Classic, except:

• Varying grades of figured maple carved-top (Premium Plus better than Plus, Premium Birdseye better than Birdseye). Some Premium Plus models made in Custom Shop.

• No pickguard on earliest, then pickguard with inscribed "1960" included in case but not mounted, then pickguard mounted.

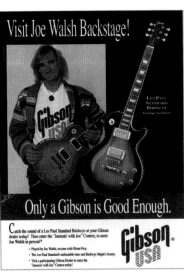

1996 Les Paul Classic Premium Plus Limited Edition Trans Blue

1993 press advertisement

LES PAUL STANDARD 1992-1993

174

1996 Les Paul Classic
Premium Plus Custom Shop
Green Quilt

1997 Les Paul Classic
Premium Plus Custom Shop
Trans Purple

1997 Les Paul Classic
Premium Plus Limited Edition
Trans Black

LES PAUL STANDARD 1993-

STANDARD 58 PLAINTOP REISSUE 1994–99, 2003–current

Similar to Standard 58 reissue *except plain (un-figured) maple top. Aged versions available, known as* Custom Authentic *(2003–05) and* VOS *Vintage Original Spec (2006–current).*
Custom Shop.

STANDARD CENTENNIAL 1994

Similar to Standard second version, *except brown sunburst, four-digit serial number on tailpiece, first digit (1) in diamonds.*
Custom Shop.

 1991 catalogue page

LES PAUL STANDARD 1994

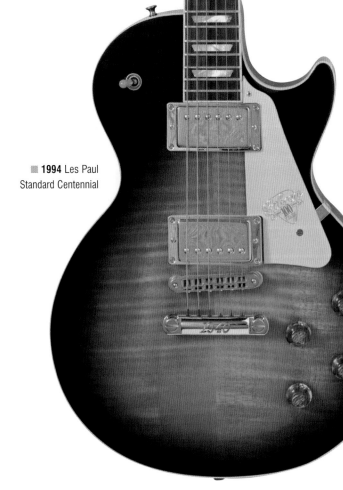

1994 Les Paul Standard Centennial

CUSTOM SHOP CREATIONS

Gibson's workshops have almost always been open to taking custom orders from artists or dealers, but only in recent decades has the idea of a self-contained Custom Shop come to be. A Custom Shop of sorts existed in the Kalamazoo plant in the 1960s, and something more akin to the modern notion of the term was established in the Nashville factory between 1983–88.

The Custom Shop as it exists today got its start in 1993, however, when Gibson allocated a dedicated premises and staff to the operation in order to capitalize on the growing trend for models that were more finely crafted and a bit more special than the standard production guitars the leading manufacturers were turning out.

Over the course of the next ten years the Custom Shop – for a time referred to as Custom-Art-Historic – played a bigger and bigger part in Gibson's production, moving beyond special orders and art guitars (one-off showpieces) to manufacture "standard custom" models. Today Gibson Custom, as the department is known, offers a range of lines that are in continual production, although more limited than the standard production lines of Gibson USA.

The bulk of these fall under the umbrella of the Historic Series, which carries the standard-issue Custom reissue models (non-Signature or Limited Edition guitars). In 2006 the accuracy of these reproductions was cranked up a notch when Gibson morphed many Les Pauls and two early Les Paul/SGs from the Historic Series into the VOS (Vintage Original Spec) Series. At the time of writing, the VOS line included the '54 goldtop (still available, although not included in the catalogue); '56 goldtop; '57 goldtop; two and three-pickup '57 Customs; '57 and '58 Les Paul Juniors; single and double-cutaway '60 Les Paul Specials; '58, '59, and '60 Sunburst Standards; and early-'60s-style SG Standard and Custom. While Gibson has tended to boast that each subsequent series of reissue models over the years has offered "the most accurate reproductions yet," as have so many makers, it seems the VOS Series really has landed squarely in that territory. A comprehensive list of revised specs helped to make these guitars more historically accurate, among them the use of a long-tenon neck joint, solid non-weight-relieved mahogany back (where applicable), accurate top-arch carve, vintage-style fret wire, correct headstock taper, historically correct binding, and more accurate pickup and control routings.

ES and archtop models fall under their own Custom Shop division, while reproductions of many Firebirds, the SG Special, the Flying V, and Explorer are classified as 'Limited Models' under the SG/Designer heading. Alongside these, many more exclusive Custom Shop models appear in the Signature and Inspired By lines. The former offers, unsurprisingly, Signature models based on famous guitars played by the likes of Jimmy Page, Pete Townshend, Joe Perry, and Neil Schon, while the latter carries models that are modified or hot-rodded according to the specifications of a range of artists. Among these are the Dave Grohl DG-335, Elliot Easton SG, Warren Haynes Model (a Les Paul Standard), Peter Frampton Les Paul Special, and others.

■ **1989** press advertisement

■ **1999** press advertisment

■ **1983** Les Paul Standard
one-piece top Custom Shop

CUSTOM SHOP

CUSTOM SHOP

2008 Slash Les Paul
VOS Custom Shop

2001 Les Paul Standard
Custom Shop

 **1995** press advertisement

ELITE DIAMOND SPARKLE 1995–97
Diamond soundholes.
- Bound carved-top body, diamond soundholes, sparkles.
- Bound ebony fingerboard, pearl rectangular markers, split-diamond headstock inlay.
- Two metal-cover humbucker pickups.
- Four knobs (two tone, two volume) plus selector switch.
- Six-saddle bridge plus separate tailpiece.
- Gold-plated hardware.

Early examples known as Bantam Elite.
Custom Shop.

1995 Jimmy Page Les Paul

LES PAUL STANDARD 1995

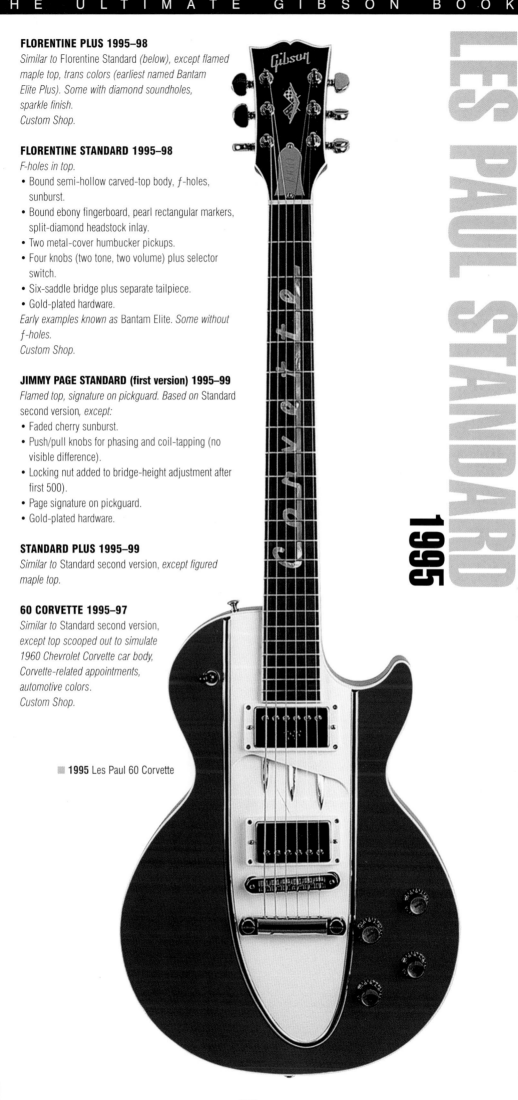

FLORENTINE PLUS 1995–98

Similar to Florentine Standard *(below), except flamed maple top, trans colors (earliest named Bantam Elite Plus). Some with diamond soundholes, sparkle finish.*
Custom Shop.

FLORENTINE STANDARD 1995–98

F-holes in top.
- Bound semi-hollow carved-top body, *f*-holes, sunburst.
- Bound ebony fingerboard, pearl rectangular markers, split-diamond headstock inlay.
- Two metal-cover humbucker pickups.
- Four knobs (two tone, two volume) plus selector switch.
- Six-saddle bridge plus separate tailpiece.
- Gold-plated hardware.

Early examples known as Bantam Elite. *Some without f-holes.*
Custom Shop.

JIMMY PAGE STANDARD (first version) 1995–99

Flamed top, signature on pickguard. Based on Standard second version, *except:*
- Faded cherry sunburst.
- Push/pull knobs for phasing and coil-tapping (no visible difference).
- Locking nut added to bridge-height adjustment after first 500).
- Page signature on pickguard.
- Gold-plated hardware.

STANDARD PLUS 1995–99

Similar to Standard second version, *except figured maple top.*

60 CORVETTE 1995–97

Similar to Standard second version, *except top scooped out to simulate 1960 Chevrolet Corvette car body, Corvette-related appointments, automotive colors.*
Custom Shop.

■ **1995** Les Paul 60 Corvette

LES PAUL STANDARD 1995

CATALINA 1996–98

Opaque colors, pearl Custom Shop logo on headstock.
Similar to Standard second version, except:
- Semi-hollow body; Black, Yellow, Red, or Turquoise.
- Ebony fingerboard with compound radius; pearl crown markers; pearl Custom Shop logo inlaid on headstock.

Custom Shop.

ELEGANT 1996–2000

Abalone crown markers, figured top.
- Bound semi-hollow carved-top body; figured maple top; Natural, stains, or sunbursts.
- Bound ebony fingerboard with compound radius, abalone pearl crown markers, pearl "Gibson" logo on headstock, metal tuner buttons.
- Two covered six-polepiece humbucker pickups.
- Four controls (two volumes, two tones) plus three-way selector.
- No pickguard.
- Six-saddle bridge plus separate bar tailpiece.

Custom Shop.

 1997 Les Paul Elegant

LES PAUL STANDARD 1996

LES PAUL STANDARD

1996

1998 press advertisement

JOE PERRY 1996–2000
Black stain finish on flamed top; white pearloid pickguard. Similar to Standard second version, *except:*
• Unbound carved figured-maple top; production version has "Joe Perry" logo near bridge; Blackburst.
• Unbound rosewood fingerboard; Custom Shop run has "Joe Perry" pearloid inlay on headstock (production version has "Les Paul Model").
• Two coverless humbucker pickups; four controls (two volume, two tone; push/pull tone knob to activate mid-boost on production version) plus selector.
• White pearloid pickguard.
• Black hardware.
Limited-edition Custom Shop run (1996) numbered with JP prefix. Production version (1996–2000) with regular eight-digit serial.

KORINA 1996
Korina (wood type) back and neck. Similar to Standard second version, *except:*
• Figured maple top, Korina back and neck.
Custom Shop.

1996 Joe Perry Les Paul Custom Shop

STANDARD 58 REISSUE 1996–99, 2001–current

Based on Standard first version *from 1958 period, with figured maple top (but less figure than 59 reissues). Over the years, more "accurate" features: longer neck tenon, smaller headstock. "R8" stamped in control cavity. Cherry sunburst finish; then Vintage Red or Butterscotch finish; Butterscotch only from 2001. Known by various names through the years, including* Standard 58 Figuredtop. *Aged version available, known as* Custom Authentic *(2002). Custom Shop.*

STANDARD TIE DYE 1996, 2002

Similar to Standard second version, *except simulated tie-dye top finish (each instrument unique). 1996 production around 100.*

STUDIO GEM 1996–97

Similar to Studio, *except:*
- Single-coil pickups with cream plastic covers.
- Gold-plated hardware.
- Rosewood fingerboard, crown markers.
- Gemstone finishes.

1999 Les Paul Standard 58 Figuredtop Reissue

LES PAUL STANDARD
1996

ULTIMA 1996–2000

Abalone top border, fancy fingerboard inlay.
- Bound semi-hollow carved-top body with abalone pearl border; flamed maple top; Natural, stains, or sunbursts.
- Bound ebony fingerboard, four optional inlay patterns: Flame, Tree Of Life, Harp, Butterfly; Custom Shop logo inlaid on headstock; pearl tuner buttons.
- Bound semi-hollow carved-top body with abalone pearl border; flamed maple top; Natural, stains, or sunbursts.
- Two covered six-polepiece humbucker pickups.
- Four controls (two volumes, two tones) plus three-way selector.
- No pickguard.
- Six-saddle bridge plus separate bar tailpiece, optional trapeze tailpiece.
- Gold-plated hardware.

Custom Shop.

1999 press advertisement

1999 Les Paul Historic
1959 Reissue 40th Anniversary

1996 Les Paul Ultima

185

SLASH 1997

Slash snakepit logo carved into top, snake inlay on fingerboard, Cranberry finish.
Custom Shop; production 50.

SLASH SIGNATURE 2004–current

Plain maple top, aged nickel-plated hardware, coverless Seymour Duncan humbuckers, Fishman Powerbridge pickup, three volume controls, one master tone, three-way pickup selector, three-way mini-toggle for bridge pickup; Antique Tobacco Sunburst with dark walnut back; initial Pilot Run from Custom Shop, with Custom Authentic aging and numbered with SL prefix, followed by regular production version (known as USA Slash Les Paul Standard) in limited run of 1,600.

SLASH #1 STANDARD 2008

Three-piece top, Seymour Duncan humbuckers; Faded Heritage Cherry Sunburst with VOS Vintage Original Spec aging treatment.
Custom Shop.

CUSTOM SHOP STANDARD 1997–2005

Similar to Standard second version, except coverless pickups (one with zebra-coil, one with black-coil), vintage-style inked serial number, with first digit corresponding to year of manufacture (as with Les Paul Classic).
Custom Shop.

2001 Les Paul
Standard 59 Figuredtop

LES PAUL STANDARD 1997

■ **1993** Gibson Historic poster signed by company personnel

■ **2001** Les Paul 1958 Reissue

■ **2003** Les Paul 1959 Reissue

187

1999 press advertisement

OXBLOOD 1997–2008

Similar to Goldtop 54 reissue, *except Oxblood finish,
coverless humbucker pickups.*
Custom Shop. See also Jeff Beck *p.206.*

OLD HICKORY 1998

"Old Hickory" on fingerboard.
• Bound carved-top tulip poplar body from tree felled
  by 1998 tornado in Nashville.
• Bound hickory fingerboard; "Old Hickory" fingerboard
  inlay; image of President Andrew Jackson ("Old
  Hickory") on headstock.
• Two metal-cover humbucker pickups.
Custom Shop.

SMARTWOOD EXOTIC 1998–2002

*"Smart Wood" on truss-rod cover, thin
body with carved top. Similar to* The Paul,
except:
• Wood certified by Rainforest Alliance.
• Curupay fingerboard, dot markers,
  "Smart Wood" on truss-rod cover.
• Gold-plated hardware.
• Top cap of ambay guasu, banara, curupay,
  or peroba wood.
• Natural finish, optional SL matte
  urethane finish.

1999 Les Paul Standard
59 Flametop Aged

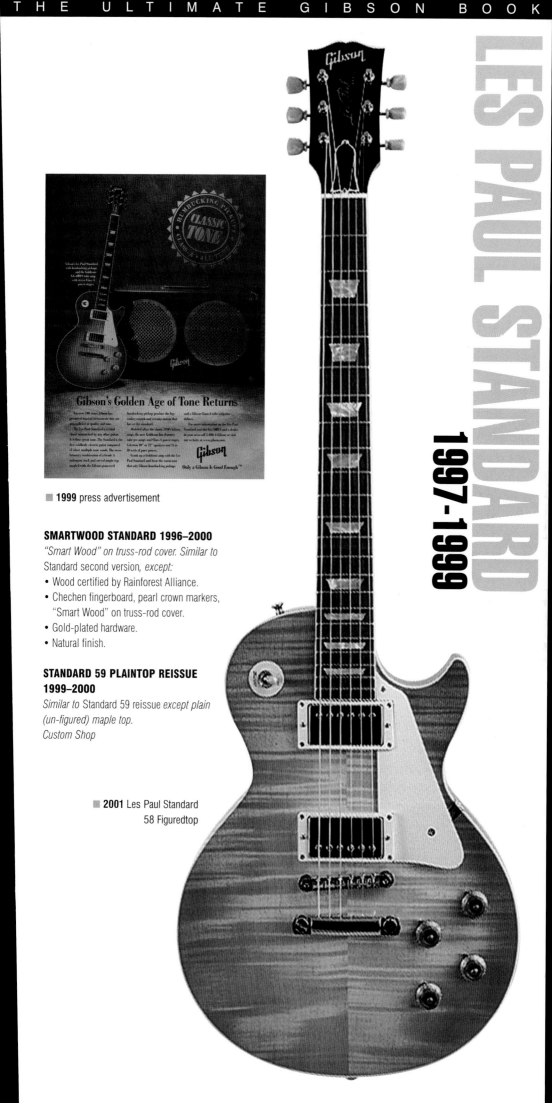

1999 press advertisement

SMARTWOOD STANDARD 1996–2000

"Smart Wood" on truss-rod cover. Similar to Standard second version, *except:*

- Wood certified by Rainforest Alliance.
- Chechen fingerboard, pearl crown markers, "Smart Wood" on truss-rod cover.
- Gold-plated hardware.
- Natural finish.

STANDARD 59 PLAINTOP REISSUE 1999–2000

Similar to Standard 59 reissue *except plain (un-figured) maple top.*
Custom Shop

2001 Les Paul Standard
58 Figuredtop

STANDARD LITE 1999–2000

Unbound double-cutaway carved-top body, crown markers, gold-plated hardware.

- Unbound carved-top body with shape of Special double-cut; maple top cap; sunbursts or colors.
- Unbound rosewood fingerboard, three-quarter-size crown markers; 24¾-inch scale-length; standard Gibson headstock shape.
- Two metal-cover humbucker pickups.
- Two knobs (tone, volume) plus selector switch.
- Wrap-over tailpiece.
- Gold-plated hardware.

For a similar guitar with chrome-plated hardware and dot markers, see DC Studio *p.272.*

ZAKK WYLDE BULLSEYE 1999–current

Bullseye finish. Based on Custom second version, *except:*

- Black/white Bullseye (concentric circles) top finish; White finish on back of body and headstock.
- Two plastic-covered poleless EMG pickups.
- Unfinished maple neck; engraved gold-plated truss-rod cover; Zakk Wylde decal on back of headstock.
- No pickguard.

Numbered with ZW prefix. Custom Shop.

ZAKK WYLDE ROUGH TOP 1999–2000

Rough maple top (very little sanding), crown markers, nickel-plated hardware, Natural finish; numbered with ZW prefix.
Custom Shop.

■ **2000** Les Paul Standard Raw Power

LES PAUL STANDARD 1999-2000

CLASSIC MAHOGANY 2000–07
Mahogany top cap, zebra-coil pickups (one black coil, one white). Similar to Classic, *except:*
• Mahogany top cap; Natural, Trans Red, or sunbursts.
• "Zebra" pickup coils (one black, one white coil).
Also Guitar Of The Week models 2007, production 400 each: antiqued appointments, Faded Cherry; antiqued appointments, scroll logo, Vintage Sunburst.

GARY MOORE 2000–current
Zebra-coil neck pickup, black-coil bridge pickup, "Gary Moore" on truss-rod cover.
Similar to *Standard second version*, except:
• Unbound carved-top of figured maple; Lemonburst.
• Unbound rosewood fingerboard; "Gary Moore" on truss-rod cover.
• Two coverless humbucker pickups (black-white coils in neck position, black coils in bridge position).
• No pickguard.

GARY MOORE SIGNATURE BFG 2009–current
Similar to BFG, *except two 60s knobs, one 50s knob, distressed hardware; satin Lemonburst.*

JIM BEAM 2000–03
Ornamentation motif from Jim Beam whiskey. Similar to Studio, *except:*
• Top overlay with "Jim Beam" and medal graphic.
• Unbound ebony fingerboard; medal graphic with letter B on headstock.
Custom Shop.

STANDARD RAW POWER 2000–01
Similar to Standard second version, *except plain top, chrome-plated hardware, Natural satin finish.*

STUDIO GOTHIC 2000–01
Similar to Studio, *except:*
• Ebony fingerboard, moon-and-star marker at 12th fret.
• Black hardware.
• Flat Black finish.

STUDIO MAHOGANY
See Vintage Mahogany *entry p.203.*

■ **1999** Zakk Wylde Bullseye Les Paul

■ **2000** Gary Moore Les Paul

191

■ **2001** press advertisement

CLASS-5 2001–08
Similar to Standard 59 reissue, *except weight relief holes (not tone chambers) to lighten weight (not visible); non-traditional finishes (Amber, Cranberry, Tangerineburst, Trans Blue, Trans Black).*
Custom Shop.

STANDARD KORINA QUILT 2001
Quilt maple top, Korina back and neck.
Custom Shop.

LES PAUL STANDARD 2001

■ **2001** Les Paul Class-5

■ **2001** press advertisement

STARS AND STRIPES 2001–08
US flag in metallic finish on top, '60s neck profile, pearl crown markers.
Custom Shop.

STUDIO PLUS 2001–05
Similar to Studio, except figured top, Translucent Red or Desert Burst (brown) finish; gold-plated hardware.

LES PAUL STANDARD

2001

■ **2001** Les Paul Junior Special Plus

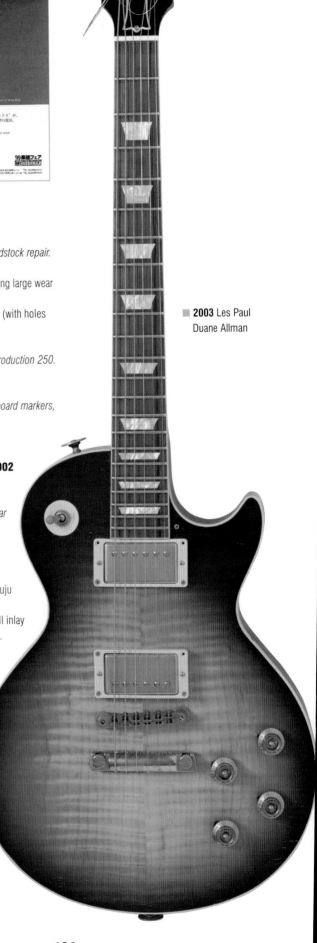

2000 press advertisement

GARY ROSSINGTON 2002
Screws in headstock simulating broken headstock repair.
Similar to Standard 59 reissue, except:
- Finish wear aged by Tom Murphy, including large wear spot on back; aged Sunburst.
- Two screws in headstock, Schaller tuners (with holes from original Klusons).
- Aged nickel-plated hardware.

Numbered with GR prefix. Custom Shop; production 250.

SPIDER-MAN LES PAUL 2002
Spider-man graphic on body, crown fingerboard markers, signed by Stan Lee and Les Paul.
Custom Shop; production 15.

STANDARD 60 PLAINTOP REISSUE 2002
Similar to Standard 60 reissue except plain (un-figured) maple top.
Custom Shop; production 5, made for Guitar Center (US dealer).

VOODOO 2002–04
Voodoo-doll inlay at fifth fret.
- Unbound carved-top swamp ash body; Juju finish (black with red wood filler).
- Unbound ebony fingerboard, voodoo-doll inlay at fifth fret, white-outline headstock logo.
- Two coverless humbucker pickups with red and black coils.
- Four controls (two volume, two tone) plus three-way selector.
- No pickguard.
- Six-saddle bridge plus separate bar tailpiece.
- Black-plated hardware.

2003 Les Paul
Duane Allman

CRAZY HORSE 2003

Similar to Standard second version, *except unbound fingerboard; features from customized Ford Bronco vehicle, including tire tread.*
Custom Shop; production 25.

DUANE ALLMAN 2003

"DUANE" on back. Similar to Standard 59 reissue, *except:*
- Finish aged by Tom Murphy.
- Grover Rotomatic tuners.
- "Ribbon" flame on maple top; DUANE spelled out in fretwire on body back.

Numbered with DALLMAN prefix.
Custom Shop.

JOE PERRY BONEYARD 2003–08

"Joe Perry" on truss-rod cover, Boneyard logo on headstock. Similar to Standard second version, *except:*
- Flamed top, weight-relieved body, no pickguard; Green Tiger finish with Custom Authentic aging.

- Aged fingerboard markers, "Joe Perry" on truss-rod cover, Boneyard (hot sauce) logo on headstock.
- Six-saddle bridge; separate bar or Bigsby tailpiece.
- Aged nickel-plated hardware.

Early examples are numbered as "Pilot Run"; later examples are numbered with BONE prefix.
Custom Shop.

SMARTWOOD STUDIO 2003–08

Carved top, green "leaf" on truss-rod cover
- Unbound carved-top of certified muirapiranga wood, mahogany back; Natural.
- Unbound muirapiranga fingerboard, dot markers, green "leaf" on truss-rod cover.
- Two metal-cover humbucker pickups.
- Four controls (two volume, two tone) plus three-way selector.
- No pickguard.
- Gold-plated hardware.

■ **2002** Gary Rossington Les Paul

■ **2001** Dickey Betts '57 Redtop Les Paul

MUSIC RISING 2005

Hand-painted multi-color top. Similar to Standard second version, *except:*

- Top hand-painted in Mardi Gras colors.
- All plastic parts replaced by wood parts.
- Music Rising logo on pickguard.

Custom Shop; production less than 300, sold at Guitar Center retail stores.

NEAL SCHON 2005–08

Double-slashed-diamond fingerboard markers.

- Multiple-bound carved-top mahogany body; Green Gold, Alpine White, or Ebony.
- Bound ebony fingerboard, pearl diamond markers with double slash, six-piece slashed-diamond headstock inlay, locking nut, sculpted heel.
- One coverless poleless humbucker pickup (neck) and one covered humbucker (bridge).
- Four controls (two tone, two volume), two mini-switches (on/off for neck pickup, octave effect), three-way selector.
- Floyd Rose vibrato.
- *Custom Shop.*

 **2005** Les Paul Music Rising

LES PAUL STANDARD 2005

■ **2007** Les Paul BFG

■ **2007** Les Paul BFG

■ **2006** Les Paul Pete Townshend Deluxe No.1

199

90TH ANNIVERSARY SUPREME 2005
Signed by Les Paul under final lacquer coat.
Custom Shop; production 90.

BFG 2006–08
Unsanded top with router furrows.
- Unbound carved-top with router furrows, chambered mahogany back; various trans(parent) colors.
- Unbound rosewood fingerboard, no markers, no truss-rod cover.
- One plastic-cover six-polepiece single-coil pickup (neck) and one coverless zebra-coil humbucker pickup (bridge).
- Three wooden controls (one tone, two volume) plus three-way selector and kill-switch toggle.
- No pickguard.
- Six-saddle bridge plus separate bar tailpiece.
- Gun metal hardware with Trans Cherry, distressed black chrome with Black, or trans gold.

GODDESS 2006–08
Two coverless pickups with clear bobbins.
- Bound carved-top; Violet Burst, Sky Burst, Rose Burst, Ice Burst, or Ebony.
- Bound ebony fingerboard, crown markers, "Goddess" on truss-rod cover, decal logo.
- Two coverless humbucker pickups with clear bobbins.
- One volume, one tone, three-way selector.
- No pickguard.
- Wrap-over bar bridge/tailpiece.

GT 2006
Monochrome finish with flames.
- Round carved-top, mahogany back, extended strap buttons; finishes with flame graphic (also Fire Engine Red finish with no flame graphic, 2007 Guitar Of The Week, production 400).
- Bound ebony fingerboard, mirror crown markers, "GT" on truss-rod cover, locking tuners, pearl logo.
- Two metal-cover humbucker pickups.
- Four push/pull knobs, high-pass tone filter, coil taps on both pickups, three-way selector.
- No pickguard.
- Six-saddle bridge plus separate bar tailpiece.

BUDWEISER 2002
Similar to Studio, except Budweiser beer graphics.
Custom Shop; production 50.

■ **2006** Les Paul Studio Premium Plus

HD.6X-PRO 2006

No fingerboard inlays; oblong black pickup between bridge-position pickup and bridge.
- Silver-bound carved-top body; Blue Metallic top.
- Unbound ebony fingerboard; carbon-fiber block markers, pearl "Gibson" logo on headstock, knurled metal cylinder tuner knobs.
- Two metal-cover humbucking pickups and one hex-output pickup; standard quarter-inch jack plus microphone input jack and ethernet output jack; onboard digital converter requires BOB (breakout box).
- Four controls (two volume, two tone) plus three-way selector.
- No pickguard.
- Six-saddle bridge plus separate bar tailpiece.
- Platinum-plated hardware.

MENACE 2006–08

Fist inlay on fingerboard.
- Carved top with 'tribal' routs, mahogany back; Black.
- Unbound ebony fingerboard, brass fist inlay at fifth fret (no other markers), brass frets, custom multi-color logo on headstock.
- Two coverless humbucker pickups with brass stud poles.
- Four controls (two volume, two tone) plus three-way selector.
- No pickguard.
- Six-saddle bridge plus separate bar tailpiece.
- Black-plated hardware.

PETE TOWNSHEND DELUXE #9 2006

"9" on top. Similar to 70s-period Deluxe, *except:*
- "9" decal on top below bridge; Heritage Cherry Sunburst.
- Two metal-cover mini-humbuckers and one coverless DiMarzio humbucker.
- Four knobs (three volume, one master tone), three-way selector, two mini toggles (phase and tap for DiMarzio).
Numbered with PETE prefix.
Custom Shop; production 75.

STUDIO PREMIUM PLUS 2006–08

Figured maple top, gold-plated hardware, cream truss-rod cover, transparent finishes.

■ **2006** Les Paul HD.6X-Pro

LES PAUL STANDARD

2006

VIXEN 2006–08
"Vixen" on truss-rod cover.
- Unbound carved-top thin mahogany body with rib-cage scarf on back; opaque colors.
- Unbound rosewood fingerboard, small diamond markers, "Les Paul Model" on headstock, decal logo.
- Two covered humbucker pickups.
- Two controls (tone and volume) plus three-way selector.
- No pickguard.
- Wrap-over bar bridge/tailpiece.

WARREN HAYNES STANDARD 2006–current
Mini-switch between tone controls.
Similar to Standard 58 reissue, except:
- Plain-top finish.
- Schaller extended strap buttons; faded Haynes Burst.
- Mini-switch between tone controls for pre-amp control.
- Tone Pro locking bridge.
Custom Shop.

CLASSIC ANTIQUE 2007–08
Figured top, crown headstock inlay (does not say "Les Paul"), antiqued parts, Honeyburst or Vintage Sunburst.

CLASSIC CUSTOM 2007–08
Single-ply antiqued binding, ebony fingerboard, crown headstock ornament, gold-plated hardware; Ebony finish standard (Silverburst or White available as Guitar Of The Week models 2007; production 400 each).

CLASSIC CUSTOM P-90 2007
Guitar Of The Week model 2007; two plastic-cover six-polepiece single-coil pickups; Antique Ebony. Production 400.

CLASSIC CUSTOM 3-PICKUP 2007
Guitar Of The Week model 2007; three DiMarzio coverless humbucker pickups with double-white coils, gold-plated hardware; Cherry Sunburst. Production 400.

KEITH RICHARDS STANDARD 2007
Aged sunburst finish, Bigsby. Similar to Standard 58 reissue, except:
- Finish aged by Tom Murphy, Bigsby tailpiece.
- Aged nickel-plated hardware.
Custom Shop; production 25, made for Vintage World (US dealer).

ROBOT LTD 2007–08
White knob with LED light in neck tone control, metal tuner buttons, bound fingerboard. Some numbered with RG prefix. The Robot name describes an auto-tune system available on the models noted here. See also Dark Fire entry p.204.

2007 Les Paul Robot Limited Edition

ROBOT STUDIO 2007–current
*White knob with LED light in neck tone-control, metal
tuner buttons, unbound fingerboard.*

STANDARD 58 CHAMBERED VOS 2007–08
*Similar to Standard 58 reissue except chambered semi-
hollow body (lighter weight but no visible difference),
Vintage Original Spec aging treatment.
Custom Shop.*

STANDARD 58 50TH ANNIVERSARY 2007–08
*Similar to Standard 58 reissue except 50th
Anniversary banner on pickguard, Cherry Sunburst;
aged by Tom Murphy.
Custom Shop; production 200.*

STANDARD FADED 2007–08
*Coverless zebra-coil humbuckers, no "Les Paul Model"
on headstock, 50s neck; satin Heritage Cherry
Sunburst, Tobacco Sunburst, or Honey Burst.
Custom Shop.*

STANDARD PREMIUM PLUS 2007
Highly figured top.

STANDARD UN-BURST 2007
*Natural finish, double-white pickup coils. Similar to
Standard second version, except:*
- *Natural finish.*
- *Two coverless DiMarzio humbuckers with double-
  white coils.*

Guitar Of The Week model 2007, production 400.

STUDIO BFG 2007
*Guitar Of The Week, plastic-cover six-polepiece single-
coil pickup (neck) and zebra-coil humbucker (bridge),
three knobs, three-way selector, kill-switch toggle;
Ebony finish.
Production 400.*

STUDIO FADED MAPLE TOP 2007–08
Faded Heritage Cherry Sunburst finish.

VINTAGE MAHOGANY 2007–08
*Carved mahogany top, nickel-plated hardware, Worn
Brown or Worn Cherry. Also known as Studio
Mahogany.*

■ **2007** Les Paul Robot Ltd

■ **2007** Les Paul Robot Ltd

AXCESS STANDARD FLOYD ROSE 2008–current

Floyd Rose trem with locking nut. Similar to Traditional, *except:*
- Locking nut, plain truss-rod cover, contoured neck heel.
- Additional control plate in middle of back, contoured back with ribcage cutout; Ice Tea Burst or Gun Metal Gray.
- Two coverless humbucker pickups.
- Push/pull on bridge-pickup volume control for coil tap.
- Floyd Rose tremolo.

Custom Shop.

DARK FIRE 2008–current

Robot auto-tuners, "Dark Fire" on truss-rod cover.
- Dark-bound carved-top, Robot-style master tone knob with LED lights (controls effects), chambered mahogany body, gloss top finish, satin back.
- Unbound ebony fingerboard, small block carbon-fiber markers, "Dark Fire" on truss-rod cover, 'flowerpot' headstock inlay, does not say "Les Paul".
- One covered six-polepiece single-coil pickup (neck), one covered humbucker pickup (bridge), carbon-fiber pickup covers, piezo bridge pickup.
- Four knobs (two volume, one tone, one multi-purpose with LED lights), rotary pickup selector switch.
- Transparent pickguard.
- Six-saddle bridge plus separate flat-plate tailpiece.
- Brushed chrome hardware.

■ **2008** Dark Fire

LES PAUL STANDARD 2008

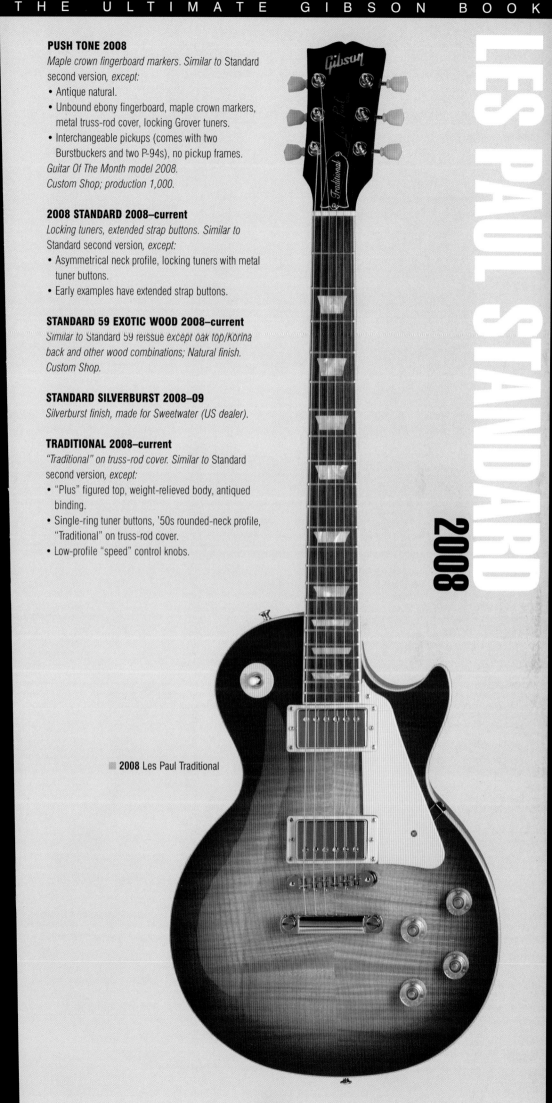

PUSH TONE 2008

Maple crown fingerboard markers. Similar to Standard second version, *except:*
- Antique natural.
- Unbound ebony fingerboard, maple crown markers, metal truss-rod cover, locking Grover tuners.
- Interchangeable pickups (comes with two Burstbuckers and two P-94s), no pickup frames.
Guitar Of The Month model 2008.
Custom Shop; production 1,000.

2008 STANDARD 2008–current

Locking tuners, extended strap buttons. Similar to Standard second version, *except:*
- Asymmetrical neck profile, locking tuners with metal tuner buttons.
- Early examples have extended strap buttons.

STANDARD 59 EXOTIC WOOD 2008–current

Similar to Standard 59 reissue *except oak top/korina back and other wood combinations; Natural finish. Custom Shop.*

STANDARD SILVERBURST 2008–09

Silverburst finish, made for Sweetwater (US dealer).

TRADITIONAL 2008–current

"Traditional" on truss-rod cover. Similar to Standard second version, *except:*
- "Plus" figured top, weight-relieved body, antiqued binding.
- Single-ring tuner buttons, '50s rounded-neck profile, "Traditional" on truss-rod cover.
- Low-profile "speed" control knobs.

2008 Les Paul Traditional

LES PAUL STANDARD 2008

AXCESS STANDARD 2009–current

Plain truss-rod cover, contoured neck heel, contoured back. Similar to Traditional, except:

- Contoured back with ribcage cutout; Ice Tea Burst or Gun Metal Gray.
- Plain truss-rod cover, contoured neck heel.
- Two coverless humbucker pickups.
- Push/pull on bridge-pickup volume control for coil tap.

Custom Shop.

JEFF BECK 1954 OXBLOOD 2009

Brown finish, cream backplates. Similar to Goldtop 54 reissue, except:

- Cream control plates on back; chocolate brown finish all over body.
- No "Les Paul Model" on headstock, metal tuner buttons.
- Two coverless humbucker pickups.

Custom Shop; production 50 custom-aged and signed; 100 with Vintage Original Spec aging treatment.
See also Oxblood entry p188.

■ **2009** Jeff Beck 1954 Oxblood

LES PAUL STANDARD 2009

LES PAUL STANDARD 50th ANNIVERSARY

It took Gibson seven years to perfect the Les Paul Standard, from the first Goldtop in 1952 to the humbucker-equipped Cherry Sunburst finish of 1959. Ironically it took more than twice as long to perfect the reissue of the 1959 Les Paul, starting around 1980 with custom orders from knowledgeable vintage dealers, on to the introduction of the Custom Shop "R9" in 1993, and, finally, a limited run of 500 guitars in 2009 to celebrate the 50th anniversary of the 1959 Les Paul Standard.

A figured maple top—highly prized by collectors—was a must on the 50th Anniversary model. From the nickel-plated ABR-1 tune-o-matic bridge and the milled edges of the pickguard to the length of the neck tenon and the routing on the floor of the control cavity, all elements were "correct"—faithfully measured and replicated from original '59s. For the final touch—the finish—Gibson chose Heritage Cherry Burst and Heritage Dark Burst to replicate two of the most popular variations of the original guitar's Cherry Sunburst finish.

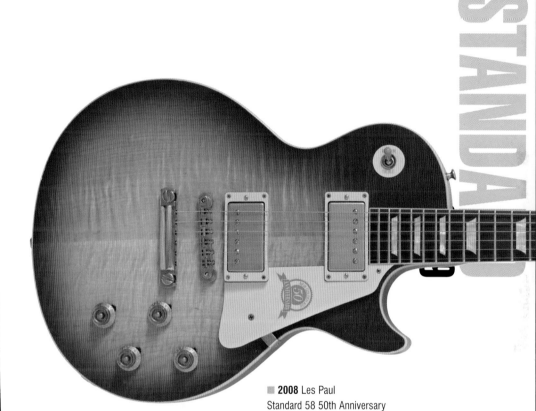

■ **2008** Les Paul
Standard 58 50th Anniversary

■ **2008** Les Paul 2008 Standard

2009 Zakk Wylde
Buzzsaw Les Paul

2009 Zakk Wylde Bullseye
Les Paul

LES PAUL STANDARD 2009

MICHAEL BLOOMFIELD 1959 STANDARD 2009

Grover tuners, two holes in top. Similar to Standard 59 reissue, except:
- Two holes in top below bridge; Bloomfield Burst finish.
- Grover Rotomatic tuners with metal kidney-bean buttons; "Les Paul" on truss-rod cover.
- Neck-pickup volume control with metal cap.

Custom Shop; production: 100 custom aged; 200 with Vintage Original Spec aging treatment.

STANDARD 59 50TH ANNIVERSARY 2009

Similar to Standard 59 reissue except Heritage Cherry Burst or Heritage Dark Burst.
Custom Shop; production 500.

STUDIO RAW POWER 2009–current

Unbound maple fingerboard, three-piece maple neck, dot inlays except for crown inlay at 12th fret, solid maple body, metal-covered humbuckers, chrome or gold-plated hardware.

50TH ANNIVERSARY KORINA TRIBUTE 2009

Offset-V headstock shape. Similar to Standard 59 reissue, except:
- Korina body.
- Korina neck, unbound fingerboard, dot markers, molded plastic logo, offset-V headstock shape.
- Three humbucker pickups.
- Four controls (three in line and one offset), slotted selector switch.

Custom Shop.

■ **2009** Les Paul Florentine

■ **2009** Michael Bloomfield 1959 Standard

BILLY GIBBONS PEARLY GATES LES PAUL STANDARD 2009

Replica of Gibbons' 1959 Les Paul Standard, finish chipped on bass side at waist, Seymour Duncan Pearly Gates humbuckers.
Production: 250 with VOS (Vintage Original Spec) aging treatment, 50 aged to replicate original Pearly Gates, 50 with replica aging and Gibbons signature.

2009 Billy Gibbons Pearly Gates Les Paul Standard

LES PAUL STANDARD 2009

BUCKETHEAD LES PAUL 2010–current
White finish, red knob on upper bass bout, one red knob and two white knobs on lower treble bout, selector switch near control knobs, two uncovered humbuckers with white coils, ebony fingerboard, no inlays, no peghead ornament or "Les Paul" silkscreen.

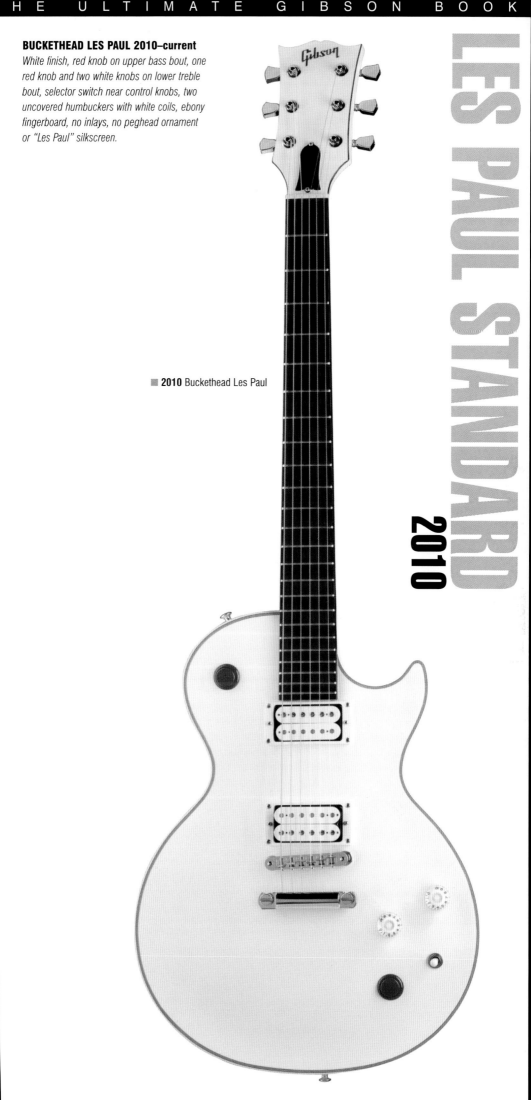

■ **2010** Buckethead Les Paul

LES PAUL STANDARD 2010

2010 Les Paul
Standard Axcess

2010 Les Paul Piezo

LES PAUL STANDARD

**DON FELDER HOTEL CALIFORNIA 1959
LES PAUL 2010–current**
*One BurstBucker 1 humbucker in bridge
position, one BurstBucker 2 in neck position,
Nashville wide-travel tune-o-matic bridge,
chrome-plated hardware, aged Felder Burst
finish (VOS Vintage Original Spec aging
treatment optional), some signed by Felder.*

■ **2010** Don Felder Hotel California
1959 Les Paul

LES PAUL STANDARD 2010

SAMMY HAGAR RED ROCKER CHICKENFOOT
LES PAUL 2010–current

Flame maple top with Cabernet finish, Cherry finish on back and sides, zebra-coil BurstBucker 3 in bridge position, '57 Classic humbucker in neck position, red "R" on truss rod cover, "chickenfoot" (rectangular peace symbol) on peghead.

2010 Sammy Hagar Red Rocker Chickenfoot Les Paul

LES PAUL STANDARD 2010

LES PAUL STUDIO 2010

■ **2010** Les Paul Studio 60s Tribute
Worn Honey Burst

■ **2010** Les Paul Studio 60s Tribute
Worn Ebony

■ **2010** Les Paul Studio 60s Tribute
Worn White

THE ULTIMATE GIBSON BOOK

CHAD KROEGER BLACKWATER LES PAUL 2010–current

Flame maple top with Trans Black finish, GraphTech Ghost piezo bridge pickup, black barrel knobs, "Blackwater" on truss rod cover, chrome-plated hardware.

BILLY MORRISON LES PAUL 2010–current

White finish, black logo and crown ornament on peghead, gold-plated hardware, Seymour Duncan 59 and Seymour Duncan JB zebra-coil humbuckers.

LOU PALLO LES PAUL 2010–current

Ebony top finish, natural back and sides, block inlays, signature at 12th fret, P-90 single-coil in neck position, uncovered Dirty Fingers humbucker in bridge position.

■ **2010** Chad Kroeger Blackwater Les Paul

LES PAUL STANDARD 2010

DUSK TIGER LES PAUL 2010–current

Exotic top, metal top plates, black poleless pickups.
- Highly figured exotic wood top, curving metal pickguard plates and pickup surrounds, tune-o-matic bridge, Robot stopbar tailpiece, Firewire jack.
- Bound ebony fingerboard, block inlays, Robot auto tuning system.
- Two black-covered poleless humbuckers, piezo in bridge, two bonnet knobs, one barrel knob, one Robot control knob, rotating selector switch for piezo blend.

Production: 1,000 announced.

LES PAUL STANDARD 2010 LIMITED 2010–11

P-90 and humbucker, Robot tuners
- Tune-o-matic bridge, Robot stopbar tailpiece, Fireball 3-tone sunburst finish, locking jack, extended strap buttons.
- Bound ebony fingerboard, block inlays, "Limited Edition" on peghead, Robot auto tuning system.
- Metal-covered soapbar P-90H single-coil in neck position, piezo in bridge, BurstBucker 3 in bridge position, two bonnet knobs, one barrel knob, one Robot control knob, rotating selector switch for piezo blend.

■ **2010** Dusk Tiger Les Paul

LES PAUL STANDARD
2011

SG/LES PAUL JUNIOR 1961–63

Beveled-edge two-cutaway body; one pickup.

- Beveled-edge two-cutaway body; Cherry.
- Unbound rosewood fingerboard, dot markers; "Les Paul Junior" on headstock; plastic tuner buttons.
- One plastic-cover six-polepiece single-coil pickup.
- Two controls (volume, tone); jack on body face.
- Black laminated plastic pickguard.
- Wrap-over bar bridge/tailpiece; optional separate vibrato tailpiece.

Production: 1961 2,151 (includes some Les Paul Junior models); 1962 2,395; 1963 2,318 (includes some SG Junior models).

1961 SG/Les Paul Junior

SG/LES PAUL 1961

SG/LES PAUL 1961

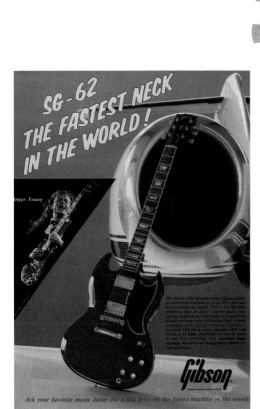

■ **1961** SG/Les Paul Standard

SG/LES PAUL STANDARD 1961–63

Beveled-edge two-cutaway body; two humbucker pickups.

- Beveled-edge two-cutaway body; Cherry.
- Bound rosewood fingerboard, crown markers; thistle-style inlay on headstock; "Les Paul" on truss-rod cover; plastic tuner buttons.
- Two metal-cover humbucker pickups.
- Four controls (two volume, two tone) plus three-way selector; jack on body face.
- Black laminated plastic pickguard.
- Six-saddle bridge plus separate sideways-action vibrato tailpiece.

Some examples with standard-action vibrato tailpieces, some of which have inlaid decorative block in body face masking holes intended for sideways-action vibrato unit. Some examples in White or Sunburst.
Production: 1961 1,662; 1962 1,449; 1963 1,445 (includes some SG Standard models).

SG/LES PAUL STANDARD REISSUE 2000–current

Reissue based on original version but with optional Maestro vibrato (long cover but not side-pull); Faded Cherry, White, or TV Yellow. Known by various names since 1986, including 62 SG Standard, 61 SG Standard, and Les Paul/SG 61 Reissue (1993–95).

SG/LES PAUL STANDARD REISSUE 2000–current

The only one with "Les Paul" on the truss-rod cover. "Les Paul" was dropped from the model name in 2004, but the model continues in current production with "Les Paul" on the truss-rod cover. Aged versions available, known as Custom Authentic (2000–03), VOS Vintage Original Spec (2006–current).
Custom Shop.

■ **1962** SG/Les Paul Standard

SG/LES PAUL 1961

CRACKING NECKS AND SHIFTING SPECS

The SG's modern double-cutaway design that gave players such excellent access to the upper frets worked in conjunction with a craze for thin neck profiles in the early 1960s to produce a major neck ache for Gibson, especially regarding the two-pickup variants of these models. Gibson had already moved the rhythm pickup a little further from the end of the fingerboard than it had been on the Les Paul of 1958–60, in order to provide a little more un-routed wood in the position of this fragile joint, but many models, and SGs in particular, were still proving alarmingly prone to both neck and headstock breaks when dropped.

During the course of the decade Gibson experimented with moving the neck pickup around slightly to improve strength in this area (the different positions are particularly noticeable on 1960s SG Specials), but the maker also sought a couple of other solutions. In late 1965, Gibson reduced the headstock pitch (back angle) from 17 degrees to 14 degrees in an attempt to make this thin joint less prone to breakage. In late 1969, a volute, or thickened wedge, was added behind the nut for further strength at the region where the neck becomes the headstock. The volute was retained until 1981, although the shallower headstock pitch was returned to its original 17 degrees around 1973, and many players today consider the slightly steeper angle— although only a difference of three degrees—to contribute to a more toneful guitar, thanks to the increased break angle of the strings over the nut that it creates.

Another altered dimension, although one that had more to do with fashion and feel than strength, was the change of the nut width of most models from 1¹¹⁄₁₆ inches to 1⅝ inches between late 1965 and around 1968. Although a shift of only ¹⁄₁₆-inch, it's enough that most players can readily feel the difference, and those who prefer a little more real estate for fingering at the low end of the fretboard often steer clear of these guitars made between 1966–68.

■ **1961** press advertisement

■ **1963** SG/Les Paul Standard
owned by Eric Clapton

SG SPECIAL 1961–63

Two black soapbar P-90 pickups, bound fingerboard, dot inlay.

- Beveled-edge two-cutaway body; Cherry or White.
- Bound rosewood fingerboard, pearl dot inlays, pearl logo.
- Two black plastic-covered single-coil pickups.
- Four controls (two volume, two tone) plus three-way selector; jack on body face.
- Black laminated plastic pickguard.
- Wraparound bridge or Maestro vibrola.

SG/LES PAUL SPECIAL / SG SPECIAL REISSUE 2000–2003

Based on 1961-63 SG Special, two black soapbar P-90 pickups, bound fingerboard, dot inlay. Despite Gibson's name for this model, the 1961–63 version was never called or labelled "Les Paul". The model continued after 2003 as the more accurately named SG Special Reissue.

■ **1963** SG Special

SG/LES PAUL 1961

1963 press advertisement

1961 SG Special

SG/LES PAUL CUSTOM 1961–63

Beveled-edge two-cutaway body; three pickups.
- Beveled-edge two-cutaway body; White only.
- Bound ebony fingerboard, block markers; split-diamond inlay on headstock; "Custom" on truss-rod cover.
- Three metal-cover humbucker pickups.
- Four controls (two volume, two tone) plus three-way selector; jack on body face.
- White laminated plastic pickguard, plus small white plastic plate reading "Les Paul Custom".
- Six-saddle bridge plus separate sideways-action vibrato tailpiece.
- Gold-plated hardware.

Some examples with standard-action vibrato tailpieces, some of which have inlaid decorative block in body face masking holes intended for sideways-action vibrato unit.
Production: 1961 513 (includes some Les Paul Custom models); 1962 298; 1963 264 (includes some SG Custom models).

SG/LES PAUL CUSTOM REISSUE 1987–90, 1998–current

Reissue based on original version, but with six-saddle bridge plus separate bar tailpiece; optional Maestro vibrato (long cover but not side-pull). Also available (2006–current) with VOS Vintage Original Spec aging treatment.

SG/LES PAUL CUSTOM 30TH ANNIVERSARY 1991–92

Anniversary model based on SG/Les Paul Custom Reissue but split-diamond inlay on headstock has "30th Anniversary" in bar and "1961, 1991" in diamond sections. Yellow finish. Custom Shop.

1961 SG/Les Paul Custom

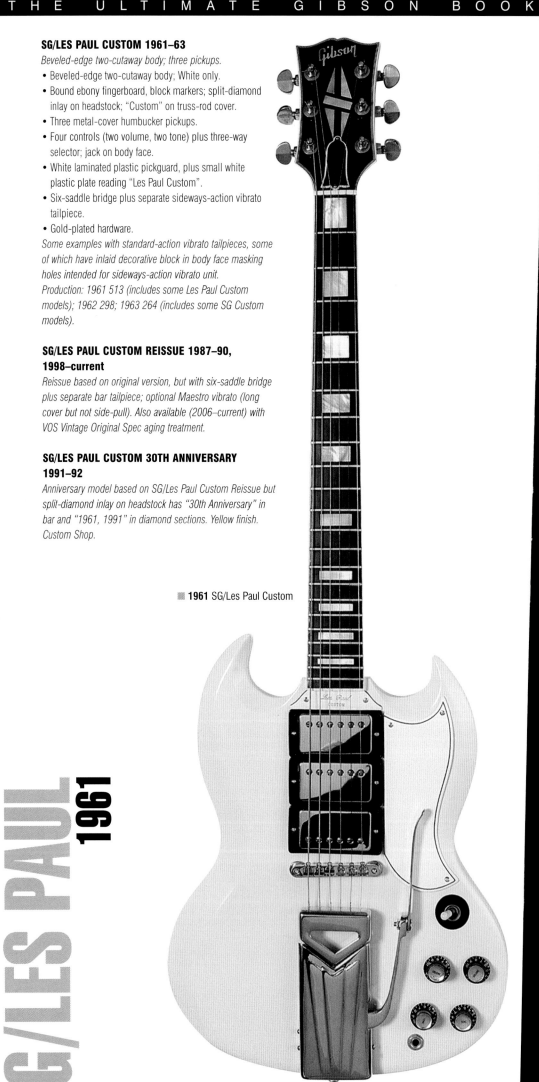

SG/LES PAUL 1961

1991 press advertisement

1961 SG/Les Paul Custom

SG TV 1960–67

Double-cut solidbody, pointed horns, Yellow finish, one P-90 pickup.

- Solid mahogany double-cutaway body, pointed horns, Maestro vibrato optional (standard 1965–70), TV Yellow finish.
- Unbound rosewood fingerboard, dot inlay.
- One "dog-ear" P-90 pickup (soapbar 1966–67).

Production: 3,480.

SG JUNIOR 1963–70, 1991–93

Double-cut solidbody, pointed horns, one P-90. Also see Les Paul Junior 1961–63.

- Double-cutaway solid mahogany body, pointed horns, Maestro vibrato optional (standard 1965–70), Cherry finish.
- Unbound rosewood fingerboard, dot inlays, decal logo.
- One "dog-ear" P-90 pickup (soapbar 1966–70), two knobs.

Production: 12,133 (1964–70, also see Les Paul Junior 1961–63).

■ **1972** press advertisement

SG STANDARD 1963–70, 1972–80, 1983–86, 1988–current

Double-cut solidbody, pointed horns, trapezoid inlays.

- Double-cutaway solid mahogany body (walnut 1981), pointed horns, pickguard does not surround pickups (larger pickguard surrounds pickups 1966–86, small pickguard 1988–90, large pickguard from 1991), tune-o-matic bridge (rectangular bridge base 1972–73), Maestro vibrato (up-and-down pull) with lyre and logo on coverplate (no vibrato 1972–75, Bigsby optional 1976–80).
- Mahogany neck (walnut 1981), bound rosewood fingerboard (unbound 1972–81), trapezoid inlay (small blocks 1972–80, dots 1981, small blocks 1983–86, trapezoids from 1988), crown peghead inlay, pearl logo, no *Les Paul* on truss-rod cover.
- Two humbucking pickups with metal covers (black plastic covers 1973–80, no covers 1981), four knobs, selector switch by pickguard (near knobs 1980–86; near edge of body from 1988), jack into top (into side 1980–89; into top from 1991).

Production: 16,677 (1964–70, also see Les Paul Standard 1961–63); 17,394 (1971–79).

SG DELUXE 1971–72, 1981–84, 1998–2000

Double-cut solidbody, pointed horns, semi-curcular control plate or three Firebird mini-humbuckers.

- Solid mahogany double-cutaway body, pointed horns, non-beveled cutaways, triangular Les Paul Standard-style pickguard flush with top (large SG-style pickup from 1981), tune-o-matic bridge (large base 1981–84), Gibson Bigsby vibrato (no vibrato 1998, Maestro Bigsby-style from 1999), Natural, Cherry, Walnut (Ebony, Ice Blue, Hellfire Red 1998–2000).
- Bound rosewood fingerboard (unbound ebony from 1998), small block inlay (some with dots 1971–84, all with dots 1998–2000), decal logo.
- Two humbucking pickups (three Firebird-style mini-humbucking pickups with no polepieces from 1988)), four knobs (two knobs, six-way rotary switch 1998–2000), semi-circular control plate (no control plate from 1998).

Production: 7,615.

SG PRO 1971, 1973–74

Double-cut solidbody, pointed horns, two P-90s, semi-circular control plate.

- Double-cutaway solid mahogany body, pointed horns, wing-shaped pickguard (Les Paul Standard-style) mounted on top, tune-o-matic bridge with rectangular base, Gibson Bigsby vibrato, Cherry, Walnut, or Natural Mahogany finish.
- Single-bound rosewood fingerboard, dot inlays, pearl logo.
- Two black soapbar P-90 pickups with mounting rings, semi-circular control plate.

Production: 2,995.

SG-100 1971

Double-cut solidbody, pointed horns, oblong pickup, oblong control plate.

- Double cutaway with pointed horns, solid poplar body (some mahogany), metal bridge cover with engraved *Gibson*, some with triangular Les Paul-type pickguard, some with large SG-type pickguard, Cherry or Walnut.
- Unbound rosewood fingerboard, dot inlays, standard Gibson peghead shape.
- Oblong Melody Maker type pickup, large pickup mounting plate, oblong control plate.

Production: 1,229.

SG MODEL 1960-1978

SG I 1972–73

Double-cut solidbody, pointed horns, black mini-humbuckers.

- Double cutaway with pointed horns, beveled edges, mahogany body, triangular wing-shaped pickguard, wraparound bridge/tailpiece, Cherry or Walnut finish.
- Dot inlays, standard Gibson peghead shape.
- Black plastic-covered mini-humbucking pickup with no poles, two knobs, semi-circular control plate.

Production: 2,331.

SG I JUNIOR PICKUP 1972

P-90 pickup.
Production: 61.

SG II 1972

Two pickups, two knobs, two slide switches, Cherry or Walnut finish.
Production: 2,927.

SG III WITH HUMBUCKERS 1975

Humbucking pickups.
Production: 61.

SG III 1972–73

Two pickups, two slide switches, tune-o-matic bridge, Cherry Sunburst finish.
Production: 953.

SG-100 JUNIOR 1972

P-90 pickup.
Production: 272.

SG-200 1971

Two pickups, two slide switches, Cherry, Walnut or black finish.
Production: 2,980.

SG-250 1971

Two pickups, two slide switches, Cherry Sunburst finish.
Production: 527.

SG STUDIO 1978

Double-cut solidbody, pointed horns, bound fingerboard, dot inlays, two humbuckers.

- Solid mahogany double-cutaway body, pointed horns, no pickguard, some with satin finish.
- Bound rosewood fingerboard, dot inlays.
- Two humbucking pickups, three knobs, one toggle switch.

Production: 931.

■ **1988** SG 90 Double

THE SG 1979–80 / SG STANDARD 1981
Double-cut solidbody, pointed horns, walnut body, exposed-coil pickups.
- Double-cutaway walnut solidbody, pointed horns, tune-o-matic bridge, small pickguard, chrome-plated hardware, Natural finish.
- One standard humbucking pickup, one Super humbucking Velvet Brick pickup, no pickup covers, four knobs.
- Walnut neck, ebony fingerboard, dot inlays, decal logo or routed logo with no inlay ("Firebrand" branded logo 1980, pearl logo 1981).

THE SG / THE SG DELUXE 1979–84
Double-cut solidbody, pointed horns, exposed-coil pickups.
- Solid mahogany double-cutaway body, pointed horns, tune-o-matic bridge, small pickguard.
- Walnut neck, ebony fingerboard, dot inlays, chrome-plated hardware.
- One standard humbucking pickup, one Super humbucking "velvet brick" pickup, no pickup covers, black mounting rings, four knobs.

SG EXCLUSIVE 1979
Double-cut solidbody, pointed horns, block inlays, rotary coil-tap control.
- Solid mahogany double-cutaway body, pointed horns, white pickguard, Ebony finish.
- Bound rosewood fingerboard, block inlays, pearl logo, crown peghead inlay.
- Two humbucking pickups with or without covers, coil-tap controlled by rotary knob.
Production: 478.

The Firebrands. Hot new brands at a price that doesn't burn.

FIREBRAND by *Gibson*

■ **1980** press advertisement

SG ARTIST 1981 / SG-R1 1980
Double-cut solidbody, pointed horns, 2 switches, active electronics.
- Thicker body than standard SG, no pickguard.
- Unbound ebony fingerboard, dot inlays, crown peghead inlay.
- Two humbucking pickups, active solid-state electronics, four knobs (two numbered 0-5-0), three-way toggle, two-way toggle.

SG 400 1985–86
Double-cut solidbody, pointed horns, three pickups, three mini-switches.
- Solid mahogany double-cutaway body, pointed horns, vibrato, black hardware.
- Bound rosewood fingerboard, dot inlays.
- 400-series electronics, one Dirty Fingers humbucking pickup, two single-coil pickups, master tone and master volume knob, three mini-switches for on/off pickup control, push/pull volume control for coil tap.

SG R-1: *See* SG Artist *below.*

SG REISSUE 1986–87 / SG '62 REISSUE 1988–90 / LES PAUL SG '61 REISSUE 1993–97 / SG '61 REISSUE 1998–current
Double-cut solidbody, pointed horns, trapezoid inlays.
- Double-cutaway solid mahogany body, pointed horns, tune-o-matic bridge, small pickguard, nickel-plated hardware, Heritage Cherry finish.
- Bound rosewood fingerboard, trapezoid inlays, crown peghead inlay, plastic keystone tuner buttons.
- Two humbucking pickups, four knobs, selector switch near pickguard, jack in top.

SG ELITE 1987–89
Double-cut solidbody, pointed horns, block inlays, locking nut.
- Solid mahogany double-cutaway body, pointed horns, tune-o-matic bridge, TP-6 fine-tune tailpiece, gold-plated hardware, Pearl White or Metallic Sunset finish.
- Bound ebony fingerboard, block inlays, locking nut, crown peghead inlay.
- Two Spotlight humbucking pickups, coil tap switch.

SG '62 SHOWCASE EDITION (April. 1988 guitar of the month)
EMG pickups, Blue finish.
Production: 200 for U.S., 50 for overseas.

SG 90 SINGLE 1988–90
Double-cut solidbody, pointed horns, strings through body.
- Pearloid pickguard, strings mounted through body, Floyd Rose vibrato optional, Alpine White, Metallic Turquoise, or Heritage Cherry finish.
- Unbound ebony fingerboard, 25½-inch scale, two-piece split-diamond inlay, crown peghead inlay, pearl logo.
- One humbucking pickup with black cover.

SG 90 DOUBLE 1988–90
One oblong single-coil pickup mounted diagonally in neck position, one black-covered humbucking pickup in bridge position, two knobs, push/pull for coil tap, selector switch between knobs.

SG CUSTOM SHOWCASE EDITION OCTOBER 1988
EMG pickups, Ferrari Red finish.
Production: 200 for U.S., 50 for overseas.

10th ANNIVERSARY SG CUSTOM 2003–04
Diamond White Sparkle finish, white pickguard, ebony fingerboard, pearl block inlays, 10th Anniversary at 12th fret, gold-plated hardware.
Production 40.

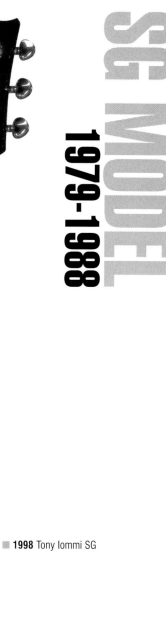

SG MODEL 1979-1988

1987 press advertisement

1998 Tony Iommi SG

SG 62 SHOWCASE EDITION
See SG Standard.

30TH ANNIVERSARY SG CUSTOM 1991
30th Anniversary *engraved on peghead inlay, TV Yellow finish (darker than traditional TV Yellow). Production: No more than 300.*

1967 SG CUSTOM 1991
Large 4-point pickguard, Wine Red finish.

SG STANDARD CELEBRITY SERIES
(August 1991)
Black finish, white knobs, white pickguard, gold-plated hardware.

LES PAUL SG '67 CUSTOM 1992–1993
Large four-point pickguard, Wine Red or Classic White finish.

SG STANDARD KORINA 1993–94
Korina (African limba wood) body, 3-piece sandwich body with rosewood center laminate, gold-plated hardware, Antique Natural finish. Production: 500.

GENERATION SWINE SG SPECIAL 1997
Promotional guitars for Motley Crue's Generation Swine *CD and tour, Ebony finish, red pickguard with "Generation Swine" logo. Production: 5 given away at Guitar Center stores, 1 given away nationally.*

■ **2000** Angus Young Signature SG

SG MODEL 1991-2005

townshend. that's who.

the pete townshend signature sg
new from gibson custom

Gibson's Custom, Art & Historic Division proudly introduces its most recent signature model, the Pete Townshend Signature SG. True Townshend fans will recognize this guitar as a faithful replica of the SG that Pete used during the Who's "Live at Leeds" concert in 1970.

The production of this model is limited to 250 units and a portion of the proceeds will go to Pete Townshend's Double O Charity to benefit young people globally.

Each guitar comes complete with a hand-signed and hand-stamped certificate of authenticity, an exclusive flight case, a Custom Shop hardshell SG case, and a protective cloth cover emblazoned with the artist's signature. Townshend's signature is also replicated on the

back of each individually numbered headstock.

To find your nearest Custom, Art & Historic Dealer, call 800-987-2284, ext. 900, or visit our website at www.gibsoncustom.com and join the Gibson Custom Club.

The World's Finest Guitars

■ **2000** press advertisement

SG-Z 1998
Double-cut solidbody, pointed horns, Z-shaped tailpiece.
• Double cutaway with pointed horns, tune-o-matic bridge, Z-shaped tailpiece with strings through body, small pickguard.
• Bound rosewood fingerboard, split-diamond inlay, 3-piece reverse-Z pearl peghead inlay, black chrome hardware, Platinum or Verdigris finish.
• One stacked-coil and one standard humbucking pickup, two knobs, selector switch between knobs.

TONY IOMMI SG 1998, 2001–05
Two custom-wound humbuckers with no polepieces, ebony fingerboard, iron cross inlays, chrome-plated hardware, left-handed or right-handed, Ebony finish.

SG CLASSIC 1999–2001
Double-cut solidbody, pointed horns, two pickups, Classic on truss-rod cover.
• Double-cutaway mahogany solidbody, pointed horns, tune-o-matic bridge, large pickguard.
• Bound rosewood fingerboard, dot inlays.
• Two P-90 pickups, four knobs.

SG SPECIAL GOTHIC 1999–2000 / SG GOTHIC 2001–02
Two exposed-coil humbuckers, satin Ebony finish, ebony fingerboard, moon-and-star inlay at 12th fret (no other inlay), black hardware.

SG SUPREME 1999–2004, 2007–current

ANGUS YOUNG SIGNATURE SG 2000–current
Based on SG Standard, large pickguard, two humbucking pickups (one custom-wound), Maestro vibrato with lyre and logo engraved in cover, "devil signature" ornament on peghead, nickel-plated hardware, aged Cherry finish.

SG VOODOO 2002–04
Double-cut solidbody, pointed horns, voodoo doll on fingerboard.
• Single-cutaway swamp ash solidbody, carved top, Juju finish (black with red wood filler), black hardware.
• Ebony fingerboard, voodoo doll inlay at 5th fret (no other inlays), red logo.
• Two humbucking pickups with red/black coils.

SG SPECIAL FADED 2002–current
Worn Cherry or Worn Brown finish, two exposed-coil humbuckers, unbound rosewood fingerboard, decal logo.

GARY ROSSINGTON SG 2003
Early 1960s SG Standard specs, Maestro vibrola, aged and faded Cherry finish.
Production: 250.

SG ELEGANT QUILT TOP 2004–06
Double-cut solidbody, pointed horns, quilted maple top.
• Mahogany double-cutaway with pointed horns, quilted maple top, gold-plated hardware.
• Bound rosewood fingerboard, abalone trapezoid block inlays.
• Two humbucking pickups, four knobs, selector switch.

SG SPECIAL REISSUE 2004–current
Small pickguard, two soapbar P-90 pickups.

SG SUPREME '57 HUMBUCKER 2005–2006
Double-cut solidbody, pointed horns, curly maple top, split-diamond inlays.
• Double cutaway with pointed horns, mahogany back, flamed maple top cap, gold-plated hardware, Fireburst finish (three-tone Sunburst shaded from bottom of body to horns).
• Bound ebony fingerboard, split-diamond inlay, bound peghead, five-piece split-diamond (SG Custom style) peghead inlay.
• Two P-90A soapbar pickups with black covers ('57 Classic humbuckers from 2005), 4 knobs.

JUDAS PRIEST SG 2005–current
Large chrome pickguard, 1 EMG and 2 Gibson 57 Classic exposed-coil humbuckers, custom stud-mounted bridge tailpiece, bound rosewood fingerboard, dot inlay, Custom Authentic Ebony finish, certificate signed by K.K. Downing and Glenn Tipton.
Production: 30 (sold as a set with Judas Priest Flying V).

SG SPECIAL NEW CENTURY 2006–current
Two exposed-coil humbuckers, full-body mirror pickguard, ebony fingerboard, mirror dot inlays, Ebony finish.

SG MENACE 2006–current
Double-cut solidbody, pointed horns, brass knuckles on fingerboard.
- Double-cutaway solid mahogany body, pointed horns, tune-o-matic bridge, tribal body routings, black hardware, Flat Black finish.
- Unbound ebony fingerboard, brass knuckles inlay at 5th fret, no other inlay, special headstock logo, gold-tinted frets.
- Two Smoky Coil humbucking pickups with brass studs, four knobs, one switch.

SG GT 2006–current
Double-cut solidbody, pointed horns, white center section.
- Double-cutaway solid mahogany body, pointed horns, tune-o-matic bridge, massive chrome tailpiece, opaque finishes with white center section, chrome-plated hardware.
- Bound ebony fingerboard, mirror trapezoid inlays, GT on truss-rod cover, no peghead ornament.
- Two humbucking pickups, four knurled knobs, one switch, locking cable jack, push/pull for coil tap, high-pass tone filter.

SG GODDESS 2006–current
Double-cut solidbody, pointed horns, red logo.
- Double-cutaway solid mahogany body, pointed horns, chrome-plated hardware.
- Bound ebony fingerboard, trapezoid inlays, Goddess on truss-rod cover, no peghead ornament, red logo.
- Two exposed-coil humbucking pickups with transparent bobbins, one volume, one tone, three-way switch.

2007 SG Special Faded

SG MODEL 2006

SG MODEL 2006

2007 SG 61 Reissue

2008 SG Standard Reissue

■ **2008** SG Les Paul Robot

■ **2008** SG Les Paul Robot

SG MODEL 2007

SG SPECIAL FADED 3 PICKUP 2007–current
Three humbuckers, two knobs, one rotary selector switch, plain truss-rod cover, Worn Ebony or Worn White finish.

SG SELECT 2007–current
Double-cut solidbody, pointed horns, trapezoid inlays, flame maple top.
- Double-cutaway solid mahogany body, pointed horns, flame maple top and back, gold-plated hardware.
- Three-piece flame maple neck, bound rosewood fingerboard with antiqued binding, trapezoid inlays, metal truss-rod cover, crown peghead inlay, metal tuner buttons, pearl logo.
- Two humbucking pickups, four knobs, one switch.

SG-3 2007–current
Double-cut solidbody, pointed horns, three humbuckers.
- Double-cutaway solid mahogany body, pointed horns, small pickguard does not surround pickups, gold-plated hardware.
- Bound rosewood fingerboard with antiqued binding, trapezoid inlays, crown peghead inlay, plastic keystone tuner buttons plastic.
- Three humbucking pickups, two knobs, six-position rotary selector switch with pointer knob.

■ **2009** SG Carved Top

SG MODEL 2007

ELLIOT EASTON CUSTOM SG 2007–current

Two humbucking pickups, Maestro vibrola with Tiki-man engraved on cover, small pickguard, chrome-plated hardware (Pelham Blue finish) or gold-plated (Classic White finish), left or right-handed.

SG SELECT 2007–08

Flame maple top and back, two humbuckers, three-piece flame maple neck, metal truss rod cover, gold-plated hardware.

ROBOT SG SPECIAL 2008–current

With auto-tuning system.

SG SPECIAL EMG 2007

2 black-covered EMG humbucking pickups, large black pickguard, SG on truss rod cover, decal logo, Black finish.
Production: 400.

SG STANDARD 3-PICKUP 2007

Three blade pickups (single-coil), two knobs, six-way selector with pointer knob, satin Natural finish.
Production: 400.

SG DIABLO 2008

Carved mahogany body, two humbuckers, two knobs, selector switch between knobs, 24 frets, trapezoid inlays, bound rosewood fingerboard, gold-plated hardware.
Production: 1,000 with Red metallic finish, 1,000 with Silver metallic finish.

SG CARVED TOP AUTUMN BURST 2009

Carved maple top cap, two humbuckers, two knobs, one switch, unbound rosewood fingerboard, trapezoid inlays, crown peghead inlay, chrome-plated hardware.
Production: 350.

■ **2009** SG Special

SG MODEL 2007-2009

SG MODEL 20 2009

■ **2009** SG Les Paul Special Raw Power

■ **2009** SG Zoot Suit

■ **2009** Robby Krieger 1967 SG Standard

SG ZOOT SUIT 2009–current

Multi-laminate birch body with each laminate dyed a different color, 486R and 500T coverless humbuckers with clear coils, two clear knobs, one switch, ebony fingerboard, no inlay, SG on truss rod cover, two-tone peghead.

ROBBY KRIEGER SG STANDARD 2009–10

Two '57 Classic humbuckers, large pickguard surrounds pickups, Maestro vibrola with long engraved coverplate, black witch hat knobs, aged Dark Cherry finish.
Production: 50 aged to replicate Krieger's 1967 SG Standard, 100 with VOS (Vintage Original Spec) aging treatment.

SG SPECIAL RAW POWER 2009–11

Solid maple body, two uncovered humbucking pickups, large pickguard surrounds pickups, tune-o-matic bridge, three-piece maple neck, unbound maple fingerboard, dot inlays except for trapezoid at 12th fret, SG on truss rod cover, decal logo.

■ **2010** SG Standard

SG MODEL 2009-2011

SG MODEL 2010-2011

■ **2010** SG Standard Reissue VOS

■ **2010** 50th Anniversary SG 12 string

■ **2011** Melody Maker SG

■ **1964** EDS-1275 Double 12

EDS-1275 1962

GOIN' SOUTH

Whatever players and collectors might think of Norlin-era Gibsons today, the guitars were selling well in the early 1970s, and the boom required further expansion of Gibson's manufacturing facilities. The troublesome labor disputes of the early 1970s inspired owner Norlin to attain this increased capacity by building a new 100,000 square foot factory in Nashville, TN, which opened in the summer of 1975.

Over the course of the next few years Gibson's general production was weighted more and more toward Nashville, and by the late 1970s and early '80s the Kalamazoo factory was largely relegated to custom and limited instruments, such as the Les Paul Heritage 80, Flying V, and Explorer.

Gibson ceased production at Kalamazoo entirely in June 1984 and relocated the company's corporate and manufacturing structures to Nashville. Between the opening of the Nashville plant and the closure of the Kalamazoo plant, Norlin reported pretax losses attributable to its holdings in the musical instrument industry of $145 million, and it appeared by the mid 1980s that Gibson was plummeting toward out-and-out closure and liquidation.

Meanwhile, three former Gibson managers – Jim Deurloo, Marv Lamb, and J.P. Moats – had refused to make the journey south, leased part of the former Gibson factory in Kalamazoo, and formed the Heritage guitar company in April 1985.

EDS-1275 DOUBLE 12 1962–68, 1974–current

Six-string neck and twelve-string neck.
- Double cutaway SG-style solidbody with pointed horns, no soundholes, tune-o-matic bridges, unbound, nickel-plated hardware (gold on Alpine White finish from 1988).
- Twelve-string and six-string necks, 24¾-inch scales, bound rosewood fingerboards, double-parallelogram inlay, pearl logo (decal from 1977).
- Two humbucking pickups for each neck, two knobs per neck, four knobs on lower treble bout, one switch between tailpieces, one switch on upper treble bout).
Production: 110 (1958–68); 1,145 (1974–79).

EDS-1275 CENTENNIAL (May 1994 guitar of the month)

Ebony finish, serial number in raised numerals on tailpiece, numeral 1 of serial number formed by row of diamonds, letter i of logo dotted by inlaid diamond, gold medallion on back of peghead, gold-plated hardware, limited run of no more than 101 serial numbered from 1894–1994; the package includes a 16x20-inch framed photograph and gold signet ring.

EDS CUSTOM

Any combination of guitar, bass, mandolin, or banjo necks was available by custom order.

EBSF-1250 1962–68

Bass neck and six-string neck
- SG-style solid mahogany body pointed horns, beveled edges.
- Four-string bass neck and six-string guitar neck, rosewood fingerboards, double-paralellogram inlays.
- Two humbucking pickups for each neck, four knobs on lower treble bout, one switch between tailpieces, one switch on upper treble bout, fuzz-tone on bass.
Production: 22.

EMS-1235 DOUBLE MANDOLIN 1962–68

Short six-string guitar neck and standard six-string guitar neck.
- Double pointed cutaways, hollow maple body with carved spruce top, no soundholes (SG-style solidbody with pointed cutaways from c1962), tune-o-matic bridge for standard neck, height-adjustable bridge for short neck.
- Standard guitar neck and short six-string neck with 15½-inch scale, bound rosewood fingerboards, double-parallelogram inlay, no peghead ornament.
- One humbucking pickup for short neck, two humbucking pickups for standard neck, four knobs on lower treble bout, one switch between tailpieces, one switch on upper treble bout.
Production: 61.

JIMMY PAGE EDS-1275 DOUBLE NECK 2007

Mahogany solidbody, pointed horns, two exposed-coil humbucking pickups on 6-string neck, VOS (Vintage Original Spec) finish treatment.

Production: 25 aged to match Page's original and signed by Page; 250 additional.

■ **1964** EDS-1275 Double 12 owned by Steve Howe

EDS-1275
2007-2010

EDS-1275

2007-2010

■ **2010** EDS-1275 Don Felder
Hotel California

FIREBIRD I, REVERSE-BODY 1963–65, 1991–92 / 1963 FIREBIRD I 2000–current

Solidbody with treble horn larger than bass horn, one mini-humbucker.

- Angular body, nine-piece mahogany/walnut neck-through-body with mahogany side wings, three-ply white-black-white pickguard with beveled edge, wraparound bridge with raised integral saddles, no vibrato (a few with Firebird III vibrato), nickel-plated hardware (gold-plated, 1991–92).
- Unbound rosewood fingerboard, dot inlays, six tuners all on treble side of peghead, beveled peghead edge, Kluson banjo-style tuners, logo on truss-rod cover.
- One mini-humbucking pickup with no polepieces, two knobs.

Production: 1,377 (1963–65, includes some non-reverse).

FIREBIRD III, REVERSE-BODY 1963–65 / 1964 FIREBIRD III 2000–current

Solidbody with treble horn larger than bass horn, two mini-humbuckers, dot inlays.

- Treble horn larger than bass horn, nine-piece mahogany/walnut neck-through-body with mahogany side wings, three-ply white-black-white pickguard with beveled edge, wraparound bridge with raised integral saddles, simple spring vibrato with flat arm.
- Single-bound rosewood fingerboard, dot inlays, tuners all on treble side of peghead (all on bass side, 1965), Kluson banjo-style tuners (some with right-angle tuners, 1965), logo on truss-rod cover.
- Two mini-humbucking pickups with no polepieces, three-way toggle switch.

Production: 2,546 (1963–65, includes some non-reverse).

■ **1963** Firebird I Reverse Body

FIREBIRD 1963

FIREBIRD V, REVERSE-BODY 1963–65, 1986–87 / FIREBIRD REISSUE 1990 / FIREBIRD V 1991–current / 1964 FIREBIRD V CUSTOM SHOP 2000–current

Solidbody with treble horn larger than bass horn, two mini-humbuckers, trapezoid inlays.

• Treble horn larger than bass horn, nine-piece mahogany/walnut neck-through-body (seven-piece from 1990) with mahogany side wings (all mahogany body with solid finish colors from 2002), three-ply white-black-white pickguard with beveled edge, tune-o-matic bridge, Deluxe vibrato with metal tailpiece cover engraved with Gibson and leaf-and-lyre (Kahler vibrato or stopbar tailpiece optional, 1986–87; no vibrola from 1990).

• Single-bound rosewood fingerboard, trapezoid inlays, tuners all on treble side of peghead (all on bass side, 1965, 1991–current), Kluson banjo-style tuners (some with right-angle tuners, 1965), logo on truss-rod cover.

• Two mini-humbucking pickups with no polepieces, three-way toggle switch.

Production: 925 (1963–65, includes some non-reverse).

FIREBIRD V 12-STRING 1966–67
Standard headstock with six tuners per side.
Production: 272.

■ **1963** press advertisement

■ **1964** Firebird V Reverse Body

■ **1963** Firebird V Reverse Body

FIREBIRD VII, REVERSE-BODY 1963–65, 1991–93, 2003–current / 1965 FIREBIRD VII CUSTOM SHOP 2000–current

Solidbody with treble horn larger than bass horn, three mini-humbuckers, block inlays.

- Treble horn larger than bass horn, nine-piece mahogany/walnut neck-through-body with mahogany side wings (all-mahogany body with red metallic finish, 2002–current), three-ply white-black-white pickguard with beveled edge, tune-o-matic bridge, Deluxe vibrato (tubular lever arm with plastic end cap, metal tailpiece cover engraved with Gibson and leaf-and-lyre decoration), gold-plated hardware (chrome-plated 1991–93).
- Single-bound ebony fingerboard, block inlay beginning at first fret, tuners all on treble side of peghead (all on bass side, 1965), beveled peghead edge, large Kluson banjo-style tuners, logo on truss-rod cover.
- Three mini-humbucking pickups with no polepieces, three-way toggle switch, pearl block inlay (aged inlay 1991–93).

Production: 303 (1963–65, includes some non-reverse).

1963 Firebird VII Reverse Body owned by Phil Manzanera

FIREBIRD 1963

SOARING BACKWARDS ... AND FORWARDS: THE FIREBIRD

Not as rare as the Flying V and Explorer, nor as highly prized as the 1958–60 Les Paul, the 'reverse-bodied' Firebirds of the early 1960s are nevertheless very high up on the desirability ladder for vintage Gibson guitars. The model illustrates another of Gibson's efforts to out-rock'n'roll the likes of Fender and Gretsch, and carries the kinds of curves and colorful finishes that indicate a keen rivalry with Leo's creations in particular. Many makers of the day were looking to the chrome-and-tailfins panache of Detroit in the golden era of the auto industry for their esthetic inspiration. Gibson went right to the source for the look of its new model by hiring car designer Ray Dietrich. The result was an instrument that, once again, conveyed a musical style that was a few years ahead of its time. The lower bout had something of the offset flare of the Explorer, although with more rounded corners, while the recessed bass-side upper bout and elongated treble-side horn slightly invoked a flipped-over Fender Jazzmaster, hence the "reverse-bodied" nickname that the model took on between its arrival in 1963 and the redesign in 1965. In addition, the Firebird had a reversed 6-on-a-side headstock shaped like a stylized falcon head, with "banjo" tuners that had their buttons extending toward the back of the headstock so as not to spoil the look.

Also arguably lifted from Fender, although again originally inspired by the car industry, was the custom color palette that Gibson made available to the Firebird range. To dress up the model, which came standard in Tobacco Sunburst, customers could order their Firebird (or any Gibson, technically) in Ember Red, Cardinal Red, Polaris White, Golden Mist, Silver Mist, Heather, Pelham Blue, Frost Blue, Kerry Green, or Inverness Green.

Beyond the colors and the body and headstock lines, the Firebird was constructed differently from any Gibson that had gone before. Its solid mahogany body was made from two "wings" glued to a slightly raised center block that extended the length of the neck—what has become known as a through neck—and its pickups were a variation of the bright, cutting mini humbuckers that Gibson had inherited from Epiphone, although without the protruding adjustment screws. The Firebird I had a single pickup at the bridge, dot position markers, and a wraparound bridge; the III had two pickups, dots, and a Maestro vibrola; the V had two pickups, Maestro, and trapezoid inlays; and the VII had three pickups, Maestro, block inlays and gold-plated hardware.

A few years after its arrival, the Firebird would find its way into the hands of Brian Jones of The Rolling Stones, Phil Manzanera of Roxy Music, bluesman Johnny Winter, and others, but it failed to set the world of rock'n'roll alight in its day, and sales were meager. Gibson redesigned the model in 1965 – an update also driven in part by Fender's objection to the similarity of the reverse-bodied versions to the offset-waist body of the Jazzmaster and Jaguar, which Fender had patented. The result was a less dramatic, though still fairly distinctive guitar. Funnily enough, the "right way around" body of the new non-reverse Firebirds, as they have come to be known, got all the horns and bulges closer to the positions they held on the Fender guitars, but they were now slightly "melted" … slightly humbled, it might seem. The through-neck construction was dropped in favor of a more standard, and no doubt simpler, traditional glued-in neck joint, the I and III models now had P-90 pickups, and all in the range carried simpler dot neck inlays. As has so often happened in the evolution of Gibson guitars, the change rendered the original reverse-bodied Firebirds forever after more desirable in the eyes of vintage guitar fanatics.

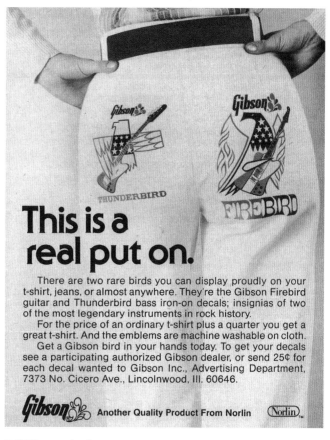

■ **1977** press advertisement

FIREBIRD (V) 1972–73

LE limited edition medallion, logo embossed on pickup covers.
Production: 366.

FIREBIRD 76 1976–78

Solidbody with treble horn longer than bass horn, Firebird with stars on pickguard.

- Reverse body, tune-o-matic bridge, red-and-blue Bicentennial Firebird figure (with stars) on pickguard near switch, gold-plated hardware, Sunburst, Natural Mahogany, White, or Ebony finish.
- Neck-through-body, unbound rosewood fingerboard, dot inlays, straight-through banjo tuners with metal buttons.
- Two mini-humbucking pickups, four knobs, selector switch.

Production: 2,847.

FIREBIRD 1980

- One-piece neck-through-body, unbound rosewood fingerboard, dot inlays, Cherry, Ebony, or Natural finish.

FIREBIRD II 1981–82

Solidbody with treble horn longer than bass horn, two full-size humbuckers, TP-6 tailpiece.

- Reverse body shape, maple body with figured maple top cap, tune-o-matic bridge, TP-6 fine-tune tailpiece, bound top, large backplate for electronics access, Antique Sunburst or Antique Fireburst finish.
- Three-piece maple neck, unbound rosewood fingerboard, dot inlays, pearl logo at tip of peghead.
- Two full-size humbucking pickups, active electronics, four black barrel knobs, selector switch, two mini-switches for standard/active, and brightness control.

FIREBIRD V CELEBRITY SERIES 1991–93

Reverse body, Black finish, white pickguard, gold-plated hardware.

FIREBIRD VII CENTENNIAL (September 1994 guitar of the month)

Vintage Sunburst finish, serial number in raised numerals on tailpiece, numeral 1 of serial number formed by row of diamonds, letter i of logo dotted by inlaid diamond, gold medallion on back of peghead, gold-plated hardware, limited run of no more than 101 serial numbered from 1894–1994, package includes 16x20 framed photograph and gold signet ring.

FIREBIRD STUDIO 2004–current

Solidbody with treble horn longer than bass horn, smaller than standard Firebird.

- Mahogany body shorter than standard Firebird, tune-o-matic bridge, stopbar tailpiece, chrome or gold-plated hardware.
- Set neck, unbound rosewood fingerboard, dot inlays, reverse headstock, logo on truss-rod cover.
- Two standard humbucking pickups, four knobs.

JOHNNY WINTER SIGNATURE FIREBIRD V 2008–09

Replica of Winter's 1963 Firebird V, stopbar tailpiece, holes in top from removal of vibrato, pickwear and arm wear through top finish, belt-buckle wear through back finish, signature and limited-edition number on back of peghead.
Production: 100.

FIREBIRD V 2010 2010–current

405R and 495T humbuckers, Nashville tune-o-matic, stopbar tailpiece, nickel-plated hardware, Steinberger gearless tuners.

1965 FIREBIRD V 2010-current

Based on 1964 version, Maestro vibrola.

FIREBIRD 1972-2010

■ **1963** catalogue spread

■ **2010** Firebird V
reverse Body

■ **1999** Firebird VII Historic
Collection Reverse Body

FIREBIRD I, NON-REVERSE 1965–69

Bass horn larger than treble, two P-90s.

- Bass horn larger than treble horn, wraparound bridge with raised integral saddles, white pickguard with red Firebird logo, short-arm vibrato with tubular lever and plastic tip.
- Set neck, unbound rosewood fingerboard, dot inlays, non-beveled peghead, right-angle 6-on-a-side tuners.
- Two black soapbar P-90 pickups, black selector slider.

Production: 1,590 (1966–69, also some in 1965).

FIREBIRD III, NON-REVERSE 1965–69

Bass horn longer than treble, three P-90s.

- Bass horn larger than treble horn, wraparound bridge with raised integral saddles, white pickguard with red Firebird logo, vibrato with tubular arm.
- Set neck, unbound rosewood fingerboard, dot inlays, non-beveled peghead, right-angle 6-on-a-side tuners.
- Three black soapbar P-90 pickups, black selector slider.

Production: 1,535 (1966–69, also some produced in 1965).

FIREBIRD V, NON-REVERSE 1965–69

Bass horn longer than treble, two mini-humbuckers.

- Bass horn larger than treble horn, wraparound bridge with raised integral saddles, white pickguard with red Firebird logo, Deluxe vibrato with tubular arm, metal tailpiece cover engraved with Gibson and leaf-and-lyre decoration.
- Set neck, unbound rosewood fingerboard, dot inlays, non-beveled peghead, right-angle 6-on-a-side tuners.
- Two mini-humbucking pickups (no polepieces), black selector slider.

Production: 492 (1966–69, also some produced in 1965).

FIREBIRD VII, NON-REVERSE 1965–69

Bass horn longer than treble, three mini-humbuckers.

- Bass horn larger than treble horn, tune-o-matic bridge, white pickguard with red Firebird logo, Deluxe Vibrato with tubular arm, metal tailpiece cover engraved with Gibson and leaf-and-lyre decoration, gold-plated hardware.
- Set neck, unbound rosewood fingerboard, dot inlays, non-beveled peghead, right-angle 6-on-a-side tuners.
- Three mini-humbucking pickups (no polepioeces), black selector slider.

Production: 283 (1966–69, also some produced in 1965).

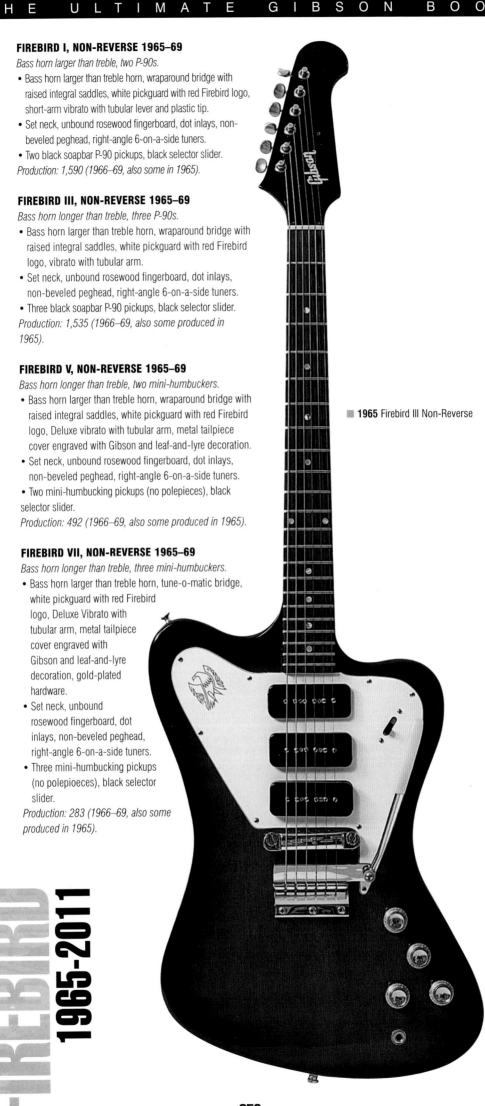

1965 Firebird III Non-Reverse

FIREBIRD
FIREBIRD
1965-2011

NON-REVERSE FIREBIRD 2002–04

Solidbody with bass horn longer than treble, humbuckers with polepieces, uniform finish.
- Bass horn larger than treble horn, tune-o-matic bridge, Cardinal Red, Walnut, or Pthalo Blue finish.
- Set neck, unbound rosewood fingerboard, dot inlay.
- Two humbucking pickups with two rows of polepieces, four knobs.

NON-REVERSE FIREBIRD PLUS 2002

Solidbody with bass horn longer than treble, humbuckers with polepieces, swirl finish.
- Mahogany solidbody, bass horn longer than treble horn, Blue, Red, or Green swirl finish, some with brushed aluminum pickguard.
- Unbound ebony fingerboard, dot inlays, peghead finish matches body.
- Two humbucking pickups, four knobs, some with coil-tap.
Production: 60 of each color.

FIREBIRD VII NON-REVERSE 2003–04

3 mini-humbucking or 3 P-90 pickups, gold-plated hardware, unbound rosewood fingerboard, dot inlays, Limed TV finish.

FIREBIRD X (2010)

Non-reverse body shape, three selector switches, digital electronics.
- Body shape similar to non-reverse, tune-o-matic bridge, covered stop tailpiece.
- Set neck, unbound fingerboard of highly figured wood, abalone trapezoid inlays, standard Gibson headstock shape with three tuners per side, bound headstock, oversized truss rod cover with *Firebird X Limited Edition*, pearl logo.
- Three covered mini-humbucking pickups with no polepieces, two metal knobs and one lighted bonnet knob for Robot auto-tune control, two switches on lower treble bout, one switch on upper bass horn, digital processor.

FIREBIRD X LIMITED EDITION 2011

Similar to Firebird X but with maple fingerboard, black dot inlays with X at fifth fret, swirl-pattern top finish.
Production: 1800.

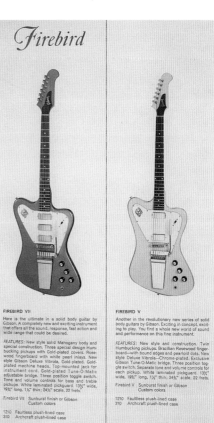

1965 press advertisement

1965 Firebird I Non-Reverse

CHANGING OWNERSHIP AND THE NORLIN DECLINE

A major portion of Gibson company history had already rolled under the bridge before the electric guitar had even come to be. The first big transition came in the very early days of the company, when founder Orville Gibson sold the rights to the Gibson name and patent to a small group of businessmen in 1902, who subsequently formed the Gibson Mandolin Guitar Manufacturing Company Ltd. The firm grew steadily through the first part of the century until guitar production was halted during World War II, and in 1944 was sold again to the massive Chicago Musical Instrument Company (CMI), which continued to cultivate the Gibson brand as one of the leading stringed instrument manufacturers in the world.

The next, and perhaps most infamous, change of ownership came in December of 1969, when Gibson was acquired by Ecuadorian Company Limited (ECL). The company changed its name to Norlin just a few months later, using the first three letters from ECL chairman Norman Stevens's name and the last three from that of CMI head M.H. Berlin. For many players and collectors, Norlin's ownership – which lasted from late 1969 to early 1986 – was to Gibson what CBS's was to Fender, and marks an era of rationalized production from a parent company perceived as unsympathetic to the craft and nuance of musical instrument manufacturing. Gibson continued to be a major name in the guitar industry under Norlin, but aspects of instrument manufacture under the conglomerate—from the conception of new models, to the standards of existing favorites, to the quality control of the entire production range—are considered by many to represent a dark period in Gibson history. Many models of the late 1970s and early '80s—various Limited Edition and "custom made" Les Pauls in particular—reclaim a measure of the CMI glory years, and certainly plenty of others are perfectly playable utilitarian guitars. But, on the whole, Norlin-era guitars are not the most admired of Gibsons.

L-5S 1973–84

Single-cut solidbody, flowerpot peghead inlay.
- 13½-inch wide, single cutaway, carved maple top, contoured back, large rectangular tune-o-matic bridge, large L-5 style plate tailpiece with silver center insert (stopbar from 1975, TP-6 from 1978), no pickguard, 7-ply top binding and 3-ply back binding with black line on side, maple control cavity cover, gold-plated hardware, Natural, Cherry Sunburst, or Vintage Sunburst finish.
- Five-piece maple/mahogany neck, 24¾-inch scale, 17 frets clear of body, bound ebony fingerboard with pointed end, abalone block inlays, five-ply fingerboard binding with black line on side, 22 frets, five-ply peghead binding, flowerpot peghead inlay.
- Two large oblong low-impedance pickups with metal covers and embossed logo (humbuckers from 1974), four knobs.
Production: 1,813 (1973–79).

1974 press advertisement

L-6S/L6-S CUSTOM: 1973–75 L-6S; 1975–79
L-6S CUSTOM

Single-cut solidbody, narrow peghead.
- 13½-inch wide, 1⅞-inch deep, single cutaway, maple body, large rectangular tune-o-matic bridge, stop tailpiece.
- Unbound maple fingerboard with Natural finish, unbound ebony fingerboard with Tobacco Sunburst finish, small block inlay (dots from 1975), 24 frets, 18 frets clear of body, 24¾ -inch scale, narrow peghead with similar shape to snakehead L-5 of late 1920s.
- Two five-sided humbucking pickups with no polepieces (rectangular from 1975), three knobs (volume, midrange and tone), six-position rotary tone selector switch for parallel and phase selection, chrome-plated hardware, Natural or Cherry finish.
Production: 12,460.

L-6S DELUXE 1975–80

Single-cut solidbody, strings through body, five-sided pickups.
- 13½-inch wide, 1⅞-inch deep, single cutaway, maple body, beveled top around bass side, large rectangular tune-o-matic bridge, strings anchor through body, string holes on a line diagonal to strings.
- Two five-sided humbucking pickups with black covers, three screws in pickup mounting rings, two knobs, three-way pickup selector switch.
- Unbound rosewood fingerboard, small block inlay (dots from 1978), metal tuner buttons.
Production: 3,483 (1975–79).

MIDNIGHT SPECIAL 1974–79

Thin single-cut solidbody, two humbuckers with no polepieces.
- Solid maple body, single-cutaway, non-beveled top around bass side, large rectangular tune-o-matic bridge, strings anchor through body on a diagonal line, chrome-plated hardware.
- Bolt-on maple neck, maple fingerboard, decal logo, metal tuner buttons.
- Two humbucking pickups with metal covers and no polepieces, two knobs, two-way tone switch, jack into top.
Production: 2,077.

■ **1973** press advertisement

SIGNATURE 1974–78
Semi-acoustic with two f-holes and offset cutaways.
• Bound semi-acoustic thinline body with two f-holes and offset cutaways; Gold or Sunburst.
• Bound rosewood fingerboard, crown markers; "Les Paul Signature" on headstock; plastic tuner buttons.
• Two rectangular plastic-cover low-impedance humbucker pickups.
• Two controls (volume, tone) plus three-position impedance rotary switch, two-way phase rotary switch, and three-way selector; one jack on side of body for normal high-impedance output, plus second jack on body face for low-impedance output; built-in impedance transformer.
• Cream plastic pickguard.
• Six-saddle bridge plus separate bar tailpiece.
Earliest examples with two round-end plastic-cover low-impedance humbucker pickups, and two side-mounted jacks.
Production: 1973 3; 1974 1046; 1975 118; 1976 150; 1977 123; 1978 20; 1979 3.

OTHER LES PAULS 1973-1974

■ **1974** Les Paul Signature

MARAUDER 1975–81

Single-cut solidbody, humbucker and blade pickups.

• 12¾ -inch wide, Les Paul-shape single cutaway, maple
  or mahogany body, large pickguard covers entire upper
  body and extends around lower treble bout.
• Bolt-on maple neck, unbound rosewood fingerboard
  (maple from 1978), dot inlays, triangular peghead
  with rounded top, decal logo.
• Humbucking pickup in neck position, blade pickup in
  bridge position, pickups set in clear epoxy, two
  knobs, rotary tone selector switch between knobs
  (some with switch on cutaway bout, 1978).
Production: 7,029 (1975–79).

MARAUDER CUSTOM 1976–77

*Three-way selector switch on cutaway bout, bound
fingerboard, block inlays, Tobacco Sunburst finish.
Production: 83.*

S-1 1976–79

Thin single-cut solidbody, 3 pickups.

• 12¾-inch wide, Les Paul-shape single cutaway,
  rectangular tune-o-matic bridge, stop tailpiece, large
  pickguard covers entire upper bodyuy and extends
  around lower treble bout.
• Bolt-on neck, maple fingerboard (some early with
  rosewood), dot inlays, triangular peghead with
  rounded top.
• Three single-coil pickups with center bar, pickups set
  in clear epoxy (black pickup covers from 1978), two-
  way toggle on cutaway bout (selects bridge pickup
  alone), four-position rotary switch for pickup
  selection, two knobs (volume, tone).
Production: 3,089.

1976 S-1

S-1 SERIES 1975-1976

HIT AND MISS MODELS (MOSTLY MISS)

Like many guitar manufacturers in the late 1970s and early '80s, Gibson struggled to find a foothold in a music world more and more dominated by electronics—and by synthesizer-based keyboards in particular—and consequently threw out a lot of oddball and generally modernistic designs that just didn't stick (and no, they didn't become classics a decade down the road either, unlike the Flying V and Explorer of the Modernistic Series launched in 1958).

Ironically, the first raft of ill-received Gibson electrics of the era came early on, in 1969, with the return of the namesake of Gibson's most legendary model.

Upon re-signing his endorsement deal with Gibson, Les Paul had urged the company to issue models that incorporated the low-impedance pickups that Paul had long favored himself. These appeared in 1969 as the Les Paul Personal and Professional models, which were replaced by the similar Les Paul Recording model in 1971. These guitars were generally considered ugly, their controls confusing, and they never found favor with musicians, in their day or after. The final incarnation of these remained in the catalog until 1979. The semi-acoustic Les Paul Signature of 1973 didn't fare much better (although most felt the guitar at least looked a little better than its siblings), nor did the original low-impedance L-5S, nor indeed the version with standard high-impedance humbuckers that followed it. Other dodos of the era were the L-6S, bolt-neck Marauder and S-1, laminated-bodied V-II, active-electronics-equipped RD Series, wood-and-plastic-bodied Sonex 180, and pig-ugly Corvus. That said, some of these clunkers didn't do too badly: Gibson sold more than 7,000 Marauders between 1975–'79, and more than 3,000 S-1s over a similar time frame.

■ **1976** press advertisement

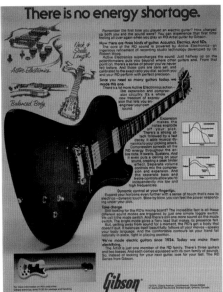

There is no energy shortage.

RD CUSTOM 1977–78 / 77 CUSTOM 1979
Solidbody with longer treble horn, maple fingerboard.
- Double cutaway, 14⅝-inch wide, upper treble horn longer than upper bass horn, lower bass horn larger than lower treble horn, tune-o-matic bridge, chrome-plated hardware, large backplate, Natural or Walnut finish.
- 25½-inch scale, maple fingerboard, dot inlays, model name on truss-rod cover, decal logo.
- Two humbucking pickups, active electronics, four knobs (standard Gibson controls), three-way pickup selector switch, two-way mini switch for mode selection (neutral or bright).

Production: 1,498 (1977–79).

RD STANDARD 1977–1978
Solidbody with longer treble horn, dot inlays, two humbuckers.
- Double cutaway, 14⅝-inch wide, upper treble horn longer than upper bass horn, lower bass horn larger than lower treble horn, tune-o-matic bridge, chrome-plated hardware, Natural, Tobacco Sunburst, or Walnut finish.
- 25½-inch scale, rosewood fingerboard, dot inlays, model name on truss-rod cover, decal logo.
- Two humbucking pickups, four knobs, one selector switch.

1979 RD Artist

RD SERIES
1977-1981

RD ARTIST/79 1979–80 / RD 1981
Solidbody with longer treble horn, winged-f on peghead.
* Double cutaway, 14⅝-inch wide, upper treble horn
  longer than upper bass horn, lower bass horn larger
  than lower treble horn, tune-o-matic bridge, TP-6
  tailpiece, large backplate, gold-plated hardware.
* Three-piece mahogany neck, 24¾-inch scale, bound
  ebony fingerboard (some unbound), block inlays,
  multiple-bound peghead, winged-*f* peghead inlay,
  pearl logo.
* Two humbucking pickups, active electronics, four
  knobs (standard Gibson controls), three-way pickup
  selector switch, three-way switch for mode selection
  (neutral, bright, front pickup expansion with back
  pickup compression.
Production: 2,340 (1977–79).

RD ARTIST/77 1980
25½-inch scale.

RD ARTIST CMT 1981
*Maple body, bound curly maple top, gold speed knobs,
TP-6 fine-tune tailpiece, maple neck, 24¾-inch scale,
bound ebony fingerboard, block inlays, chrome-plated
hardware, Antique Cherry Sunburst or Antique Sunburst
finish.*
Production: 100.

GK-55 1979–80
Les Paul shape, bolt-on neck, TP-6 tailpiece.
* Single cutaway mahogany solidbody, flat top,
  rectangular tune-o-matic bridge, TP-6 tailpiece or
  stop tailpiece, no pickguard, Tobacco Sunburst finish.
* Bolt-on neck, unbound rosewood fingerboard, dot
  inlays, model name on truss-rod cover, decal logo.
* Two Dirty Fingers pickups (exposed coils), four knobs.
Production: 1,000.

KZ-II 1980–81
*Double-cut solidbody, rounded horns (different from Les
Pauls), two humbuckers.*
* Double-cutaway solidbody, with Melody Maker style
  rounded horns, made in Kalamazoo factory, tune-o-

matic bridge, chrome-plated hardware, Walnut stain
with satin non-gloss finish.
* Dot inlays, metal tuner buttons, standard Gibson
  peghead size, *KZ-II* on truss-rod cover.
* Two humbucking pickups.

SONEX-180 1980 / SONEX-180 DELUXE 1981–83
*Single-cut solidbody, bolt on neck, exposed-coil
pickups.*
* Les Paul body size and shape, beveled edge on bass
  side, Multi-Phonic body (wood core, resin outer
  layer), tune-o-matic bridge, pickguard covers three-
  quarters of body, chrome-plated hardware.
* Bolt-on three-piece maple neck, rosewood
  fingerboard, dot inlays, metal tuners, decal logo.
* Two exposed-coil Velvet Brick humbucking pickups,
  three-way selector switch.

SONEX-180 DELUXE LEFT HAND 1982
Left-handed.

SONEX-180 CUSTOM 1980–82
Coil-tap switch, ebony fingerboard.

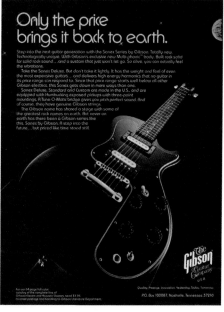

■ **1981** press advertisement

■ **1979** RD Artist

SONEX ARTIST 1981–84

Active electrionics, two standard humbuckers, three mini-switches (bright, compression, expansion), TP-6 tailpiece, no pickguard, Artist on truss-rod cover.

GGC-700 1981–82

Single-cut solidbody, flat top, oversized black pickguard.

- Single-cutaway solidbody, flat top, beveled edge on bass side, tune-o-matic bridge, large black pickguard covers three-quarters of body, chrome-plated hardware.
- Unbound rosewood fingerboard, dot inlays, decal logo *The Gibson Guitar Company*, metal keystone tuner buttons.
- Two humbucking pickups with exposed zebra coils, four black barrel knobs, selector switch near bridge, coil-tap switch, jack into top.

VICTORY MV-2 OR MV-II 1981–84

Double-cut solidbody, extended pointed horns, peghead points to bass side.

- Maple body, 13-inch wide, asymmetrical double cutaway with extended horns, horns come to a point, wide-travel Nashville tune-o-matic bridge, chrome-plated hardware, Candy Apple Red or Antique Fireburst finish.
- Three-piece bolt-on maple neck, bound rosewood fingerboard, dot inlay positioned near bass edge of fingerboard, 6-on-a-side tuner arrangement, peghead points to bass side, decal logo and *Victory* decal near nut.
- Velvet Brick zebra-coil neck pickup, special design black-coil humbucking bridge pickup, two knobs, coil-tap switch, three-position slide switch.

VICTORY MV-10 OR MV-X 1981–84

Two zebra-coil humbucking pickups and one stacked-coil humucking pickup (middle position), two knobs, master coil-tap switch, five-position slide switch, bound ebony fingerboard, Antique Cherry Sunburst, Candy Apple Red, or Twilight Blue finish.

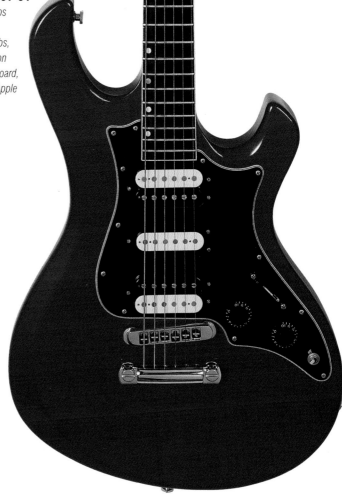

■ **1981** Victory MV-X

OTHER MODELS
1981-1987

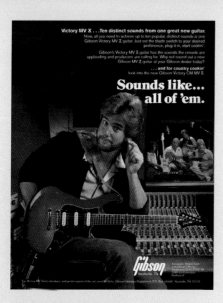

■ **1981** press advertisement

CHET ATKINS CE (STANDARD) 1982–2005
Single-cut solidbody classical, nylon strings.
- 14½-inch wide, single cutaway, chambered mahogany back, spruce top (cedar optional 1994–95), simulated round soundhole, soundhole insert with signature and prewar script logo, rectangular bridge, multiple-bound top with brown outer layer, gold-plated hardware.
- 25½ -inch scale, unbound rosewood fingerboard (ebony from 1996), 1.8-inch nut width (also specified as 1¹³⁄₁₆ -inch and 1⅞-inch), slotted peghead, scalloped top edge of peghead, no logo (standard "dove wing" with logo from 1993).
- Transducer pickup, roller knobs recessed into upper bass side, individual trim pots accessible internally.

CHET ATKINS CEC 1982–2005
Ebony fingerboard, 2-inch wide at nut.

CHET ATKINS CE SHOWCASE EDITION (July 1988 guitar of the month)
Vintage Sunburst finish. Production: 200 for U.S., 50 for overseas.

CHET ATKINS CEC – TRUE CEDAR 2000–2005
Cedar top, ebony fingerboard, 2-inch wide at nut, Natural finish.

CHET ATKINS CGP 1986–87
Asymmetrical solidbody, two mini toggles, bolt-on neck.
- Contoured mahogany body, flat-mount bridge/ tailpiece with individual string adjustments, Kahler Flyer vibrato optional, gold-plated hardware, Wine Red finish.
- Bolt-on maple neck, ebony fingerboard, 25½ scale.
- Two single-coil pickups tapped for normal and high output, two knobs (volume and tone), two mini-toggles for ohm tap, three-way selector switch.
Production: Catalogued, but few if any produced.

CHET ATKINS SST 1987–2005
Single-cut solidbody acoustic, steel strings, Chet Atkins signature on body.
- Single cutaway, spruce top, mahogany body with Chromyte (balsa) center, simulated round soundhole, soundhole insert with signature and prewar script logo (no soundhole from 1993, signature decal near fingerboard from 1993), rectangular ebony bridge (belly bridge from 1993), bound top, gold-plated hardware, Antique Natural, Alpine White, or Ebony finish.
- Mahogany neck, 21 frets, 25½-inch scale, unbound ebony fingerboard, dot inlay (star inlay from 1993), 1¹¹⁄₁₆-inch nut width, solid peghead, scalloped top edge of peghead (standard "dove wing" peghead from 1991), no peghead logo or ornament (prewar-style script logo from 1991, star inlay from 1993).
- Transducer bridge pickup with built-in preamp, two knobs on top (knobs on rim from 1993).

■ **1987** Chet Atkins SST

Our new solid body Chet Atkins Classic Electric.

Nothing we can say will prepare you for this experience. Let your music tell the story.

Gibson

Making history. Yesterday, today, tomorrow.

1983 press advertisement

CHET ATKINS SST 12-STRING 1990–94
Star fingerboard inlay, scalloped top edge of peghead, prewar script logo, gold-plated hardware, Antique Natural, Alpine White, Wine Red, or Ebony finish.

CHET ATKINS SST W/FLAME-TOP 1993–95
Flamed maple top, Antique Natural, Heritage Cherry Sunburst, or Translucent Amber finish.

CHET ATKINS SST CELEBRITY SERIES 1991–93
Gold-plated hardware, Ebony finish.

CHET ATKINS SST 12-STRING BRETT MICHAELS EDITION 1992–93
Antique Gold finish. Production: 2.

CHET ATKINS STUDIO CLASSIC 1991–93
Single-cut solidbody acoustic, fleur de lis on peghead.
• Single cutaway, hollow mahogany back, fan-braced spruce top, controls on rim, no soundhole, flared bridge ends, abalone top border, cocobolo wood

bindings, top inlaid at end of fingerboard with rosewood and abalone fleur-de-lis (no top inlay, 1993), gold-plated hardware, Antique Natural finish.
• 26¼-inch scale, V-end ebony fingerboard (asymmetrical with treble-side extension, 1993), 2-inch nut width, small *CGP* inlay at 7th fret, no other fingerboard inlay, slotted peghead, peghead narrows toward top, rosewood peghead veneer, prewar style *The Gibson* logo in pearl (postwar logo, 1993), small fleur-de-lis peghead inlay.
• Under-saddle pickup, controls on rim.

CHET ATKINS STUDIO CE 1993–2000, 2004–05
Single-cut solidbody acoustic, nylon strings, Chet Atkins signature on body.
• Single cutaway (deeper cutaway from 2004), hollow mahogany back (sound port from 2004), spruce top (cedar from 2004), no soundhole, flared bridge ends (moustache bridge from 2004), gold-plated hardware, Antique Natural finish.
• 26-inch scale, unbound ebony fingerboard with treble-side extension, 1¹³⁄₁₆-inch nut width, slotted peghead, decal logo.
• Under-saddle pickup, controls on rim (slider controls on circular plate on upper bass bout from 2004), individual string volume controls accessible internally, signature on upper bass bout near fingerboard, multiple-bound top with black outer layer.

CHET ATKINS STUDIO CEC 1993–2000, 2004–05
2-inch nut width.

SPIRIT I 1982–87
Double-cut solidbody, rounded horns, carved top, one humbucker.
• Combination bridge/tailpiece with individual string adjustments, tortoiseshell celluloid pickguard, chrome-plated hardware, silver finish standard,.
• Three-piece maple neck, 24¾-inch scale, unbound rosewood fingerboard, 22 frets, dot inlays, plastic keystone tuner buttons, decal logo.
• One exposed-coil humbucking pickup with creme coils, two barrel knobs.

When you're ready for the spotlight ... you're ready for a Gibson.®

Now you can afford to step into the lights with the best . . . a Gibson.
The Invader,™ the Corvus,™ and the Challenger™—the Gibson American Series of authentic American made, high quality Gibson guitars. Ready to rock when you are.
Prices start at $299.*

Gibson®

The first name in guitars.
Yesterday, today, tomorrow.

Gibson, P.O. Box 100087, Nashville, TN 37210
Giessenweg 67A 3044 AK Rotterdam, The Netherlands
*Manufacturers suggested retail price

1984 press advertisement

SPIRIT I XPL 1985–86

One pickup with cream coils, Kahler Flyer vibrato, bound top, bound fingerboard, Explorer-style peghead with 6-on-a-side tuner arrangement.

SPIRIT II 1982–87

Curly maple top optional (1983), two pickups, three knobs, selector switch below knobs, no pickguard, bound top.

SPIRIT II XPL 1985–86

Two pickups, three knobs, selector switch below knobs, bound top, bound fingerboard, Explorer-style peghead with 6-on-a-side tuner arrangement.

FUTURA 1982–84

Solidbody shaped like battle axe, 6-on-a-side tuners, set neck.
- Neck-through-body, cutout along entire bass side of body, cutout on upper treble side, deep cutout from bottom end almost to bridge, Gibson/Kahler Supertone vibrato optional, large tailpiece with individually adjustable saddles, gold-plated hardware, Ebony, Ultra Violet, or Pearl White finish.
- Rosewood fingerboard, dot inlays, 6-on-a-side tuners.
- Two humbucking pickups with no visible poles, two knobs.

FUTURA REISSUE 1996 / MAHOGANY FUTURA 2002–04

Angular body, V-shaped peghead (unrelated to solidbody Futura, this is a reissue of Explorer prototype).
- Mahogany body, body shape similar to Explorer but with sharper angles and narrower treble horn.
- Unbound rosewood fingerboard, dot inlays, V-shaped peghead.
- Two humbucking pickups, three knobs.
Production: 100 (1996); 15 in each of four metallic colors (2002–2004).

CORVUS I 1982–84

Solidbody shaped like battle ax, 6-on-a-side tuners, bolt-on neck.
- Solidbody with cutout along entire bass side of body, cutout on upper treble side, deep V-shaped cutout from bottom end almost to bridge, chrome-plated hardware, silver finish.
- Bolt-on maple neck, 24¾-inch scale, unbound rosewood fingerboard, dot inlays, 6-on-a-side tuners, decal logo.
- One humbucking pickup with black cover and no visible poles, pickup dipped in epoxy, two knobs, combination bridge/tailpiece with individual string adjustments.

CORVUS II 1982–84

Two pickups, three knobs.

CORVUS III 1982–84

Three high-output single-coil pickups, two knobs, five-way switch.

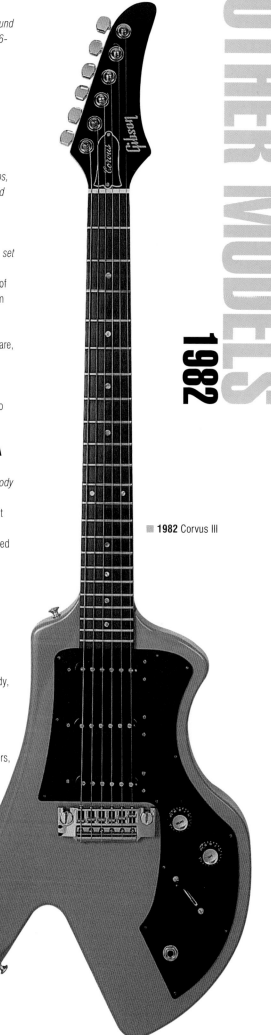

OTHER MODELS 1982

■ 1982 Corvus III

The American Series
Quality you can afford.

American made instruments from the premier fretted instrument manufacturer— Gibson. Starting at $299.

The Challenger, the Corvus and the Invader.

from *Gibson*

Making history.
Yesterday, today, tomorrow.

1983 press advertisement

CHALLENGER I 1983–84
Single-cut solidbody, bolt-on neck, standard peghead.
- Single-cutaway solidbody, flat top, pickguard surrounds pickup(s), combination bridge/tailpiece with individual string adjustments, chrome-plated hardware, silver finish standard.
- Bolt-on maple neck, unbound rosewood fingerboard, dot inlays, standard peghead shape, decal logo.
- One humbucking pickup with black cover and no visible poles, two knobs.

CHALLENGER II 1983–84
Two pickups, three knobs.

INVADER 1983–89 (prototypes from 1980)
Single-cut solidbody, bolt-on neck, stopbar tailpiece.
- Single-cutaway mahogany solidbody, beveled bass-side edge, tune-o-matic bridge, stop tailpiece, chrome-plated hardware.
- Bolt-on maple neck, ebony fingerboard, dot inlays, standard Gibson peghead shape, decal logo.
- Two ceramic magnet humbucking pickups with exposed zebra coils, four knobs, three-way selector switch.
INVADER VARIATIONS 1988–89:
- One narrow pickup, two knobs, Kahler vibrato, set maple neck, ebony fingerboard, dot inlays, crown peghead inlay, black chrome hardware.
- Two humbucking pickups with black plastic covers and no visible polepieces, two knobs, one switch, Kahler Flyer vibrato, pearloid pickguard covers most of treble-side body, jack in pickguard, set neck, unbound ebony fingerboard, dot inlays, Explorer-style peghead, 6-on-a-side tuners, black chrome hardware.

MAP-SHAPE 1983
Body shaped like United States.
- Mahogany body shaped like United States, combination bridge/tailpiece with individual string adjustments, Natural Mahogany finish standard; 9 made with American flag finish.
- Three-piece maple neck, ebony fingerboard, dot inlays, crown peghead inlay, pearl logo, metal tuner buttons.
- Two humbucking pickups, four knobs, one switch.
Production: Promotional model for dealers only.

SPECIAL I 1983–85
Double-cut solidbody, pointed horns, one humbucker.
- Solid mahogany double-cutaway body, pointed horns, combination bridge/tailpiece with individual string adjustments.
- Unbound rosewood fingerboard, dot inlays, *Special* on truss-rod cover.
- One exposed-coil humbucking pickup, two knobs, jack into top.

BLACK KNIGHT CUSTOM 1984
Single-cut solidbody, bolt-on neck, 6-on-a-side tuners.
- Single-cutaway solidbody, flat top with beveled edges, four knobs, three-way selector switch near knobs, Kahler vibrato, black chrome-plated hardware, Ebony finish.
- Bolt-on neck, rosewood fingerboard, dot inlays, 6-on-a-side tuner arrangement.
- Two humbucking pickups.

EXP 425 1985–86
Angular solidbody, humbucker and two single-coils.
- Angular solid mahogany body, no pickguard, black hardware, Kahler vibrato.
- Ebony fingerboard, 6-on-a-side tuner arrangement.
- One humbucking and two single-coil pickups, no pickup covers, two knobs, three mini-toggle switches.

Q-100 (ALPHA SERIES) 1985
Double-cut asymmetrical solidbody, bolt-on neck.
- Double-cutaway body shape similar to Victory MV, tune-o-matic bridge, optional Kahler Flyer vibrato, chrome-plated hardware without Kahler, black chrome hardware with Kahler, Ebony or Panther Pink finish.
- Bolt-on neck, ebony fingerboard, dot inlays, 6-on-a-side tuner arrangement.
- One Dirty Fingers humbucking pickup.

Q-200 1985
One HP-90 single-coil pickup in neck position, one Dirty Fingers humbucking pickup in bridge position, coil tap, Kahler Flyer vibrato, Ebony, Alpine White, Ferrari Red, or Panther Pink finish.

Q-300/Q-3000 1985

Three HP-90 single-coil pickups, two knobs, selector switch, "mid" switch, Kahler Flyer vibrato, Ebony or Red finish.

Q-4000 1985 / 400 1986

One humbucking pickup, one Dirty Fingers humbucking pickup and two single-coil pickups, master tone and master volume knob, three mini-switches for on/off pickup control, push/pull volume control for coil tap, Kahler Flyer vibrato, earliest with neck-through-body, Ebony, Ferrari Red, or Panther Pink finish.

XPL CUSTOM 1985–86

Angular solidbody, cutout in lower treble horn.
- Solidbody somewhat similar to Explorer but with sharply pointed horns, cutout at lower treble horn, bound curly maple top, locking nut vibrato system, bound top, Cherry Sunburst or Alpine White finish.
- Dot Inlays, 6-on-a-side tuner configuration.
- Two Dirty Fingers exposed-coil humbucking pickups, two knobs, one switch.

XPL STANDARD 1985

Solidbody with shape similar to small Firebird, two exposed-coil humbuckers.
- Solidbody, "sculptured" edges, small Firebird shape, tune-o-matic bridge or Kahler Flyer vibrato, chrome-plated or black chrome hardware, Ebony, Kerry Green, or Alpine White finish.
- 6-on-a-side tuner configuration.
- Two Dirty Fingers exposed-coil humbucking pickups.

■ **1985** Q-300 Alpha Series

OTHER MODELS 1983-1985

A BRIGHT NEW ERA

Following the rapid decline of the company in the final years of Norlin's ownership, and the closure of the Kalamazoo plant in 1984, Gibson was sold to former Harvard Business School classmates Henry Juszkiewicz, David Berryman, and Gary Zebrowski in January 1986 for $5 million. After the virtually inevitable teething troubles that new regimes are bound to experience, and the cool reception given to a raft of non-Gibsony new models, Gibson's new leaders began steadily reclaiming the brand.

Much of the return to strength came in recognizing the appeal of the classic models of the 1950s and early '60s, and in providing appropriately accurate reissues of these – a trend that was foreshadowed by the success of the Heritage Series of the early 1980s, and further confirmed by the Historic Collection in the early 1990s (Fender, meanwhile, was following much the same reissue-paved road back to liquidity in its post-CBS years). Saved from what most analysts agree was the brink of extinction by three businessmen who, for a change, showed a keen interest in guitars, Gibson was not only out of the woods but on the way to becoming the biggest and strongest company it had ever been.

A raft of well-targeted new models also helped to get Gibsons back into the hands of players again. On one side of the coin, guitars such as the well-received SG Reissue of 1986 addressed guitarists' continuing desires for the great Gibsons of days gone by, while a number of new variations on old themes—such as the ES-335 Studio, Les Paul Studio Lite, Les Paul Custom Lite, Explorer 90, and Flying V 90—updated the legends to suit contemporary playing needs.

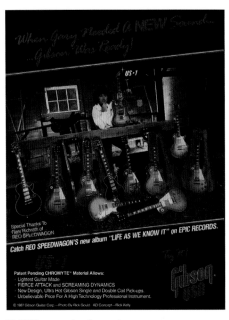

1987 press advertisement

US-1: 1986–90
Double-cut solidbody, Strat-like shape, split-diamond inlays.
- Double cutaway solidbody similar to Fender Stratocaster, maple top, mahogany back, Chromyte (balsa) core, tune-o-matic bridge or Kahler locking nut vibrato system, bound top and back, gold-plated hardware with tune-o-matic bridge, black chrome hardware with Kahler vibrato.
- Maple neck, 25½-inch scale, bound ebony fingerboard, split-diamond inlays, bound peghead, 6-on-a-side tuner arrangement, large raised plastic logo (pearl from 1987), mini-Grover tuners.
- Three humbucking pickups (two with stacked-coil design) with no visible poles, three mini-switches for on/off pickup control, two knobs (push/pull volume control for coil tap).

CHET ATKINS PHASAR 1987
Double-cut asymmetrical solidbody, two narrow humbuckers.
- Asymmetrical double cutaway solidbody.
- Rosewood fingerboard, 25½-inch scale, dot inlays, 6-on-a-side tuner arrangement.
- Two narrow humbucking pickups with no visible poles, two knobs.

Production: 6 (3 with vibrato, 3 without).

SR-71 1987–89
Double-cut solidbody, Strat-like shape, set neck, designed by Wayne Charvel.
- Body shape similar to Fender Stratocaster, Ebony, Nuclear Yellow, or Alpine White finish.
- Glued-in maple neck, 25½-inch scale, 6-on-a-side tuner arrangement, point on treble side of peghead, prewar script logo, Custom Shop model, 250 made, limited edition number on truss-rod cover.
- One humbucking and two single-coil pickups, Floyd Rose locking nut vibrato system.

Production: 250.

U-2/MACH II 1987–90
Double-cut solidbody, Strat-like shape, raised plastic peghead logo.
- Asymmetrical double-cutaway solidbody similar to Fender Stratocaster, basswood body, contoured back.
- 25½-inch scale, unbound rosewood fingerboard, 24 frets, dot inlays, unbound peghead, 6-on-a-side tuner arrangement, large raised plastic logo.
- Two single-coil pickups and 1 HPAF humbucking pickup, two Spotlight humbucking pickups optional, Floyd Rose vibrato, two knobs, three mini-switches, bound top, maple neck, black chrome hardware.

WRC 1987–89
Double-cut solidbody, Strat-like shape, three mini switches, designed by Wayne Charvel.
- Alder body similar to Fender Stratocaster, beveled lower bass bout, Floyd Rose or Kahler vibrato, Ebony, Honeyburst, or Ferrari Red finish.
- Bolt-on maple neck, 25½-inch scale, ebony fingerboard, dot inlays, 6-on-a-side tuner arrangement, point on treble side of peghead, WRC or WC on truss-rod cover, prewar script logo (earliest with Charvel decal on peghead).
- One humbucking pickup and two stacked-coil humbucking pickups with black covers and no polepieces, three on/off mini-switches, push/pull volume control for coil tap.

U-2 SHOWCASE EDITION (Nov. 1988 guitar of the month)
EMG pickups.
Production: 200 for U.S., 50 for overseas.

WRC SHOWCASE EDITION (Sept. 1988 guitar of the month)
Three EMG pickups (one humbucking, two single-coil), three knobs, four toggle switches, Kahler vibrato, Sperzel tuners.
Production: 200 for U.S., 50 for overseas.

M-III STANDARD 1991–95
Solidbody, swooping double cutaway with extended bass horn.
- Double-cutaway poplar solidbody, extended bass horn, Floyd Rose vibrato.
- 25½-inch scale, 24 frets, maple neck and fingerboard, black arrowhead inlay flush with bass side, peghead points to bass side, 6-on-a-side tuner arrangement with tuners all on treble side, logo reads upside down to player.
- Two ceramic magnet humbucking pickups with no covers in neck and bridge positions, NSX single-coil pickup with slug polepieces in middle position, two-way toggle switch and five-way slide switch for ten pickup combinations.

M-III STANDARD 1991–95
No pickguard, Translucent Red or Translucent Amber finish.

M-III STEALTH 1991
Black limba wood body, Floyd Rose vibrato, black chrome hardware, satin neck finish.

M-III-H STANDARD 1991–92
Two humbucking pickups, no pickguard, Translucent Red or Translucent Amber finish.

M-III DELUXE 1991–92
Laminated body of maple/walnut/poplar, same electronics as M-III Standard, Floyd Rose vibrato, maple neck and fingerboard, arrowhead inlay flush with bass side, Antique Natural finish.

M-III-H DELUXE 1991
Five-ply body with walnut top, curly maple back and poplar core, two humbucking pickups, six-way switch, no pickguard, satin (non-gloss) neck finish, Antique Natural finish.

M-III 1996–97
Mahogany body, three humbucking pickups, Ebony or Wine Red finish.

1988 US-1

OTHER MODELS 1986-1991

267

M-IV S STANDARD 1993–95
Steinberger vibrato, black chrome hardware, Ebony finish.

M-IV S DELUXE 1993–95
Steinberger vibrato, Natural finish.

NIGHTHAWK CUSTOM 1993–98
Single-cut solidbody, strings through body, trapezoid inlay.
- Single cutaway, mahogany back, flat maple top, low profile bridge, strings through body, optional Floyd Rose vibrato (1994), gold-plated hardware, Antique Natural, Fireburst, or Translucent Amber finish.
- 25½-inch scale, ebony fingerboard, trapezoid inlay.
- One Firebird mini-humbucking pickup in neck position, one NSX single-coil pickup in middle position, one slant-mounted humbucking pickup, master volume, push/pull master tone, five-way switch, optional two-pickup version with no single-coil and no push/pull tone control.

NIGHTHAWK SPECIAL 1993–98
Rosewood fingerboard, dot inlays, gold-plated hardware, Ebony, Heritage Cherry or Vintage Sunburst finish.

NIGHTHAWK STANDARD 1993–98
Rosewood fingerboard, double-parallelogram inlay, gold-plated hardware, optional two-pickup version with no single-coil and no push/pull tone control, optional Floyd Rose vibrato (1994), Fireburst, Translucent Amber, or Vintage Sunburst finish.

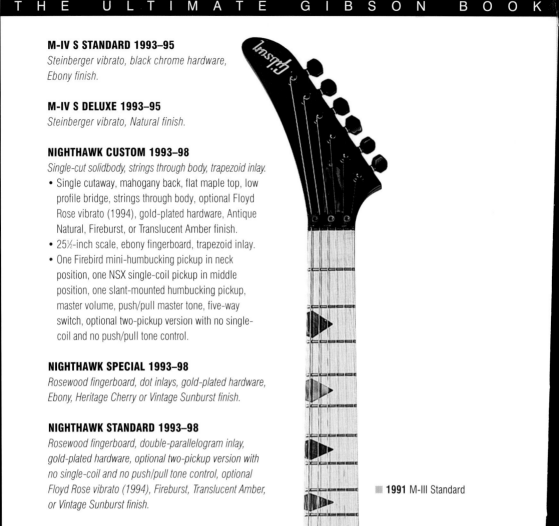

■ **1991** M-III Standard

OTHER MODELS 1993

1993 Nighthawk Special

2009 Nighthawk Special

Joe Louis Walker
Picks Gibson!

Because Only a Gibson is Good Enough.

Gibson
USA

1995 press advertisement

ACCESS ALL FRETS: LES PAUL GOES DOUBLE-CUT

Having been subject to a range of updates over the years, the classic Les Paul design received what was arguably its most significant modification in 40 years with the release of the Les Paul DC Pro in 1997. The guitar featured two humbuckers (P-90s optional) and the carved maple top and mahogany back that have come to characterize the breed (although the body was now weight-relieved, courtesy of a series of unseen chambers). However, an extra sweep of the saw gave it a second cutaway, resulting in a new yet somehow very familiar dual-horned design. The slightly more rounded and very slightly asymmetrical cutaway horns followed an outline closer to those of the double-cutaway Les Paul Junior and Special circa 1960, and the design was further streamlined by moving the selector switch down to the lower bout and including only master volume and tone controls, rather than the individual controls of the Les Paul Standard. Alongside the DC Pro, Gibson released the Les Paul DC Studio, which followed the low-frills theme of the Les Paul Studio released in 1983. The following year the (to be shortlived) Les Paul DC Standard joined the lineup.

Double-cutaway Les Paul-style guitars from other makers had been popular since the 1970s, most notably perhaps from makers Hamer and Yamaha, so this seemed an obvious and long-overdue arrival from Gibson with the aim of squelching the competition. The timing of the Les Paul DC range was probably inspired more by the success of Paul Reed Smith guitars, however, whose double-cutaway but otherwise fairly Les Paul-ish models had carved out a big share of the marketplace for themselves. In fact, the outline of the DC's body most closely resembled that of PRS's Santana model, still a special-order instrument at that time.

After PRS issued its own Singlecut model in 2000, which had a single-cutaway body that more closely resembled the classic Les Paul body lines, Gibson filed a lawsuit claiming trademark infringement against the Les Paul. After initially being upheld by a court in Nashville, with an order handed down for PRS to stop sales of the Singlecut, the decision was eventually reversed and Gibson's final appeal denied by the United States Supreme Court in June 2006.

ALL AMERICAN I 1995–97 / SG-X 1998–2000

SG body, one humbucker.
- Solid mahogany double-cutaway body, pointed horns, tune-o-matic bridge, chrome-plated hardware, Ebony finish.
- Unbound rosewood fingerboard, dot inlays, decal logo.
- One exposed-coil humbucking pickup two knobs, coil tap.

ALL AMERICAN II 1995–97

Double-cut solidbody, pointed horns (not as pointed as SG).
- Double cutaway with pointed horns (not SG-shape, similar to early 1960s Melody Maker), vibrato, Ebony or Deep Wine Red finish.
- Unbound rosewood fingerboard, dot inlays, *II* on truss-rod cover.
- Two oblong single-coil pickups with non-adjustable polepieces, two knobs, one switch.

GRACELAND 1995–96

Thinbody acoustic guitar shape, ELVIS *on fingerboard.*
- Acoustic J-200 body shape, thin body, poplar back, spruce top, multiple top binding, tune-o-matic bridge, pickguard with modern-art design from Elvis Presley's custom J-200 acoustic, gold-plated hardware.
- Maple neck, bound ebony fingerboard, *ELVIS* and two stars inlaid on fingerboard.
- Two black soapbar pickups.

BLUESHAWK 1996–2003

Single-cut solidbody, Varitone rotary control, diamond inlay.
- Single cutaway, mahogany back, flat maple top, semi-hollow poplar body, *f*-holes, Maestro Bigsby-style optional 1998.
- 25½-inch scale, unbound rosewood fingerboard, diamond inlay, stacked-diamond peghead inlay, pearl logo, gold-plated hardware, Ebony or Cherry finish.
- Two special Blues 90 pickups with cream soapbar covers and non-adjustable poles, two knobs (with push/pull to disable Varitone), slide switch, six-position Varitone control, combination bridge/tailpiece with individual string adjustments, strings through body, single-bound top.

THE HAWK 1996–97

Single-cut solidbody, Hawk *on truss-rod cover.*
- Nighthawk body shape, single cutaway mahogany solidbody (no top cap), no binding, Ebony or Wine Red finish.
- 25½-inch scale, unbound rosewood fingerboard, dot inlays, model name on truss-rod cover, American flag decal on back of peghead.
- Two humbucking pickups, two knobs, one switch.

LES PAUL-DC 1995-1996

LANDMARK 1996–97

Single-cut solidbody, flat top, strings through body, Firebird mini-humbuckers.

- Single cutaway, mahogany back, flat maple top, low profile bridge, strings through body, bound top, combination bridge/tailpiece with individual string adjustments.
- 25½-inch scale, unbound rosewood fingerboard, dot inlays, pearl logo, gold-plated hardware, Glacier Blue, Sequoia Red, Mojaveburst, Navajo Turquoise, or Everglades Green finish.
- Two Firebird mini-humbucking pickups, two knobs, three-way slide switch with coil-tap capability.

DC PRO 1997–98

Double-cutaway carved-top body, non-standard headstock with straight string-pull (no "Les Paul" on headstock or truss-rod cover).

- Bound carved-top body with shape of Special double-cut; flamed maple top; sunbursts or translucents.
- Unbound ebony fingerboard, dot markers; 24 ¾-inch scale-length (25 ½-inch scale optional); headstock with straight string-pull.
- Optional pickup and bridge configurations: two plastic-cover single-coil pickups with wrap-over bridge; two metal-cover humbucker pickups with wrap-over bridge or with separate bridge and tailpiece.
- Two controls (volume, tone) plus three-way selector.
- Nickel-plated hardware.

Custom Shop.

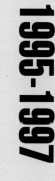

■ **1997** Les Paul DC Pro

$2,189*
(suggested retail)

Gibson introduces a *new* standard in
double-cutaway guitars

Creating a new Les Paul Standard is no easy task. It requires the best American craftsmanship and innovation to design a guitar coveted by the world's most influential musicians.

It also takes traditional Les Paul features such as a carved maple cap, mahogany body, and humbucker pickups for that unmistakable tone.

With a double-cutaway body, chambered back, and streamlined electronics, the new DC Standard is faster and lighter than ever been before.

And we had to show off our AAA flamed, lacquer finished Maple tops with these five new translucent colors: Amber Serrano, Black Pepper, Red Hot Tamale, Green Jalapeno, Blue Diamond

The DC's most incredible feature—a hot price at just $2,189*. Ask any guitarist what a Standard is and he'll tell you it's a Gibson Les Paul.

For a FREE poster of the 1998 Les Paul line-up, visit us at http://lespaul.gibson.com/freeposterDC3/ or call 1-800-4-GIBSON.**

Only a **Gibson** Is Good Enough™

Amber Serrano

■ **1998** press advertisement

DC STUDIO 1997–98, 2006–08
Unbound double-cutaway carved-top body, dot markers, chrome hardware.
- Unbound carved-top body with shape of Special double-cut; sunbursts or colors.
- Unbound rosewood fingerboard, dot markers; 24 ¾-inch scale-length; standard Gibson headstock shape.
- Two metal-cover humbucker pickups.
- Two knobs (tone, volume) plus selector switch
- Wrap-over tailpiece (separate bridge and tailpiece from 1998).
- Chrome-plated hardware.

■ **1998** Les Paul DC Standard

LES PAUL-DC 1997-2003

DC STANDARD 1998–2007

Double-cutaway carved-top body, crown markers, standard Gibson headstock (no "Les Paul" on headstock or truss-rod cover).

- Unbound carved-top body with shape of Special double-cut; maple top (flamed from 2001); sunbursts or colors (sparkle finishes only in 2000, trans finishes only from 2001).
- Bound rosewood fingerboard, crown markers; 24 ¾-inch scale-length; standard Gibson headstock shape.
- Two metal-cover humbucker pickups.
- Two knobs (tone, volume) plus selector switch.
- Wrap-over tailpiece.
- Chrome-plated hardware (in 2000, hardware was chrome with Lemonburst, or gold with Tangerineburst; from 2001, hardware was gold-plated).

Listed as Standard Double Cut Plus from 2001.

THE LOG 2003

Replica of Les Paul's Log, 4x4-inch centerpiece.

- Solid 4x4-inch center block, detachable wings from full-depth archtop, homemade vibrato.
- Rosewood fingerboard with varied-pattern inlay (originally from a Larson Bros. guitar), seven-piece star-shaped peghead inlay (from 1930s Gibson L-12 acoustic), Epiphone tuners.
- Two pickups with brown oblong covers.

Production: 3.

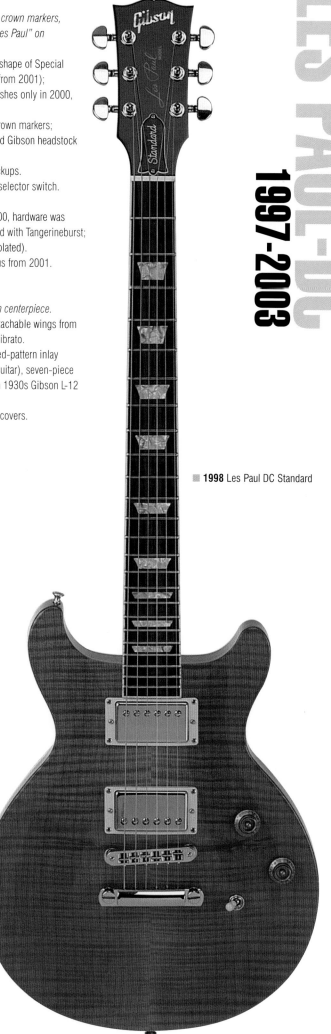

LES PAUL-DC

1997-2003

■ **1998** Les Paul DC Standard

EYE 2009

Body similar to Fender Strat with pointed horns.
- Solid mahogany body, pickguard with pointed ends, tune-o-matic bridge, Fire Engine Red finish.
- Unbound ebony fingerboard, no inlays
- 490R and 498T humbuckers with red plastic covers and no polepieces, two knobs, one selector switch.

Production: 350.

■ **2009** Eye

EYE GUITAR 2009

SHARK FIN 2010

Explorer body style with bass fin and squared-off treble fin.

- Solid mahogany body, chrome-plated hardware, Silver metallic finish.
- Unbound ebony fingerboard, dot inlays, reverse Explorer-style headstock curves to treble side with all tuners on treble side, knurled-knob tuners, black silkscreen logo.
- Uncovered 496R and 500T humbuckers, two knobs, selector switch between knobs.

■ **2010** Shark Fin

SHARK FIN 2010

JOAN JETT BLACKHEART 2010

Based on symmetrical double-cut Melody Maker.

- Pointed horns, tune-o-matic bridge, Black finish.
- Unbound ebony fingerboard, red dot inlays, signature on truss rod cover, narrow peghead, decal logo.
- One zebra-coil humbucking pickup, two knobs, one selector switch, controls and jack mounted on pickguard.

2010 Joan Jett Blackheart

BLACKHEART

2010